THE SINGLE W

The increase in numbers of single people has been described as one of the greatest social phenomena of western society. It is increasingly likely for most women that they will spend periods of their lives alone, without a committed partner relationship. In spite of the social changes that have made singleness less unusual for women, there is still a degree of social stigma attached to this status. Single women are a crucial group for study in relation to perceived changes in family life and relationships. This book provides a new understanding of what is often taken-for-granted – *female single identity*.

In an examination of extracts from her interviews with women aged 30 to 60 years and living alone, Jill Reynolds explores how single women deal with this potentially stigmatized identity. Reynolds focuses on identity and self-representation through consideration of discourse and the conversational moves made by the participants in discussion about their lives and relationships. Her analysis highlights that the culturally available and familiar resources for understanding singleness are highly polarized. Single women weave their way through the extreme contrasts of a denigrated or an empowered identity. Thus, while most participants give very positive accounts, they also pay attention to widespread social expectations that see success in life as involving a long-term committed relationship.

This book makes an important contribution to the understanding of the lives of single women and represents a challenge to the considerable literature on gender and family life which has inadequately theorized singleness. It will be of great interest to academics and students in social psychology, sociology, social work and social policy. It will also be of particular interest to students of gender studies, qualitative research, narrative studies, conversation analysis and discourse analysis.

Jill Reynolds is a Senior Lecturer in the Faculty of Health & Social Care at The Open University. Her teaching is in the areas of social work, managing health and social care and mental health. Her research interests include feminist practice, identity and singleness, meanings of care and support and training and practice issues.

WOMEN AND PSYCHOLOGY
Series Editor: Jane Ussher
School of Psychology, University of Western Sydney

This series brings together current theory and research on women and psychology. Drawing on scholarship from a number of different areas of psychology, it bridges the gap between abstract research and the reality of women's lives by integrating theory and practice, research and policy.

Each book addresses a 'cutting edge' issue of research, covering such topics as post-natal depression, eating disorders, theories and methodologies.

The series provides accessible and concise accounts of key issues in the study of women and psychology, and clearly demonstrates the centrality of psychology to debates within women's studies or feminism.

The Series Editor would be pleased to discuss proposals for new books in the series.

Other titles in this series:

THE THIN WOMAN
Helen Malson

THE MENSTRUAL CYCLE
Anne E. Walker

POST-NATAL DEPRESSION
Paula Nicolson

RE-THINKING ABORTION
Mary Boyle

WOMEN AND AGING
Linda R. Gannon

BEING MARRIED. DOING GENDER
Caroline Dryden

UNDERSTANDING DEPRESSION
Janet M. Stoppard

FEMININITY AND THE PHYSICALLY ACTIVE WOMAN
Precilla Y.L. Choi

GENDER, LANGUAGE AND DISCOURSE
Anne Weatherall

THE SCIENCE/FICTION OF SEX
Annie Potts

THE PSYCHOLOGICAL DEVELOPMENT OF GIRLS
AND WOMEN
Sheila Greene

JUST SEX?
Nicola Gavey

WOMAN'S RELATIONSHIP WITH HERSELF
Helen O'Grady

GENDER TALK
Susan A. Speer

BEAUTY AND MISOGYNY
Sheila Jeffreys

BODY WORK
Sylvia K. Blood

MANAGING THE MONSTROUS FEMININE
Jane M. Ussher

THE CAPACITY TO CARE
Wendy Hollway

SANCTIONING PREGNANCY
Harriet Gross and Helen Pattison

THE SINGLE WOMAN

A Discursive Investigation

Jill Reynolds

Routledge
Taylor & Francis Group

LONDON AND NEW YORK

First published 2008 by Routledge
27 Church Road, Hove, East Sussex BN3 2FA

Simultaneously published in the USA and Canada
by Routledge
270 Madison Avenue, New York, NY 10016

Routledge is an imprint of the Taylor & Francis Group, an Informa business

© 2008 Psychology Press

Typeset in Times by Garfield Morgan, Swansea, West Glamorgan
Printed and bound in Great Britain by TJ International Ltd, Padstow, Cornwall
Paperback cover design by Terry Foley

This publication has been produced with paper manufactured to strict environmental
standards and with pulp derived from sustainable forests.

British Library Cataloguing in Publication Data
A catalogue record for this book is available from the British Library

Library of Congress Cataloging in Publication Data
Reynolds, Jill, 1948–
The single woman : a discursive investigation / Jill Reynolds. – 1st. ed.
p. cm. – (Women and psychology)
Includes bibliographical references and index.
ISBN 978-0-415-40568-3 (hardback) – ISBN 978-0-415-40569-0 (pbk.) 1. Single women–Great
Britain. 2. Middle-aged women–Great Britain. 3. Feminism. I. Title.
HQ800.2.R485 2008
306.81′530941–dc22

2007045136

ISBN 978-0-415-40568-3 (hbk)
ISBN 978-0-415-40569-0 (pbk)

CONTENTS

Acknowledgements   viii

1   Developing a feminist discursive analysis of singleness   1

2   Contrasting models of a single identity   24

3   Working with a 'single' identity   43

4   A narrative of relationships and singleness   74

5   Choice and chance in relationships: negotiating agency   96

6   The everyday politics of singleness   122

7   Conclusions   148

Appendix 1: Methods   158
Appendix 2: Transcription conventions   166
References   167
Index   180

ACKNOWLEDGEMENTS

Many people have helped me over the long period of time from when I started the original research for my PhD thesis until this current publication. I should like to thank all the women who took part in my research project, giving generously of their time and sharing their thoughts. I am also grateful to Elaine Farmer for inspiring the interest in research on this topic and to Jane Shackman for her steadfast encouragement and positive comments on drafts.

The Faculty of Health & Social Care at The Open University has supported me through financial assistance with data recording, transcription and attendance at conferences; through responses to papers presented at school research seminars; and through the generosity of colleagues who took on additional work when I had study leave. I have also been helped by members of the cross-faculty Qualitative Work in Progress (previously discourse analysis) group with exploring different aspects of my data and reading and commenting on related papers at various stages. In particular, thanks to Margie Wetherell and Stephanie Taylor, for their steadfast commitment and support throughout the many vicissitudes of producing this work, and for their creative and inspiring ideas concerning my data and topic.

Thanks also to those secretaries and course team assistants who did the initial transcriptions, in particular Kathy McPhee, not only for her accurate typing but for her continuing interest in the project.

Thanks to Jane Ussher for her editorial guidance and encouragement and to Corinne Squire and two further anonymous reviewers for their very helpful comments.

Thanks to Dave Wallace for his companionship, for encouraging me to complete this work and for tolerating my continuing tendency to identify myself as 'single'.

Permissions

I would like to thank Judy Small for permission to quote 'The family maiden aunt', words and music by Judy Small © 1982 Crafty Maid Music; Margie

Wetherell for her help in formulating the theoretical commitments that have guided this work, and Sage Publications for granting permission to use sections of copyright material from Reynolds, J. and Wetherell, M. (2003) 'The discursive climate of singleness: the consequences for women's negotiation of a single identity', *Feminism & Psychology*, 13, 4: 489–510; Linda Blong for generous permission to quote from 'I ain't gonna be the woman that you left behind', unpublished song by Linda Woehrle Blong (1980); John Benjamins Publishing Company, Amsterdam/Philadelphia for kind permission to use sections of copyright material from Reynolds, J. and Taylor, S. (2005) 'Narrating singleness: life stories and deficit identities', *Narrative Inquiry*, 15, 2: 197–215; Blackwell Publishing for giving permission to use sections of copyright material from Reynolds, J., Wetherell, M. and Taylor, S. (2007) 'Choice and chance: negotiating agency in narratives of singleness', *Sociological Review*, Volume 55, 2: 331–351; and *Sociological Research Online* for permission to use sections of Reynolds, J. (2006) 'Patterns in the telling: single women's intimate relationships with men', *Sociological Research Online*, 11, 3.

1

DEVELOPING A FEMINIST DISCURSIVE ANALYSIS OF SINGLENESS

Introduction

I WILL NOT
[. . .] Sulk about having no boyfriend, but develop inner poise and authority and sense of self as woman of substance, complete without boyfriend, as best way to obtain boyfriend.

(Fielding 1996: 2)

'And you're not married and you don't have children. Is it really worth giving up marriage and children for your career?'

Victory laughed. Why was it that no matter what a woman accomplished in the world, if she hadn't married and had children, she was still considered a failure? [. . .]

'Every morning when I wake up,' Victory began, telling a story she'd told to interviewers many times before (but still, none of them seemed to be able to get it), 'I look around and I listen. I'm alone, and I hear . . . silence.' The girl gave her a sympathetic look. 'But wait,' Victory said, holding up one finger. 'I hear . . . silence. And slowly but surely a happiness spreads through my body. A joy. And I thank God that somehow, I've managed to remain free. Free to enjoy my life and my career.'

(Bushnell 2005: 4–5)

'I'm not hell bent on meeting anyone. My life's good. I think Bridget Jones propagates an old notion of what being alone means. I don't have a boyfriend or a husband, but I'm never alone, not unless I choose to be. I'm surrounded by people I like and love.' (Emily who is single, 32, and a theatrical agent.)

(Vernon 2005)

The extracts from romantic fiction and a newspaper article quoted above illustrate some changing ways of talking about singleness. In different ways, and to different degrees defending themselves against common images of

1

singleness for women, the speakers put forward a notion that being without a boyfriend, husband or children does not have to be a failure but can mean freedom and choice about companionship. These are strongly positive claims; yet there are traces of more negative associations of singleness in each extract.

This book investigates different meanings of singleness as understood by women in the UK in their middle years and alone. What meanings of singleness can be observed in the talk of ordinary women in conversation? How do new meanings interweave with more historical notions of the woman's place? What do the meanings conveyed through talk signify for what might be thought of as a single identity? I examine how women work with a single identity in a social context that is changing rapidly. My main focus is on identity and self-representation. The book is based on research interviews with 30 women aged between 30 and 60 years who responded to an invitation to be interviewed as a 'woman alone'.

Identity and self-representation are explored through looking at discourse, that is, language in use. In particular, I look at the discursive and conversational moves made by my participants: the kind of language that they and I used and the particular twists and turns of our conversations. Examination of how women talked about themselves and singleness shows linked but distinctive forms of 'trouble'. This is not to suggest that the individuals concerned were unusually troubled or unhappy. It is rather to draw attention to more general constraints and limitations of common ways of talking about singleness. The culturally available and familiar resources for understanding singleness are highly polarized.

I argue that the cultural context today incorporates new representations of singleness while continuing to draw on older, more devalued notions that being single is a problem for women: generally to be solved through commitment to a heterosexual relationship. For instance, works such as Candace Bushnell's (2005) *Lipstick Jungle* (from which the second extract at the opening of this chapter was taken), as well as her earlier (1996, 2004) *Sex and the City* on which the successful US television series was based, offers versions of modern women acting confidently, succeeding in business and creative arts, pursuing close same-sex friendships that seem as important as their sexual relationships, and acting with spirit and independence. While these themes contrast with traditional romantic fiction, there is some continuity in the narrative threads of such works which often involve the resolution of dilemmas in getting or holding on to a man.

The importance for a woman of finding and keeping a man is extremely well embedded in western culture, and hard for many of us (myself included) to question. In a radio interview celebrating forty years since the publication of the influential *The Female Eunuch*, Germaine Greer was asked by an audience member whether she thought her book had resulted in men preferring more spirited women. Greer wondered whether men want women at all, suggesting that as women get more demanding, men get increasingly shy of commitment and more neurotic about being entrapped. She suggested that 'if we get any more uppity, men will decide to do without us altogether' (BBC 2007). 'So have we shot ourselves in the foot?' asked the questioner. How many other listeners, like me, pondered for a moment on whether we had, and whether forty plus years of feminism were responsible for a worsening of female/male relationships?

Greer, of course, had a ready riposte: 'Ah well, that depends on whether you think what a woman really needs is a man! I think probably a woman does need a man like a fish needs a bicycle!' The position taken by Greer here is an extreme one: yet in arriving at this strong statement she had first envisaged that it was the men who will 'decide to do without us'. And on her way she told anecdotes of men or women living in her home describing men pursued by women as 'the phone rings off the wall', while women 'wait and wait'. In such representations of women as needy and men as detached, Greer recognizes some widely prevailing understandings, alongside her challenge to the orthodoxy on what a woman needs.

The strong cultural hold of a romantic ideal of fulfilment through a close and continuing intimate relationship can leave those without such a relationship feeling stranded and excluded from normality argues Trimberger (2005). If single women are in some way marginalized, this becomes an issue for their presentation of themselves and their conversational practices. My participants demonstrate rhetorical work in weaving their ways through the extreme contrasts of a denigrated or an empowered identity. These polarized ways of thinking create a 'troubled identity' for single women.

Singleness is an important topic for feminism and there is a need for sustained analysis of the marginalization of women who are not engaged in a long-term intimate partnership. There are changing cultural definitions of what it means to be 'single' and who can be included in this category. Rather than seeking to define singleness more precisely, an aim in this book is to consider the new and different associations linked to singleness as a category as well as more long-standing notions of this status.

My initial interest in singleness was because of my own experience of over twenty years of living alone, following the break-up of my marriage when I was just 25. I had not expected to be on my own for so long, and found it hard to explain this to others and to myself. Although explanations were not regularly solicited there were the occasional 'how come a nice girl like you is on her own?' kind of comments. One time, when I was away for a short break with a collection of cycling enthusiasts, a married chap in the group expressed over dinner his amazement at a collection of three single women – such remarkable beings – sitting and chatting together. We realized we were a phenomenon simply outside his experience.

Finding 'the one' for a proper relationship never seemed like the main object of life in my thirties and forties. Couple relationships with men did occur for me from time to time, and probably I did hope to encounter someone with whom I could form a lasting attachment. When I looked back I wondered whether any of the sexual relationships that I had during this period really 'counted' as relationships, since none of them had led to long-term commitment.

At the time I commenced my research I was not unhappy, and I had a strong network of friends and an active social life. Yet it seemed to me that the kind of experiences that I and other single friends had were not well represented in the media and that there was little public awareness or understanding of the lives of single women. The sexual double standard – whereby men can have multiple relationships and remain in some way glamorous, while women cannot – was still alive and well. Although from an earlier era, the images from the Eagles' song, 'Take it easy', still typified male and female sexuality (Browne and Frey 1972). The man was running down the road with seven women on his mind (all of whom he was intimately involved with) and still expecting the one he was about to meet to save him with her sweet love! The traditional male preserve of road movies had been joined by *Thelma and Louise* – vibrant, assertive women – but you knew before the weekend was out they would meet disaster and be punished by the death option out of the range of possible road movie endings.

Lucy, *Mary Tyler Moore* and a later spin-off, *Rhoda*, were some of the situation comedy programmes shown in the UK through the 1970s and 1980s featuring single professional women. Few female leads in the 1980s were allowed to appear as divorced or unconcerned about getting a man (Atkin 1991). When, in the 1990s, women began to appear as single in programmes where romance was not the driving force we were alerted as viewers to problematic areas in their lives, as in the alcoholism of the character of Christine Cagney in *Cagney and Lacey*.

Although there had been research on single women by the 1990s, for many social researchers they were still not on the radar. When I repeatedly had to correct academics at seminars and conferences when they misheard my research topic as 'single mothers', I realized that single women as a category in their own right were invisible. I was drawn to the idea of 'giving voice' to women's experience, and framing more positive accounts of the richness and variety of single lives. However, as I explored the research literature I recognized that there was no shortage of accounts of the experience of women on their own, yet these under-theorized thematic accounts added little to knowledge and understanding. Where single women were dealt with more systematically in the academic literature the focus was on their potential problems. Studies recounted women's sense of hurt and loss in 'aloneness' (Bickerton 1983; Lewis and Moon 1997).

There have been many changes in women's lives: they have greater opportunities for economic power and satisfying careers. Yet singleness for women continues to be remarkably resistant to losing an association with a discreditable identity. The steady production of self-help literature aimed at single women over the last 70 years gives a taste of popular conceptions of the issues of the time (Anderson and Stewart 1995; Bristow 2000; Hilliard 1956; Hillis 1936; Hodgkinson 1993; Lewis, K.G. 2001; Payne 1983; Roulston 1951; Smith 1952). The fictional character Bridget Jones, who appears to have a large collection of self-help books to turn to, suggests they are a 'new form of religion' (Fielding 2000: 75). In identifying the problems that self-help must tackle, authors are also conveying how single-ness is understood more generally in society. So what are the changing representations of singleness in self-help literature, and what kind of consistency has there been over the years?

Self-help for the single woman

Marjorie Hillis (1936) in her guide for the 'extra woman', *Live Alone and Like it*, aims to address women whether rich or poor and, with a dry wit, sets out a plan for being independent. She writes as a single woman. She assumes that her reader may have chosen to be modern and single, may belong to the army of lonely hearts 'with nobody to love them', or may have a fleeting solitary existence between husbands.

It is interesting to compare this work from the 1930s with one from the new millennium. Wendy Bristow's (2000) work, *Single and Loving it*, advises on how to be happy and whole when there is no other half. This author is also single, but writes after having divorced for the second time. Her assumption is that the reader who is single has arrived there after an ending to a relationship, and the book is divided into three parts to reflect what she sees as phases to singleness: 'recovery from loss, learning to be alone and dating again'.

Hillis is bracing, caustic but funny, commenting on lonely hearts:

> This is a group to which no one with any gumption need belong to for more than a couple of weeks, but in which a great many people settle permanently and gloomily.
>
> (Hillis 1936: 15–16)

Bristow, in contrast, is sympathetic and intense, advising women to recognize their periods of 'longing', whether for a lost love, or a love 'we never seem to find', but ultimately to detach from it so that 'you're in control of it, rather than it controlling you' (2000: 178). Both in their different ways are recommending that self-pity be avoided.

Hillis (1936) opens by asking the reader 'Who do you think you are?' and advises that she should stop thinking of herself as pitiable, a widow or a spinster, words 'rapidly becoming extinct'. 'A woman is now a woman, just

5

as a man is a man, and expected to stand on her own feet, as he (supposedly) stands on his' (Hillis 1936: 26). This lays down a marker for the times for today's reader of the influence of the earlier wave of feminism, changes resulting from the First World War and the notion of a 'new woman'. Hillis recommends developing a positive mental picture: 'you'll need at least two things: a mental picture of yourself as a gay and independent person, and enough spunk to get the picture across to the other person' (Hillis 1936: 19).

Bristow also asks her reader 'Who are you?', and in keeping with a present-day trend of development of the self, advises that 'You can't have an effective, fulfilling relationship with anyone unless you have one with yourself' (2000: 105). Again, where Hillis is brisk but mocking, Bristow turns to inner exploration and self-understanding.

However much these books from different eras put forward strategies for liking or loving the single state, they have in common the expectation that finding a relationship with a man is the desired end goal of the reader. The advice contains the implicit assumptions that singleness is not the norm; that no one would be single if they could avoid it, and that single women need to act in a way that overcomes other people's hostility or indifference. Living alone, it seems, is not naturally the desired state, but can be turned into a pleasant experience. It involves obstacles to be overcome and requires determination and an effective strategy.

Even more sociologically based work focuses on strategies for individual women to take to combat prejudice and myth and often has much in common with self-help literature. For instance, Carol M. Anderson and Susan Stewart (1995) talked to approximately 90 women in a midlife range (mostly between 40 and 55 years) who were either never-married, or divorced or widowed. All participants had lived alone for some years or for their adult life, although many of them were in committed relationships. The voice that predominates in the text is that of a woman who has not chosen to be single, but nonetheless survives and flourishes without a partner.

The work is interesting in demonstrating changing and conflicting representations of singleness. The authors focus on positive examples of single women in 'midlife', 'flying solo' in 'uncharted territory'. They aim to provide models of singleness for other single, and even married women, and write of challenging the myths concerning the disadvantages of the single life. The book's starting point, which is not explored in depth, is that in popular opinion single women are inevitably unhappy. Anderson and Stewart's work is not unusual in focusing on this taken-for-granted premise, and in producing examples of fulfilled single women to challenge popular opinion.

There are a number of academic studies that focus on the incidence of stress or distress among single women, generally finding that there is little to distinguish single women from the general population in relation to life satisfaction (Davies 1995; Loewenstein *et al.* 1981). Indeed, what would be unusual would be to find a contemporary academic work that argues that single women are, in general, unhappy.

Work such as Anderson and Stewart's appears to be based on the belief that by reading about positive examples of women who have 'succeeded' at being single, others will be reassured and inspired. Yet, by challenging ideas of singleness as problematic, authors also privilege such ideas, and give recognition to their force and power. There is a reliance in such work on a simplistic model of social change, which targets the single woman herself as able to resist stigmatizing attitudes and change them through her positive approach.

Anderson and Stewart say that they began their project by looking for 'successful' midlife single women, and they assumed that success would be associated with prestigious positions. Instead, they found themselves directed to women who did not match this definition. They changed their preferred participant group to women who 'felt good about themselves and their lives'. This formulation may be responsible for a rather prescriptive tone to the text, which tells the single woman what she needs to do in order to feel good about herself, drawing on the lessons from the authors' case study style presentation of findings. The approach is upbeat, presenting an idealized picture of singleness for middle-aged women, and is permeated with the metaphor of flying, for instance:

> Flying solo successfully, they say, is very much a question of attitude. Of course, women do need resources and opportunities, but securing these begins with realizing that they deserve to fly. And while all this is possible earlier in life, it is easier at midlife, as our middle years bring us the confidence and courage many of us need to give our souls the gift of flight.
>
> (Anderson and Stewart 1995: 288)

The authors advise that three main points summarize how women in their study became confident: accept who you are; dare to dream of a new destination; and take action.

This positive advice, which goes far beyond reporting on and discussing research findings, shapes, directs and tells women what they need to do in order to be single properly. The authors move from description of what women report to prescription for single women. They provide women with instructions for how singleness should be practised. The focus is on the problems of the single woman as personal ones, amenable to personal solutions. There is little recognition of the 'public issues' of singleness (Byrne and Carr 2005) and the evidence from the literature of a political and gendered dimension to singleness (Adams 1976; Bickerton 1983; Chandler 1991; DePaulo and Morris 2005a; Rosa 1994).

Changing practices in relationships

The examples discussed above give some indication of changes in the anticipated readership of books on singleness. This reflects shifts in social behaviour and in the numbers getting married, divorced, living together and remaining single. These changing practices mean it is also difficult to get precise figures on how many women might be considered single. Statistics can at best offer a snapshot; for instance, only in recent years have same-sex relationships been included in the General Household Survey under a category of cohabitation. However, the overall indications are that the proportions getting married are declining, while single households are increasing.

In 2005 in Great Britain, 49 per cent of all women over 16 years were married and 10 per cent were cohabiting: outside either of these categories are 41 per cent who were either single, widowed, divorced or separated (Office for National Statistics 2006a: Table 5.1). As a glimpse of how things have changed over time, between 1979 and 2005 the proportion of women in Great Britain who were single (that is, not including the widowed, divorced or separated) aged between 18 and 49 years more than doubled from 18 per cent to 39 per cent (Office for National Statistics 2006b: 3). In the same period, the proportion of non-married women in this age group who were cohabiting at the time of the interview increased from 11 per cent to 29 per cent. The proportion of cohabiting women who were single (again, not including the widowed, divorced or separated) increased from 8 per cent to 31 per cent in 2005 (Office for National Statistics 2006b: 3). Information from the 2001 Census shows that 30 per cent of households in England and Wales were one-person households: an increase from 26.3 per cent in 1991.

Figures from the USA are similar, showing proportions of divorced, widowed or always single growing from 28 per cent of the population in 1970 to more than 40 per cent in 2002. The number of one-person households in the USA has increased so that there are now more of these than there are households of married couples with children (DePaulo and Morris 2005a). Scase (2000) notes that by 2010 single person households will become the predominant household type in Britain too. He predicts that the increase will be pronounced among those of younger middle age, and more middle-aged people will live alone not only because of divorce and separation, but also from personal choice (Scase 2000: 24).

There are fewer married women than in the past, and correspondingly more women who remain single in the legal sense of not being married; there are also more women who are in a cohabiting relationship who account for a significant proportion of the higher number of single women. There are additionally increases in divorce, separation, lone parenthood, step-families and greater acknowledgement of same-sex relationships (Williams 2004).

Census and General Household Survey figures cannot give fully accurate information on more complex forms of relationship, but responses to an Office for National Statistics question on 'living apart together' give rise to tentative estimates that two million men and two million women in Great Britain aged under 60 have a regular partner who is living in another household (Haskey 2005). What is clear from the changes in marriage, divorce and cohabitation figures is that there are many dimensions to singleness, and that it is increasingly the case that most women experience periods of living alone at different stages in their adult lives.

Theories of contemporary relationships

A number of social theorists have provided analyses of the changing practices in contemporary relationships. Writing of the German context, Ulrick Beck and Elisabeth Beck-Gernsheim (1995) argue that there is currently a collision of interests between love, the family and personal freedom. They diagnose that the nuclear family, built around gender status, is falling apart on issues of emancipation and equal rights. In Germany, as in the UK, single person households are growing in number (Beck and Beck-Gernsheim 1995). For women, argues Beck-Gernsheim, the ties to the family have loosened as a result of improved contraception, the impact of more equal opportunities in education on young women's ambition and increased opportunities for women to work. For the first time, women are not dependent on marriage for economic security. They can choose:

> perhaps not altogether freely but more than before, whether they really want to marry or to stay single, and whether to seek a divorce rather than put up with endless conflicts if the marriage does not turn out as they hoped
>
> (Beck-Gernsheim 1998: 59)

There are, of course, questions as to why what might appear to be personal matters and decisions should take on such 'epidemic' proportions (Beck and Beck-Gernsheim 1995: 4). Beck and Beck-Gernsheim's theory is that *individualization* is driving these changes. Each historical period creates particular types of people, and in this current period needing to 'become what one *is* is the hallmark' (Bauman 2001: xv). Human 'identity' is no longer a 'given' but a 'task' (Bauman 1998: 27). 'The ethic of individual self-fulfilment and achievement is the most powerful current in modern society' (Beck and Beck-Gernsheim 2001: 22).

The possibility of leading a life that is fully one's own emerges when a society is highly differentiated, so that people are integrated into society only in their partial aspects as taxpayers, car drivers, patients, mothers,

9

sisters, pedestrians and so on (Beck and Beck-Gernsheim 2001). Beck and Beck-Gernsheim refer to a shift from family interests to individual interests as the primary drive for decision making. In the current climate, it is argued, individualization opens up all decisions for personal choice and people have to take on individual responsibility for choices instead of considering the overriding interests of the marriage. However, any freedom is only relative, since the demands of the labour market and the demands of relationships are in conflict.

Anthony Giddens (1992) also theorizes a relationship and sexual revolution. He traces the breaking of the connection of sexuality from its association with integration, reproduction, kinship and the different generations. He provides a new term, 'plastic sexuality', to describe this independent sexuality, freed from the needs of reproduction. According to Giddens, the availability of reliable contraception has brought about a revolution in female sexual autonomy and undermined the overweening importance of male sexual experience.

In Giddens's view, ordinary women as well as feminist thinkers have pioneered a move away from an ideal of romantic love, based on the primacy of the marital relationship as a lasting shared commitment. In its place is an ideal of 'confluent love', based on equality in emotional give and take and an expectation that the relationship will only last as long as it is satisfying to both participants. Now that more women are able to work and are no longer confined to the home, and as a result of the pressure from feminists, they expect more equal relationships that have to be worked at constantly and negotiated. The result, rather than the cause, argues Giddens, is the separating and divorcing society of today.

Giddens (1992) characterizes the changes as a 'transformation of intimacy' and proposes that trust has to be continually worked at in relationships in modern society (Giddens 2005). He suggests that the self becomes a reflexive project, involving a narrative of self. Needing to tell a story about the self is a consequence of a self less anchored in traditional structures, according to Giddens. While the changes involve freedom for women the new situation of the self is surrounded by anxieties. Women are caught in stresses and strains in achieving a new identity, especially as they are caught between the wish to have a family and the wish to have a career (Giddens 2005).

In a 'portfolio of rough and fragmentary sketches' Bauman takes up some implications from Giddens's work. He describes a world of rampant individualization, where relationships are a mixed blessing (Bauman 2003). Relationships, argues Bauman, are nevertheless seen as the central medium for satisfaction, all the more in so far as they have been found unsatisfactory to date. At the same time, we experience contradictory and forceful drives for freedom as well as a craving for belonging. Loose and revocable relationships have replaced the model of 'till death us do part' (2003: 90).

Commitment is to be avoided: instead people like to 'see how it works' in their relationships (2003: 36).

Critics of these theorists point to the lack of empirical work underpinning their arguments; a general focus on more privileged lifestyles; and the failure to engage with existing theoretical arguments (Fontana 1994; Jamieson 1999; Jiminez 1993; Lewis, J. 2001; Turner 1993). Through a review of academic research, Jamieson (1998) critically examines the notion that intimacy is at the centre of meaningful life in contemporary society. She argues that Giddens's vision of the future draws selectively from the range of available evidence, and does not sufficiently explore those aspects of the wider context that perpetuate inequalities between men and women. Jamieson distinguishes between the 'public stories' of social change and the 'everyday private practices' (Jamieson 1998: 158). She suggests that the view that 'disclosing intimacy' is increasingly sought in personal life may over-dramatize a selected aspect of the variety of ways in which people create intimacy (1998: 160). In contrast, she argues, love, practical caring and sharing of chores and domestic responsibilities remain as or more important in many types of relationship.

In a research-based exploration of changes in parenting and partnering and the implications for social policy, Fiona Williams (2004) emphasizes the interaction between changes in living and relationship arrangements and other social, cultural and demographic changes. More women participate in the labour market, growing numbers have the earning capacity to finance mortgages and live independently. Housing costs have risen. Fewer people experience lifelong marriage. A multicultural society means a diversity of family traditions and care commitments may span continents. Women having fewer children, or having them later in life or not at all, along with a longer life expectancy and an ageing society have also altered the course of lives compared with earlier generations (Williams 2004). Williams calls for a new framework for thinking about families, relationships and care and argues that a focus on intimacy tends to underplay the importance of other kinds of relationships, for instance those between children and parents or commitment to other kin and friends.

Challenges for feminism

From different analyses discussed above, it would seem likely that women who have chosen to stay single or to divorce are in the vanguard of social change. Some of the literature on the transformation of intimacy is implicitly hostile towards singleness, seeing in it the triumph of individualization and the breakdown of family and community (see Lewis, J. 2001 for a review). It might be imagined that the single woman is now positioned as a powerful player who can negotiate for relationships that meet her needs. However, there are different strands to social change that suggest other outcomes, for instance the feminization of poverty, which means some women face the choice of dependence on a male breadwinner or dependence on welfare benefits; or the work-centred focus of the professional woman (Beck and Beck-Gernsheim 1995). Oppressive poverty or the lack of time for leisure pursuits can both leave single women disengaged from relationships.

Single women negotiate their relationships in a context that still carries strong patriarchal expectations for women of a continuing sexual relationship (Bickerton 1983; DePaulo and Morris 2005a; Rosa 1994), and heteronormative assumptions that this will be with a man (Walby 1989). Byrne and Carr suggest that single people are caught in a 'cultural lag' between macro-social changes that encourage singleness as a desirable option and persistent cultural ideals that retain marriage as the ideal state (2005: 84). Throughout this book I argue that the discursive context, within which women gain and articulate their own understandings, contains highly contradictory representations of singleness. Like Jamieson (1998) I see some distinctions between the public stories of social change and everyday private practice. However, the 'practice' which forms the basis for my evidence is the practice expressed through talk. It would be difficult to gain direct knowledge of how and with whom women engage in practical expressions of intimacy. What can be examined is the way in which women talk about such activities. Talk is not simply a medium for conveying information about other practices; it is itself the subject of scrutiny. People draw upon public stories as resources for making sense of their own experiences, and in this sense the public stories are highly influential.

Single women are a crucial group for study in relation to the perceived changes in family life and relationships, and yet their experiences and situations have not attracted detailed attention from social theorists. One reason for this is that interest has often centred on what is happening to 'the family' and 'marriage' or 'relationships', and on building a picture of normality in relation to these different institutions. In constructing normality, it is often the case that groups that do not fit the image of normality (single persons, the childless) are screened out (Beck-Gernsheim 1998). Yet it is important to study women who are on their own in relation to claims about social change.

Feminist theorizing has influenced the developing analyses of the changing social context discussed above, and this is explicitly or implicitly acknowledged, although the roots and sources are not always traced in detail. Feminist practice in the latter half of the twentieth century has also contributed to the social changes that are under scrutiny. Thus feminists at the same time developed the tools for analysis and set in motion the changes.

Singleness is an important topic for feminism: however, it is a topic that has also remained at the margins of feminist theorizing. While feminism has drawn attention to the possibilities for women to live independently of men and actively shape their own lives, much of the debate has focused on the imbalance of power in relationships between men and women (Dowling 1982; Greer 1971; Hite 1993). Theorizing on what Adrienne Rich (1980) called 'compulsory heterosexuality' has been a significant challenge to the terms of the debate. However, what seems to be compulsory is not just heterosexuality but long-term partnerships of any sort within a marriage or cohabitation (Rosa 1994). There has been little sustained analysis of the marginalization of women who live alone without a long-term intimate partnership with another adult. While not all women who are alone would consider themselves to be feminists, it is likely that a better understanding of this group will have important lessons for feminism.

Changing practices in defining singleness

There is some difficulty in discussing singleness since cultural definitions change with regard to who might be considered single. These definitions in turn reflect the changing social context. There is, of course, one meaning of 'single' in the sense of categories in relation to legal marital status: here it means 'never-married' and contrasts with other non-married categories of widowed, divorced and separated. However, for purposes of research or popular writing on singleness, at different periods 'a single woman' has been taken to mean: chaste, never-married and childless (Hillis 1936); or to include the divorced and widowed, but not lesbians (whether or not they are in a couple relationship) or parents (Adams 1976); or to include all of these categories but not those currently in cohabiting relationships (Gordon 1994).

The meaning of 'singleness' is elusive. In the terms of Saussure's theory of language, it is both a 'signifier', that is, a written or spoken image, and a 'signified', the concept or meaning that is attached to the signifier (Saussure 1974: 67). The meanings of singleness, or what it is that is being signified, have differed over time, as is shown in the examples of how writers have defined singleness. There is no natural or constant connection between the word 'singleness' and the meaning that it conveys: the meanings are socially produced. Weedon has argued that the signifier 'woman' changes its meaning from 'victim' to 'object of sexual desire', according to its context (Weedon 1987: 25). In a similar way, 'singleness' has different meanings which offer different subject positions for women, for instance: 'celibate', 'solitary', 'independent', 'desperate for a man' or 'powerful'. Subject positions are the different identities that may be brought into play through different ways of talking (Davies and Harré 1990; Edley 2001), and I discuss these more fully as a tool for analysing my data in Chapter 3. The different subject positions and the meanings conveyed depend on the discursive relations within which singleness is located. Singleness is thus open to constant rereading and reinterpretation.

13

As well as changes in definitions, there are changes in the common representational practices associated with singleness: what it is that is being signified. One of the aims of this book is to consider these new and different associations now linked to the category 'single' and their relationship with continuing and more long-standing notions of the single status.

'Otherness' and systems of difference are important in language and semiotic systems for constructing identity. What the varying definitions have in common concerning who is included in discussion of singleness is that they are formed by stating what the single woman is not: not sexual, not married, not a parent, not living with a partner. Over time, the definition of singleness appears to be expanding to cover previously excluded categories, although some recently emerging work returns to a focus on single women who have not married and are not currently in a cohabiting relationship (Byrne 2000; Simpson 2003, 2006).

The question of cohabitation is complex: it is a category that can include single people (meaning not legally married), although many researchers on singleness have seen cohabitation as similar enough to marriage to exclude those living in cohabitation from their studies. In contrast there are 'living apart together' partnerships (Haskey 2005) that do not involve cohabitation. These include divorced men or women with offspring who choose not to cohabit again until the children have grown up, referred to in *The Observer Magazine* as 'semi-detached' couples. 'They may be around-the-block-a-few-times couples, busy career builders, single parents or just highly independent types' (Rice 2002).

Williams (2004) highlights some interesting articulations of what defines a partnership and the nature of the commitment in the process of creating civil partnerships. 'Emotional and financial commitments' are referred to as the basis of partnership in the proposals on civil partnerships, and in response as to whether civil partners have a duty to cohabit the proposals said:

> Cohabitation means living in a shared household. The obligation to cohabit can be achieved by separate homes, which can form one household if this is the customary arrangement for the partners concerned.
> Women and Equality Unit (2003: 37) quoted in Williams (2004: 38)

Such blurring of definitions of partnership makes problematic any common-sense categorizations of those who might be considered single and those who might not (see Roseneil 2006 for a discussion of the complexity). In the course of doing the research for this book I changed the way I categorize myself. At the time of my interviews I considered myself single: it is difficult to pinpoint the time I began to think of the man whom I was seeing regularly as a partner, but it predated our decision to live together.

As a result of the same set of legal changes as civil partnership, introduced in the UK in 2005, the words 'spinster' and 'bachelor' will no longer appear on the marriage or civil partnership certificate of anyone, but will be replaced by 'single' as the relevant marital or partnership status. Media comment has generally seen this as a positive step, viewing 'spinster' as a word with negative connotations of being no longer young and unlikely to marry (Bindel 2005; Gledhill 2005).

Age is another problematic aspect to discerning different meanings of singleness. Is singleness age-related, and if so, how do its parameters work? Is a 14-year-old single? Probably not in most people's everyday understanding, being below the age of consent, but what about a 16-year-old? What about an 85-year-old whose husband has just died? Or a woman of 70 years who has recently divorced? In relation to the midlife single woman Nancy Berke argues she is 'always already dumped', by which she means the dumping of society's judgement: 'the social insult of having something wrong with her because she never "settled down" with anyone' (Berke 2006: 242). Is there a 'proper' age for being single, and is this notion linked to expectations of marriage or partnership?

A feminist discursive analysis of singleness

Women rising valiantly above the inherent difficulties of being single, or working through grief and a sense of loss from their 'aloneness' was not the focus I wanted for my work.

I found promising theoretical insights from Margaret Adams (1976), whose work points to the social construction of singleness, and the results for those who are living lives that run counter to public understandings of femaleness and femininity. She argues that psychological theory is used to define singleness – essentially a social situation – in terms of deviance and deficiency. Her innovative work does not appear to have been built upon and developed by later authors in an effective way. In considering theory to examine the social construction of singleness, I saw the need for some exploration of discourses: regimes of talking about singleness. The available ways of representing singleness seem likely to shape how women on their own make sense of, and talk about, what they do. These discourses may well constrain the possibilities for a sense of identity that emphasizes positive aspects of singleness.

What I seek to develop in this work is a feminist discursive analysis of 'singleness'. Several theoretical commitments have guided my empirical research (Reynolds and Wetherell 2003), and I discuss them here. These commitments consist of five linked claims about 'singleness' and follow variants of discursive psychology, and social constructionist thinking about identity issues in social psychology (Wetherell 1998). These claims are that the single state is best viewed as socially constructed; that singleness is a social category; that singleness should be studied as a discourse; that singleness should also be studied as a set of personal narratives and subject positions; and finally that singleness is not just socially constructed, a social category, a discourse and a set of personal narratives and subject positions: singleness should also be a politics.

The single state is best viewed as socially constructed

The ways in which we understand the world and ourselves are not the only ways of understanding. Everything that we take for granted could be otherwise (Gergen 1999: 47). Theories of social construction collapse distinctions between material existence, social relations and systems of meaning. Foucault, for instance, argues that nothing has any meaning outside of discourse (Foucault 1972). Of course there are things that have a natural existence in the world, but it takes the system of representation that is involved in discourse to give them meaning.

This notion brings into sharp relief the shifting patterns of meaning through which singleness has been understood historically as well as the changing pattern of social arrangements and social practices for regulating relationships. It is a reminder that singleness, like marriage, is not a 'natural' fact or a natural social arrangement. It highlights the historically and culturally variable status of singleness. Consider the contrast, for instance, between the quotations at the beginning of this chapter, highlighting post-millennium celebration of the single life as proactive lifestyle choice and the extract below from an advice book by an 'unmarried woman doctor' looking at 'love and life' in the 1950s:

> The unmarried woman has to face up to herself and her life. She's got to stop expecting life to be fair. Life isn't meant to be that way at all. Life doesn't owe her a handsome adoring husband and two beautiful children full of bright sayings – life owes her nothing. She has to reorganize her thinking so that she can be grateful for the good things that happen to her and work her way through the bad things without a sense of defeat.
>
> This is the bitter, desperate adjustment that the single woman has to make. Nothing will again be as painful as the moment she realizes that she will live all her life alone; no moment will ever hurt so much.
>
> (Hilliard 1956: 68–9)

At an empirical level, this shifting social appraisal draws attention to the relativity of current relational forms. It raises questions about the other ways relationships might be constructed and why some particular modes and representations of the single state dominate social organization now.

Some representations of singleness for women, in contrast, prove particularly enduring. Janet Fink and Katherine Holden (1999) argue that the figures of the spinster and the unmarried mother have been positioned in Britain throughout the nineteenth and twentieth centuries at opposite ends of a spectrum of female deviance. They demonstrate through a review of representations in mid-Victorian fiction, interwar Hollywood melodrama and British films of the 1950s and 1960s that the portrayal of female sexuality outside marriage has remained remarkably consistent over time and genre (Fink and Holden 1999). For instance, they note that the imagery of an unmarried mother employed by artists and novelists in early Victorian England was frequently of a solitary, shabby woman excluded from polite society. The postwar films selected by Fink and Holden include *The L-Shaped Room* (1962) and they find a return to the stereotype of the nineteenth century and the related imagery focusing on the woman's sexual deviancy. While sexual behaviour may be more overt in these films, there appears to be a prohibition on enjoyment either of the sexual act or of motherhood. The films warn that pre-marital and extra-marital relationships intrinsically lack pleasure and that the birth of an illegitimate child will result, as in the nineteenth century, in the woman's marginalization by society (Fink and Holden 1999).

If singleness is a variable social construction, this has implications for how single people make sense of who they are, to themselves and to each other. It is of interest how people constitute themselves as recognizable members of particular identity categories, and how they hold each other accountable for such memberships. This leads me to my next theoretical commitment.

Singleness is a social category

I understand categories and categorization from a discursive rather than a cognitive perspective (Edwards 1997; Potter and Wetherell 1987). As Harvey Sacks has argued, categorization-in-use is revealing about social order (Sacks 1992). Sacks has drawn attention, for instance, to the workings of common understandings of singleness as age-related, in everyday conversational practices, to produce the category of 'unmarried'. 'When persons 25 years old say in assessing themselves that they're unmarried, they're told "No, you can't say that yet."' (Sacks 1992 Volume I: 68). Such responses suggest that there is indeed a recognizable age at which it is 'proper' to consider oneself as unmarried.

Categorization practices and the flexible resources these provide for constructing relationships and events at any given moment (single versus married; cohabiting versus married; living alone versus cohabiting; spinster versus bachelor; parent versus childless; wife versus mistress and so on) help provide an orderly and accountable framework in social life. The use of categories suggests an order for that moment.

Categories give different opportunities for drawing contrasts. Newspaper articles written following John Profumo's death variously described Christine Keeler as 'the woman with whom Profumo denied any impropriety in a statement to MPs', a 'showgirl', a 'call girl' as well as, more unusually, 'the laughing teenager' (Agencies 2006; Kettle and Kennedy 2006; Parris 2006). These descriptions offer contrasting categorizations and suggest correspondingly different contexts for the descriptions. A 'laughing teenager' offers an image of innocence and youth, in contrast to the complex combination of sophistication and defilement more readily associated with a 'call girl'. Depending on which categories are selected, descriptions become differently infused with value-laden or emotive associations.

Difference can also become hidden when categories are conflated within an overall category framework. The category single can be worked through many different category contrasts, and constructions of 'otherness' and 'sameness', 'outsider status' and 'insider status', to produce a wide range of accounts and evaluations (Hester and Eglin 1997). The question then arises, among all the possibilities, why are some repeated over and over?

Much of the literature treats the categorization of singleness as a natural, rather than socially constructed, phenomenon. Questions of meaning often concern finding the *correct* definition. Does the category just include the 'never-married' (Allen 1989; Peterson 1981) or what some call the 'ever single' (Reilly 1996) or does it extend to the divorced, the separated and the widowed, those who are 'single again' (Lewis and Moon 1997), and those who live in long-term partnerships but are not married? In contrast to debates on who is *really* single, my interest is in how the category is constituted. I want to re-focus research, therefore, on 'how' the social category of singleness is constructed rather than 'who' really is a member. How do the methods of categorization work and what are the institutional and identity consequences and implications of different formulations?

Singleness should be studied as a discourse

Singleness is a set of complex meanings and practices. The *discourse of singleness* produces knowledge, forms of truth and expertise (see Hall 1997b). To speak about singleness is to speak in relation to this discourse. Stuart Hall has helpfully summarized Foucault's discussion of what is included in the study of discourse (Hall 1997b: 45–46), and I have adapted his summary below to apply to single women:

1   Statements about 'singleness' or 'aloneness' which give us a certain kind of knowledge about these things, and the ways in which this knowledge works to regulate conduct.

2   Rules which prescribe certain ways of talking about these topics and exclude other ways – governing what is 'sayable' or 'thinkable' about singleness at a particular moment. What such rules expose about the workings and effects of power.

3   'Subjects' who in some way personify the discourse – the lonely spinster; the swinger; the available woman; the social network activist; the dangerous divorcee; the family helper; the fiercely independent battler; the self-reliant coper – and particular attributes we would expect these subjects to have, given the way knowledge is constructed about the topic at the time.

4   That this knowledge acquires authority and embodies the 'truth' about the topic at a historical moment, with 'truth effects' for those who live in this category. Some ways of living are considered normal and unexceptional, while others require accounting for.

5   Practices within institutions for dealing with the single. For example, an insistence that women should specify their marital status in all sorts of ordinary interactions such as placing an order with a shop, or making a dental appointment; routine expectations that husbands or partners are included in social invitations; a courtesy title of Mrs extended to women attending hospital appointments. Single women's conduct is regulated and organized according to those ideas.

6   Acknowledgement that a different discourse will arise at a later historical moment supplanting the existing one – opening up a new *discursive formation* and producing in turn new conceptions of singleness, with new authority to regulate social practices in new ways.

The last point is an important matter for Foucault. Discourse is historicized, and things only have meaning within a specific historical context. As I have already noted, singleness is not an objective fact that is the same in all historical periods. Only within a definite discursive location can singleness appear as a meaningful construct (Weedon 1987). One of the puzzles of Foucault's formulation is how the discourse changes – what opens up the way for a new discourse to supplant an old one? Although Foucault rejected the term ideology (Foucault 1980), in my view it is also helpful to see singleness as an 'ideological field', following the definition of ideology suggested by Billig which sees the processes of everyday thinking and talking as processes of ideology (Billig 1991; Wetherell and Potter 1992). The ideological field of everyday talk is a patchwork of contradictory possibilities, and speakers encounter dilemmas in trying to reconcile the different implications. If we see the processes of everyday talk as processes of ideology, then we must recognize that speakers are at the same time in charge of the language they select, and limited by its possibilities (Billig 1991). This allows single women some agency in influencing and shaping the discourse.

Both the terms 'discourse' and 'ideological field' stress that the shifting patterns of meaning which construct singleness are formed in relation to power. Singleness is a discourse regulating conduct. Discourse explains the working of power on behalf of specialist interests, and it can be used to analyse the opportunities for resistance to it. At the level of the individual it offers an explanation of where our experience comes from – we draw on the discourse to give shape to our experience – and why it is contradictory, or incoherent, and why and how it can change (Weedon 1987). I would expect to find that singleness is a discourse which naturalizes and pathologizes, creates patches of visibility and patches of invisibility and mystifies some forms of being while normalizing other forms. I anticipate that it is likely to be an ideological field organized through commonplaces, tropes and dilemmas, a highly variable and inconsistent patchwork of representation (Billig *et al.* 1988; Wetherell and Potter 1992).

Singleness needs to be studied as a set of personal narratives and subject positions

Social history, social practices and the ideological field around singleness construct different cultural slots and sets of identity possibilities. They are possibilities rather than a fixed and static model of identity controlled by an ideological field. The process of living in these slots and living with these possibilities (working with them, complying, resisting and transforming them) becomes a personal identity project for the individual single woman. As Giddens (2005) observes, the self is a reflexive project that involves creating a story about the self. However, there are limitations to what kind of self can be narrated within a particular cultural context. In developing narratives and accounts of themselves, and in making sense of their lives and life choices, people work up the discursive resources available as identity. Indeed, narratives are a way of managing identity in a shifting, fragmented and complex ideological field. In this respect categorization practices and the discursive field of singleness produce a psychology and modes of subjectivity.

Identity is a negotiated performance. I am interested in the everyday ways in which women who are alone make sense of their situations in talk and conversation. In line with previous research in discursive psychology (Marshall and Wetherell 1989; Wetherell and Potter 1992), I would expect that their accounts will be highly variable, the identity positions developed will be distributed and multiple and the contradictions and inconsistencies will be informative about the constitution of the discursive field of singleness as a whole. I would also expect some continuity in the ways that women understand 'singleness', and that it should be possible to find some patterns within and between accounts. I assume that identity is 'precarious, contradictory and in process, constantly being reconstituted in discourse each time we think or speak' (Weedon 1987: 33). The immediate situation and local context of each conversation will shape the way in which identity is performed.

As well as mapping these fragmented patterns, and discussing their psychological implications, I also aim from a feminist perspective to critically evaluate the kinds of identity resources on offer to women to negotiate their identity projects. This leads me to my final guiding principle.

Singleness should also be a politics

In other words, it is an arena in which feminists need to develop further strategies of resistance and develop a collective voice which might help women position themselves in much more enabling ways. Just as meanings of singleness change over time, it is likely that the focus of resistance will change.

For example, feminists of the second wave, such as Greer, targeted marriage as the problem for women: 'If independence is a necessary concomitant of freedom, women must not marry' (Greer 1971: 320). Greer's vision, which now seems utopian, was that women would be freer if they entered partnerships without the shackles of marriage. Feminists of her period were critical of the power relations within marriage, and some who chose not to marry perhaps also sought to undermine the social distinction between married and single, heterosexual and lesbian.

In contrast, Joan Chandler points to the privileging of all couple relationships over singleness (Chandler 1991). She suggests that all women are in the shadow of marriage, and that there are degrees of marriage, since many women who are outside conventional marriage still have some domestic connection with men. Rather than limit her focus to marriage as such, her analysis broadens out to the wide range of heterosexual relationships that are in some way influenced by the structure and social expectations of marriage. There are links, she argues, between being a wife and femininity, and between marriage and women's residual role as economically dependent:

> For all women marriage casts a long shadow, part of the way in which they are defined and categorised by their relationship to men. Wifehood is keyed into womanhood to socially stigmatise those who are unmarried. In this way the structure and ideology of marriage are central to the gendering of women.
>
> (Chandler 1991: 2)

Becky Rosa targets a slightly different problem: she argues that the monogamous couple relationship has come to be seen as the only 'natural' way of structuring society (Rosa 1994: 117). This leaves single heterosexual women, like lesbians, to dispel the myth that women should be dependent on a man. Rosa comments that single women are penalized as a result.

These contrasting politicized discussions of singleness suggest that categorization practices have proved remarkably flexible in carrying forward cultural divisions. Similar contrasts are produced whether the distinction is between married/single, heterosexual couple/single or monogamous couple/single. As what it means to be married or monogamous changes its meaning, one aspect for what it means to be single has continuity – it is defined by what it is not. There is likely to be continuing work for feminists in exploring changes and continuities in understandings of singleness and identifying the political tasks implied.

I explain and justify this set of theoretical commitments in more detail in the course of this book. I introduce briefly below the focus of my empirical work.

I have several reasons for focusing solely on women rather than including men who are on their own. Singleness is generally acknowledged to be a gendered category that works differently for men and for women (Adams 1976; Dowling 1982; Faludi 1992; Gordon 1994; Greer 1971). Just as marriage involves gender power relations (Dryden 1999), so does being single. As a feminist, I want to work with categories defined by women, for women (Cline 1993). There are arguments for working comparatively across genders, especially in the light of claims that living alone is 'bad for men' and makes them sad (Scase 2000). There may be some shifts in contrasts in the discursive context, but in this book I argue that the canonical images of lonely spinsters and eligible bachelors continue to be pervasive, despite some newer images of socially active women as compared with sad, isolated men. Detailed attention to the discursive climate for single women, which is different to that for men, is a legitimate task in itself.

Moreover, although there have been some attempts to work comparatively in relation to singleness for women and for men (Stein 1976, 1981; Wile 1940), most of this work is now out of print, and does not form a good basis for new work. There is a tradition in the main bodies of work on singleness of focusing on single women (Allen 1989; Anderson and Stewart 1995; Bickerton 1983; Chandler 1991; Clements 1998; Gordon 1994; Jeffreys 1985; Trimberger 2005), and this is helpful in reviewing the changing meanings of singleness for women. My aim is to build upon this tradition, using a feminist perspective and introducing new tools for analysis of the discursive context of singleness.

With regard to research participants I take an inclusive approach. It is not clear that there is widespread agreement over whom the label 'single' applies to, nor whether further changes may take place. Since my interest is in exploring the different meanings of singleness, I have tried not to narrow down the category in a pre-defined way that might prevent some meanings from emerging. I wanted to see how women work with the idea of 'single-ness'. My interviews were with a total of 30 women. My aim has been to treat the interviews as 'discursive events' (Wetherell *et al.* 2001) which would allow me to explore the range of interpretative resources participants drew on, and the kind of meaning-making that was going on. The analytic approach I have followed is one characteristic of critical discursive psychology (Wetherell and Edley 1999) that blends insights from the ethnomethodological and conver-sation tradition with those from Foucauldian-inspired concepts of discourse.

This book explores a number of related questions. How do women who are on their own make sense of, and talk about, singleness and relation-ships? How do new and different cultural resources employed by women in their talk interweave with more historical discourses of the woman's place? How is agency and choice understood by women in relation to their single state? What power relations structure their experience of singleness? How do women work rhetorically with stigmatized aspects of singleness? What kind of collective and personal strategies are there to help women either to fit neatly into the cultural slots for singleness or to put up some resistance to them? More detailed questions drove the analysis for particular data chapters.

2

CONTRASTING MODELS OF A SINGLE IDENTITY

Gone now the years of my halcyon twenties
And thirties are looming alarming ahead
And family members have started their sighing
Indulgently at me and shaking their heads

'Cause here I am, the family maiden aunt
Oh isn't-it-sad, marriage-hopes-are-fading aunt
The lonely-future-expectation-laden aunt
I wonder what on earth's to become of me now?
(Small 1982)

Introduction

On the day before my wedding my brother remarked to my husband-to-be that the future stages of our life were set out before him. Indicating me, my mother and my grandmother he said 'Well John, you've got the 22-year-old model, the 60-year-old model and the 91-year-old model. What do you think?'

While amused by his comment, I was alarmed at the idea that the passage of years would reveal similarities in the three of us, let alone that they might be visible right now. Considering his point now, what were these 'models' that my brother spoke of? Could they be thought of as stages in a woman's life cycle? Perhaps even as stages in singleness, for although I didn't think of it that way at the time, we were all at that moment single. My mother and grandmother were both widowed, my grandmother having been separated for some years from her husband at the time of his death (the separation never later referred to and a well-kept family secret). The message that I took from my brother's joke was that John might be heading for a future with these two further models of womanhood, rather than the one he was familiar with. He could though, perhaps more threateningly for John, have been pointing out two further examples of women on their own.

What is the single identity and is it useful to theorize it as an identity that has different, identifiable stages in a life cycle? In this chapter I turn to issues of the subjectivity of the single woman, and trace some ways in which the single identity has been theorized in the empirical social science litera-ture. Empirical work on singleness has drawn extensively on psychological and sociological frameworks developed for broader purposes of examining human experience. A rich variety of different models of identity has been employed, although at times the theoretical stance has been more implicit than explicit. The distinctive approaches used by different authors are identified in this chapter, as well as the wider range of psychological and sociological literature that underpins theoretically the different models of identity. In turn, I review life cycle, psychodynamic and experiential models of identity as applied to single women.

These models permeate western cultural traditions, and popular fiction and media representations also make use of all three. For instance, Bridget Jones (Fielding 1996, 2000), 32 years when she first appeared in a column, aged only three or four years over the next decade (Vernon 2005). Similarly, the female detectives at the centre of the respective series of works stretching over decades by Sara Paretsky (1987, 2002) and by Sue Grafton (1990, 2005) never age significantly. Grafton deals with the problem of needing her detective, Kinsey Millhone, to be of an age considered suitable for romantic adventures as well as high-risk detection work by locating all episodes in a brief period of time in the past, while V.I. Warshawski, Paretsky's central character, ages at a different rate from the years in which the books appear (life cycle). Both characters have complex childhood experiences that are drawn on to explain their adult characters and their relationships with men (psychodynamic). Each of these women also resists conventional stereotypes of singleness, showing feistiness, independence, control, warmth and achievement (experiential).

I am interested in the multiple possibilities for subjectivity that these different models offer to single women as resources for thinking and talking about themselves. As well as discussing the models, I outline the contrasting approach to theorizing a single identity that this book aims to develop.

In brief, I understand identity as something that we can only know about through looking at social practices, since the inner subjectivity remains hidden from the researcher's view. My approach aims to view single women more as social selves rather than self-contained individuals (Burkitt 1991). I regard identity as a negotiated performance that may be performed differently for different sets of circumstances. Rather than something that is fixed and unchanging, I expect the single identity to be shaped by the wider cultural resources available to the individual woman, her own personal history and the conversational turns suggested by the immediate situation. The use that I make here of the different theoretical models of identity that emerge from the empirical literature is to examine and explore how single women draw on these models in their talk and in their sense-making of their experience.

There are not precise equivalents in the purpose and usage of different models of identity. Life cycle and psychodynamic models tend to be used by authors writing of their clinical practice with single women in therapeutic settings, although some authors (for instance, Allen 1989) are more interested in developing theoretical tools for their empirical study. In contrast, experiential models are more often used by authors writing of their qualitative research or enquiry. It is rare, in this area, for one model to be used to the exclusion of all others. Most writers acknowledge the force of social and cultural expectations, and the effects of cultural representations on women's self-image. For instance, while many writers draw on psychodynamic thinking, none of these seek to suggest that all difficulties encountered by single women stem from early unconscious influences.

There are many useful insights and approaches to singleness in the literature, but my purpose here is to review a range of 'ideal types' for the explanations given in relation to identity and singleness. What do different models imply when pursued in a rigorous fashion? What does the 'single identity' mean according to different models? What different ways do they offer a woman on her own of understanding her life and her current situation?

Life cycle model

Several writers on singleness have attempted to make sense of single women's lives through the adaptation of family life cycle or developmental models (see, for instance, Lewis and Moon 1997; Schwartzberg *et al.* 1995). I have grouped different models here under the umbrella term of 'life cycle'.

Basic assumptions of life cycle models

Life cycle models are often used in literature on family therapy (see, for instance, Carter and McGoldrick 1980). Such approaches generally draw on the notion of development as a biological phenomenon, and the sets of beliefs and cultural expectations that people have about change and development. Cultures vary in how different transitions are conceptualized – the age at which children are expected to leave the parental home, for instance, or the impact on a family of childbirth. However, life cycle approaches assume that there are some universal aspects of development that present the need to adapt and change at key transitional points, such as courtship, marriage, birth of children, children leaving home and retirement.

Identity in this model is something that changes, adapts and develops appropriately according to the life circumstances. It is a social model of identity, based on cultural expectations of the individual at key life points, but with an underlying assumption that some aspects of development must be negotiated whatever the cultural context. The individual will not necessarily feel that she is acting according to social requirements, but will perceive the stages identified as having resonance in her own life. There will be a sense of comfort and fit, or lack of it, according to her ability to negotiate these stages successfully.

Literature on singleness and the life cycle model

If key transitional points involve marriage and child-rearing then the life cycle model is deficient in capturing the life stages of women parenting on their own, or who are childless. However, some writers have nonetheless attempted to extend the model and create a variation to embrace the lives of single women. Schwartzberg *et al.* (1995), writing of their clinical practice in family therapy, add their own modifications to the life cycle model, to highlight the developmental issues relevant to the single adult. They make use of the concept of differentiation of self (the process of defining one's separateness and connection to one's family) as a key to understanding the single adult's position in their nuclear family.

Schwartzberg and colleagues argue that the emotional interconnectedness of family members' lives in the present and the past is what gives meaning to people's lives. Thus in looking at the life cycle of the single adult, they advise therapists to look at the impact of other family members' life stage issues, as well as how the family as a whole accommodates to the life choices of its members. For instance, parents who have expected to see their adult children marry and have children may feel and express disappointment when this does not take place. According to this model, and indeed most common understandings, my impending marriage would be a cause for celebration, rather than an opportunity to reflect on different stages of singleness, which my brother's observation might have invited.

Since the organization of rearing children is not a key focus for the single, childless adult, Schwartzberg *et al.* argue that this particular stage division is irrelevant for them. They look, instead, for other developmental drivers that push the individual and family through time, such as relationship with work, finances, peer network and family and culture.

However, without the purposes of family and child-rearing processes, the stages suggested by Schwartzberg and colleagues look rather bleakly focused on ageing and health. The progression is:

- not yet married
- the thirties: entering the 'twilight zone' of singlehood
- midlife (forties to mid-fifties)
- later life (fifties to when physical health fails)
- elderly (between failing health and death) (Schwartzberg *et al.* 1995: 56).

While the authors warn that this should not be seen as a hierarchical progression, with one stage building on another, in their schematic depiction of the model, emotional processes are linked with specific life period stages. For instance, the thirties involve:

1   facing single status for the first time
2   expanding life goals to include other possibilities in addition to marriage (Schwartzberg *et al.* 1995: 56).

This model is so firmly rooted in the stages involved in the cycle of families, that it appears that what single people are needing to negotiate is their deviation from the normal progression of family life and child-rearing. Chandler (1991) criticizes life cycle and life course models for not being sufficiently rooted in the variability of the social context. She argues that they make assumptions about typical individuals and families.

Another life cycle approach is from Lewis (1994) and describes eight non-sequential developmental tasks for adult singles. Placing the emphasis on tasks, rather than progressive age and biology related stages, removes some of the more overt depiction of the single life as deviant. However, Lewis's non-sequential tasks become progressively more age related as we move down the list of eight (adapted from Lewis and Moon 1997: 129–30):

1   grounding (in the home, neighbourhood, career, finances, social life);
2   friendships (having close female friends, pruning close friendships – keeping them compatible with personal and professional growth, making new friendships);
3   basic needs (for daily contact, security, touch, rituals, enhanced use of free time);
4   sexual feelings (acknowledging them, numbing them, transitioning between);
5   children and other forms of nurturing (making a decision about children, nurturing self, nurturing others, being nurtured by others);
6   grieving (accepting the ambiguity, grieving lost dreams, separating a single woman's grief from her family's grief);
7   making peace with the parents (teaching them to treat the single woman as an adult, resolving old issues or finding a tolerable place for them, accepting the positive traits/styles/rituals and rejecting the rest);
8   old age (having a positive image of the single self in old age, preparing financially, maintaining friendships, considering living options, preparing for death, e.g. will, burial arrangements).

These tasks are proposed as relevant for adult single people and it is not made clear by the authors whether they are also adaptable for adults who marry – they appear fairly universal tasks in the summary given. From that point of view, this model is potentially more inclusive, and therefore less stigmatizing than that from Schwartzberg *et al.* But the model is predicated on a notion of acceptance and adjustment to the changes that come with ageing and continued singleness. Such notions of age-appropriate attitudes and behaviour have been criticized for their oppressive and ageist nature, for instance in *Growing Old Disgracefully* (The Hen Co-op 1993). There are assumptions in this model of identity that there are particular sorts of feelings that a single person can expect to have, and by implication, a 'right' way to have these feelings (grief and its resolution, acknowledgement of sexual feelings, which can then be placed in abeyance).

What happens if you've passed Schwarzberg *et al.*'s 'twilight zone' or numbed your sexual feelings as advised in Lewis's model – is that the end of all sexual activity? Fortunately we know from Jane Juska's (2003) audacious account, of breaking a period of celibacy following her personal ad in the paper, that women in their late sixties can still have adventures in sex and romance at any age.

The variations of the life cycle model have a prescriptive feel. According to the Lewis model (1994), once she has succeeded at the developmental tasks a woman will be living her life in a number of life-enhancing ways. There are cultural assumptions built into this vision of well-adjusted single life. However, because it is not obvious that they are cultural assumptions, women may define themselves as deficient if they cannot deal with the task outlined. Similarly, some women may experience as pressure the insistence of Schwartzberg and her colleagues on the individual confronting her status and defining an authentic life for herself within the single status. A woman who is not currently involved in an intimate relationship may feel required to define herself as single and plan her life accordingly. While this may suit some, others may hope that by keeping their status undefined they can maintain a range of possible options.

In summary, the problems with the application of a life cycle model to the lives of women alone are the claims that the model makes. The model purports to incorporate fundamental biological imperatives, fundamental aspects of change in roles and relationships as well as societal aspects of change and organization of relationships (Dallos 1996). It needs therefore to be universally applicable and recognizable to single women as well as their wider families. The family life cycle model as described by Carter and McGoldrick (1980) may have little personal relevance to some single women. However, it will have meaning for them as a dominant cultural storyline, or master narrative that shapes their lives, as it may be the course that they and others have expected their lives to take. They may experience the model as a source of oppression.

What kind of identity is being proposed by variants of the life cycle model? Although the notion of a person going through stages aims to incorporate change and transition in the individual life, it suggests quite a fixed and static identity, where the same basic character matures and develops but does not deviate from the track. Therapists are advised by Schwartzberg *et al.* to help the single person shift their life story from one of lack of marital status, yet the basic model does not incorporate an assumption that self presentation is fluid and that individuals can make use of shifting narratives.

Katherine Allen (1989) employs a life course variation in analysing her data from a comparison study of 30 women born in 1910, half of whom had never married or had children, while the others were widows. She claims that this builds on the strengths of the developmental approach but departs from the idea of a normative family life cycle. Nonetheless, she identifies a 'process' described by the unmarried women by which they had never married. This road to permanent singlehood is described by Allen as a 'hidden event' in the female life course (Allen 1989: 77).

In that ideas about a life cycle are embedded in the cultural context, they cannot be discarded as intellectual tools, and may be useful resources for some women. I am intrigued by Allen's (1989) notion of a hidden event, and indeed a process of not marrying, that is an essential component to an account of being single. Could it be that the expectation of marriage and family life is so strong that the women in her study may have felt required to account for their non-participation in this event and retrospectively explain the process? My own data suggest that the cultural storyline of the family life cycle is one which women may use to position themselves against, in explaining why they made the choices they did (Chapter 4). My interest is in how women may represent their lives in terms of a life cycle model, and in looking at the practical features they construct through their talk (Gubrium and Holstein 1994).

Psychodynamic models

Psychodynamic models are often shadowed in the literature on singleness, although they are rarely used explicitly or exclusively to explain and work with issues for single women.

Basic assumptions of psychodynamic models

The term 'psychodynamic' stems from the tradition developed by Freud and extended by other psychoanalysts, and goes beyond this to encompass a wide range of changing ideas about what drives social life (Thomas 1996). The perspective aims to find generalizations about psychological processes, but the data come from the clinical work of psychoanalysts. Psychoanalysts prioritize the subjectivity of the person they are studying (Frosh 1989). The

30

aim is to make the actions and emotions of the subject intelligible through causal explanations at the level of the subject's desires. However, individuals are themselves often unaware of their own purposes and meanings.

The idea of psychological defences is central: according to psychodynamic thinking, we structure our lives defensively in order to avoid anxiety. The internal versions of the world are formed very early in life, and are emotionally charged constructions (Thomas 1996). Experiences in childhood are thus very important in psychoanalytic theory, although there is a good deal of disagreement among psychoanalysts about the nature of the child's subjective world.

One criticism of psychoanalysis is the preoccupation with an individual level of explanation. The explanatory notions of psychoanalysis are always complex, but rarely enough so to incorporate the power of social forces into its frame of reference (Frosh 1989). Chodorow critiques the tendency in clinical practice to focus on the sense of self and relationship that comes from the individual family (1995). She argues that it is important to look at cultural practices as well:

> How people conceptualize themselves as gendered varies by a number of factors, including culture, history and early family development – the *specifics* of the family and its meanings [. . .] What becomes important are not just anyone's femaleness or maleness, but the psychologically and culturally *specific* meanings that gender holds *for them*.
>
> (Chodorow 1995: 100)

Feminist therapists have tried to transform the therapeutic relationship through feminist understanding that women's psychology is formed within a particular social context (Eichenbaum and Orbach 1987: 51). Eichenbaum and Orbach draw on sex-role theory within their psychodynamic model. They suggest that a woman's psychology is defined to a large extent by her designated social role as a mother. She will have been brought up to take on the social role of caregiver and nurturer. A further defining feature for Eichenbaum and Orbach is the idea that a woman has only reached adulthood when she has connected herself with a man. In order to find a man, she must make herself into someone that others will find appealing.

According to Eichenbaum and Orbach (1987) many women have difficulty in experiencing their own identity as a separate free-standing person who relates with other separate people. The argument is that women seek self-definition through relating to others. They may stay in unsatisfactory relationships for fear of a loss of self if they were to withdraw from the relationship. They seek new relationships driven not just by need for connection, but for identity.

31

Literature on singleness and psychodynamic models

We might expect an 'ideal type' psychodynamic approach to understanding women alone to emphasize:

- early experiences which influence the potential for intimacy and closeness;
- the difficulty women have experienced in separating themselves from their mothers and their subsequent need to be needed;
- distress attached to unsatisfactory relationships in the past;
- the effects of previous losses on current sense of self;
- the formation of defences to protect against such distress, which may make closeness more difficult to achieve;
- hankering after a relationship driven by the need for identity.

Quotations in the literature on singleness from women's own accounts suggest that psychodynamic thinking is often drawn on by women to make sense of their circumstances. For instance, Siegel interviewed 51 older single women comparing their motivation towards marriage with 51 demographically matched married women. One of Siegel's respondents says:

> Marriage is something that I have always wanted and never been able to put together. I go to the single-mothers groups and they say we are stronger and more independent, and that's why we don't have relationships or successful relationships with men. Then when you really get to know them, you find that most of us come from highly dysfunctional families and there are real problems there in not having successful dual relationships. I used to pick the wrong kind of guy because of unconscious factors motivating me to pick people who weren't treating me well.
>
> (Siegel 1995: 204–5)

'Picking the wrong kind of guy' is also a common theme in self-help books, which may explain why it has become a resource used by women to account for their own behaviour. Robin Norwood (1990) for instance, in her influential *Women Who Love Too Much*, proposes a syndrome of co-dependency. According to Norwood, women who have come from severely troubled families choose men who have problems and are emotionally unavailable. By doing this they unconsciously recreate and relive significant aspects of their own childhood.

Tricia Bickerton (1983), writing of her workshops at the Women's Therapy Centre, London, for 'women alone', identifies the relationship between mother and daughter as crucial to a woman's lack of self-esteem. Daughters, she says, are taught to believe that their lives depend on another, and are therefore ill-equipped to imagine life on their own. It is hard for the adult woman to understand her own needs, or go some way toward meeting them, when her identity has been formed on the basis of serving others.

Bickerton explores difficulties for some women in forming close, sexual relationships, and argues that individual reasons are important as well as social structural constraints. She suggests that women may have formed defences in childhood as necessary for survival, which they then continue to operate in adulthood. Memories of being touched may be painful or faint, and getting too close may feel terrifying. While a relationship may be desired, the fear of losing even an artificial independence may seem more disturbing. Resentment at not having a sexual partner may emerge as bitterness related to early relationships, which then deters anyone who comes too close. Unexpressed anger towards others can stop a woman from acting on her own behalf (Bickerton 1983).

This is a powerful articulation of psychodynamic theorizing on the single identity, and a description that has a number of fictional counterparts. A contemporary example is Barbara Covett, the sixty-something narrator in Zoë Heller's (2004) *Notes on a Scandal*. Her interactions with others are curt and often hostile, yet she wonders why all her friends fall out with her. There are glimpses of longing for closeness: with a younger male teacher, and with Sheba, the attractive and confused new teacher whom Barbara tries to protect and control following the scandal of the title, her affair with a schoolboy.

According to Bickerton, a woman may fear her own negative hostile emotions and imagine their devastating effect on others. There is often the fantasy that she is destructive and undeserving and must keep her distance – that being alone may be a punishment for her badness (as seems to be the case with Heller's character). Some women, argues Bickerton, will drive themselves towards perfection in the hope of finding lasting relationships, striving to achieve more, or become more attractive. She identifies this as a defence that may appear necessary to prevent collapse, but which serves to prevent any real contact being made.

Despite the force of these descriptions, there are some difficulties in combining theorizing about social and cultural expectations of women with a more classic psychoanalytic hypothesis of specific problems in the past re-emerging for women who are alone. There is circularity in the identification of potential problems rooted in the individual woman's past as a cause of her remaining single. If women are normatively likely to feel inadequate, to suffer low self-esteem, and to be driven by social expectations that maturity involves connection to a man as Eichenbaum and Orbach (1987) argue, in what way are psychodynamic processes also causative for some individual women, preventing them from forming intimate heterosexual relationships as in Bickerton's portrayal?

How can judgements be made as to the relative importance of cultural constraints and individual pathology (Reynolds 2002)? If a woman assumes her failure to achieve intimacy is because of her own pathology, but then goes on to form a satisfactory sexual relationship, how should this be understood? Has she overcome her problem, or was her earlier distress simply a normal reaction to her cultural conditioning? If all women suffer low self-esteem, would all benefit from psychotherapeutic help? The significantly higher number of women than men seeking therapy, in many clinics comprising two-thirds of all patients (Bankoff 1994), suggests that this is what many women have come to believe.

Concepts of loss and grief form another area on which therapists writing on singleness have focused as integral to the single identity. The losses discussed include the disappointment at not having children; loss of time in searching for a man; loss of assurance about the future. At no point do women know for sure that they will not marry in the future – as long as there is the hope of marriage, there is the pain of ambiguity (Lewis and Moon 1997: 126). There is also the loss of previous relationships.

Lewis and Moon (1997) report that the women in their study wanted certainty, rather than the pain of ambiguity. With the certainty that they would not meet a man, they would be able to get on with their lives. Yet some uncertainty would seem to be part of the human condition. Marriage and relationships also involve uncertainty (Duck 1994). I suggest that internalizing and externalizing the blame are both ways of dealing with uncertainty, and as long as marriage-type relationships are privileged above all others, thereby inducing a sense of failure in those not in such relationships, women will continue to move between these explanations.

There is much sensitive description of single women's concerns and fears in the literature that draws on psychodynamic traditions. It can be empowering for women to read and identify feelings that they have also experienced. The approach also offers some solutions, which adds to its attraction as a set of explanations. However, these solutions may be turning social issues into psychological problems: a major criticism of psychodynamic models.

Lewis and Moon hint at the dangers of psychologizing, as they caution that therapists should distinguish ambivalence that is unconscious. In contrast they depict some women as aware that they are acting positively to counter their family's pessimism about being single, or because they think it is politically correct, while still feeling lonely. However, Lewis and Moon seem to have fallen into a trap of dividing their subjects into those who have legitimate contradictory feelings, and those whose contradictions are still hidden from them. In reality, there is little that can distinguish those who are working with 'social contradictions', and those who are working with 'unconscious contradictions', and this is a crucial problem with the psychodynamic model of identity.

Psychodynamic models are tied to finding individual solutions to what are essentially conceptualized as psychological problems. There is thus over-emphasis on treating as dysfunctional, aspects of women's development which are also presented as normative. Calls to therapists to avoid participating in a woman's self-blame may not meet with positive effect, since a psychodynamic model does not offer guidance on distinguishing what is socially constructed and what is individual pathology.

The very nature of therapy is to help its subjects change, yet the emphasis in psychodynamic approaches on early childhood experience produces quite a pre-determined model of identity. Identity appears to be formed at a very early age, and this leaves little room for later identity-forming experiences. The influence of feminist theorizing has allowed for a conceptualization of a gendered identity, predicated in the case of women on connectedness, but this still is founded on an identity that is formed from early experiences.

A difficulty in making use of psychodynamic models for research purposes is their focus on areas of personality that may remain hidden from the individual concerned. While such explanations may be compelling and convincing, they are not verifiable. The individual herself is by definition debarred from knowing whether they are correct, and others do not have access to her subjective experience. In contrast, as the quotation from Siegel's (1995) study suggests, women may come to believe in a psychodynamic explanation of their situation, and act in accordance with such beliefs. This in itself gives such explanations considerable force.

While my data are not clinical case history, and not amenable to psychodynamic interpretation, I am interested in the use that women make of psychodynamic explanation of their situation. It may be empowering for women to draw on psychodynamic understanding and find recognition of their feelings. I wonder, though, to what extent does the use of a psychodynamic framework tend to *produce* a particular type of feeling – by giving sanction does it also give expression? In the analysis of my own data I look for ways in which my participants employ a psychodynamic way of thinking about their lives.

Experiential models

Much of the literature on singleness might be said to rely on an experiential model of identity. Unlike the other frameworks discussed, there is not a coherent body of work setting out the experiential model, but it can be argued that a lot of important work is encompassed within a broadly experiential perspective. Richard Stevens suggests that phenomenological, existential and humanistic perspectives have in common a focus on subjective experience (Stevens 1996).

Basic assumptions of experiential models

A phenomenological perspective involves trying to understand human awareness as we experience it. The basic assumption is that what people are feeling and experiencing is the most significant information. For existentialists the capacity to reflect on our own experience of being a person is vital. The basic assumption here is that there is a dynamic quality to human existence. Existentialists believe that we are able to choose our thoughts and actions and in doing so we create who we are, and search for meaning in life. Humanistic psychology focuses on finding ways to help people become more aware of their feelings and experiences. Stevens identifies three key features in these approaches to identity:

- to be a person is to experience oneself as existing in the world
- to be a person is to be an active intentional agent who engages with, and can influence, the world
- to be a person is to possess reflexive awareness (adapted from Stevens 1996: 153).

Literature on singleness and experiential models

It is not surprising that the experiential model has found a home in the growing literature on singleness. The focus on subjective experience offers the promise that women's voices and experiences can be heard without an intervening interpretation of what these experiences really mean. As Gilligan's empirical work has shown, women often have different modes of describing their relationships and identity (Gilligan 1982). In a period when women appear to be discovering new ways of living, according to some, without reliance on traditional roles and scripts (Clements 1998; Reilly 1996), it seems appropriate to explore what these new experiences have meant to those undertaking them.

The strength of the women's movement has had much to do with the sharing of experience, and efforts to formulate understanding and theory from grass-roots personal experience. Consciousness-raising groups explicitly sought to discover commonalities in women's experience, and 'the personal is political' encapsulates this approach. An experiential approach to understanding and accounting for identity can be a powerful force for change.

An experiential approach to understanding the identity of single women treats women as able to reflect on their experience of singleness and to extract meaning from this experience. It assumes that women find different meanings in the state of singleness, but that there will be nevertheless some common themes in what different women say, and that it will be possible to conceptualize from these themes to say something sensible about the state in general. There are, however, questions about how far, and when, singleness is considered by individual women to be salient for them.

An experiential approach depicts single women as able to make choices and act autonomously in the light of their experience and their feelings about their experience. It will treat their understandings as worthy of fuller exploration, and credit them with the ability to change and adapt to their singleness (see, for instance, Byrne 2003). An experiential approach will not look for meanings that are beyond the awareness or grasp of the individual women.

In a broad sense all of the qualitative and ethnographic research on single women draws on an experiential model insofar as it assumes that the women can make sense of and comment on their experience. Dalton describes an explicitly phenomenological research design she used to explore the meanings of singleness to women who have never married (Dalton 1992). Her framework has some limitations in theorizing the different meanings of singleness. Having come up with thirteen categories of meanings for singleness – such as singleness as self-reliance, as a burden, as openness, as self-acceptance and so on – she argues that women experience different aspects of singleness, but that furthermore, individuals experience all these aspects at once. However, descriptions have meaning in the contexts within which they are used, and in my view a more useful approach would be to try to understand the contexts of the women's narratives and the resources they draw on for their multiple descriptions.

There are several authors who use a form of presentation which has more in common with journalism than a research study, and use case studies of the women talked to, where they present pen pictures of individual women, supplemented by occasional direct quotes. The work by Peterson (1981), Anderson and Stewart (1995), Reilly (1996) and Clements (1998) is all of this nature, and the work is organized into a framework of themes pursued in different chapters with commentary from the authors. The authors make explicit use of their own experience as single women to a different degree, the accounts are readable, but under-theorized, with the representation of experience presented as unproblematic.

A number of authors argue that choice is central to positive experience of being single. Reilly, for instance, characterizes as 'singular' the women in her study who have made a successful journey from girlhood, and found an identity that can sustain partnership or do without it. 'The singular woman likes herself, she values her place in the world, and she makes her way through the world without apology' (Reilly 1996: 7). What such discussion points to is the way in which images of women who succeed in living alone happily are *marked* by their gender. When a category is marked, it stands out as unusual. The gender that is unmarked (in this case male) is assumed to be doing what is normal (Tannen 1995). The very notion of independence is associated with maleness, while dependence is associated with femaleness. There is therefore an implicit assumption that to be single, whether by staying in this state or as a result of relationship breakdown, is difficult, undesirable, and requires adjustment. Women who have managed to adapt well to the conditions of singleness and turn their situation to their advantage are not what might be ordinarily expected, instead they are *singular*.

The area of distinction in what I have characterized here as an experiential approach is in the emphasis on women's capacity to reflect for themselves on what they want from life and to come up with answers. This contrasts with models that may be delivered through self-help books or through therapy, but which impose a structure of stages or tasks that need to be accomplished. Reilly suggests that her stories of singular women offer all women a different kind of feminine narrative. One which is in many ways accidental and messy, but nevertheless existing in the midst of a 'culture that portrays its women as dependent and passive, as happy only in marriage, as productive only in motherhood, as potent and interesting only in youth' (1996: 200).

There are some tensions between the social scientist's need to present some patterns in their material, and the inevitable proliferation of possibilities that different stories of experience produce. Marcelle Clements (1998), for instance, presents clusters of excerpts edited down and organized into themes, preceded by an introduction in which she says she attempts less to answer the questions raised by respondents than to offer a parallel commentary. The result is hard to make sense of or evaluate, with very scanty descriptions of each speaker, which do little to locate them in the reader's mind. Tuula Gordon (1994) adopts a more conventionally academic ethnographic approach. Her theoretical discussion is illustrated by quotations from her respondents, organized in thematic chapters. However, the effect of this approach, which collects up like examples in order to support a point, is to iron out difference. Because brief quotations are taken out of context to reinforce majority views, there is in this work again little sense of what these comments might mean for an individual woman in the context of her life as a whole.

Gordon describes herself as interested in research that '*gives a voice*' (1994: 41, her emphasis). Her aim was that 'interviews and the analysis form interlocking sets of narratives: my narrative is one of selection and interpretation, but not of silencing' (1994: 41). It is an attractive idea to give a voice to women who, according also to Clements (1998), have no collective sense of themselves. Perhaps the degree to which this can be done depends on what the overall purpose is. An experiential approach can help people transform their own lives, or that at least is the supposition that informs existentialism and humanistic psychology. The kind of understanding that others can gain from the voices of a few will always be uncertain. Whether voices are presented directly or mediated and summarized, there is always a filter of selection and representation which is liable to distort or misinform.

The use of experiential models in literature on singleness has considerable strength in exploring aspects of the lives of women alone, in acknowledging the different ways in which women make sense of their experience through their individual accounts, and in drawing attention to messiness, complexity and variation in such experiences. There is, however, a tension between presenting snapshots of experience which are left to speak without inter-pretation and are under-theorized, and collating and categorizing experi-ence in ways which may distort or conceal difference. There may also be a tendency to assume that there is something pure and untainted about experience that gives access to the 'truth'. It is important to remember that what can be collected are women's reflections on their experience. These reflections are themselves the product of social interpretations. They tell us about the kinds of thoughts which women are encouraged to have as a result of the social context in which they live. Joan Scott has pointed to the theoretical and political need for experience to be deconstructed, and for the analysis to be situated:

> Experience is at once always already an interpretation *and* some-thing that needs to be interpreted. What counts as experience is neither self-evident nor straightforward; it is always contested, and always therefore political.
>
> (Scott 1991: 797)

This politicized aspect of the experiential model, also illuminated by Weedon (1987), forms the contribution of women's subjective experience to feminist politics. As such, it provides a context for my own analysis. Weedon argues that rather than subjectivity providing a coherent and authoritative inter-pretation of 'reality', a useful theory needs to make use of the subjective, and to show where women's experience comes from, and how it relates to material social practices and the power relations that structure them (Weedon 1987).

While Reilly (1996) and Clements (1998) suggest that single women are 'scriptless', without the usual structures, or any collective sense of them-selves, they do not examine this through empirical work. This requires analysis of the conversational structures employed by participants and of the wider cultural resources drawn upon in social interaction. My own work aims to fill this gap with detailed analysis of patterns in interpretative resources used by participants in my research. Are there traces of 'scripts' to be found in how women talk about singleness? In order to describe their experience of life alone, what narrative traditions can and do women draw on? Are there some commonly accepted ways of parcelling up and account-ing for experience, or are women finding new ways of describing their lives?

Developing an approach to single identity as discursively constructed

Each of the different theoretical models of identity that appear in the empirical social science literature on singleness I find in some way deficient in giving a proper account of the self that works well in thinking about singleness. Much of the theorizing involves an emphasis on the inner psychology of single women that tends to pathologize them. This focus places the responsibility for coping with or transforming singleness upon the individual. All too easily this can lead to seeing the issues of singleness as aspects of personal deficit. I aim to develop a theoretical approach that is more truly social psychological, and which recognizes more fully the public issues without always turning back to private troubles as the focus for action.

In contrast to the models I have described, the model that I seek to develop dissolves the firm division between society and the individual. Instead of assuming that individuals are separate and self-contained, and that they can be considered in a way detached from the social context, I view the self as the result of a continuously changing and fluid history of relationships (Gergen 1999; Wetherell and Maybin 1996). Bruner argues that the self has to be seen as 'distributed': made up of many daily practices such as people's work, friendships, writing, letters, diaries and daily communications, in locations well beyond the boundary of their physical bodies (Bruner 1990). Individuals are social beings, who use socially developed resources in producing their own communications and understandings. In this sense society and individual are the same thing, viewed from a different angle (Burkitt 1991).

In arguing that the individual and the social cannot be separated, Robert Connell (1987) maintains that there is no such thing as individual practice, there is only collective practice:

> A personal life is a path through a field of practices which are following a range of collective logics and responding to a range of structural conditions which routinely intersect and often contradict each other.
>
> (Connell 1987: 222)

For Connell personality *is* practice, seen from the perspective of the life history. People do experience themselves in terms of a life trajectory – but even though we may conceive of this as a life cycle, it is *not* cyclical and personal history is *not* unfolding. Instead it is something we make – a construction. Like Connell I understand 'identity' not as a consistent and fixed entity, determined from early childhood, but as something more fluid and adaptive to the changing circumstances of a life. We do not have 'identity' we have 'identity projects' (Connell 1987).

40

There are aspects of the models of identity discussed in this chapter that I make use of in developing a theoretical perspective that sees identity as a project rather than something fixed. These aspects are all linked to social practices. The notion of a set of practices around being a person seems a more fruitful way of conceptualizing singleness. Such practice can be thought of as psycho-discursive (Wetherell and Edley 1999): occurring in talk and also implicating a psychology as the speaker develops a sense of self through the different subject positions taken up. Singleness then becomes something that people *do*, while making full use of their own capacity to extract meaning from their actions and the actions of those around them. The models that I have found in the empirical literature on singleness are ones that single women may draw on in making sense of their lives and use in working on their own identity project. In this sense, they form a powerful influence on how singleness is experienced. The process is not, however, a matter of discovery of a pre-existing 'single identity' or consistent core of self. Instead it involves multiply constructed identities, or identifications, across intersecting and antagonist discourses, practices and positions (Hall 2000).

Powerful social practices regulate women's behaviour from childhood, for instance through families and schooling (Walkerdine 1990). Valerie Walkerdine looks at the cultural images available to young girls and how they use these images to position themselves. She argues that the possible positions that an individual may take are embedded in social practices. Similarly, single women are aware of the cultural representations of singleness, such as those described in the literature. My argument is that women do not accept these images uncritically, but work with the cultural material they have been given, and use it creatively in their accounts of themselves.

From the perspective of an identity project, singleness is not something that is a given and which fixes us, but is something that we work with. We do have scripts, but these are occasioned by particular contexts and for particular conversational moments. We have stories and narratives through which we make some sense of our lives – and we do this often in psychological terms. The idea of an identity project is of course also a cultural construction and ideas about what 'counts' as a good identity play their part, as well as typical discursive practices of what makes a good story. The identity project is then something that people work up in their talk. To argue this involves seeing talk as an active medium that actually creates different possible identities, rather than being simply a window into some inner 'real' self. People's talk, their discourse, is social action (Wetherell 2001).

It is through ordinary conversational practices that we become who we are, but I do not expect this to be a consistent creation through which a single authentic self is conveyed. Instead it is a patchwork of possibilities

41

that draw on familiar as well as changing cultural representations, and acquire new meanings as these resources are used in different contexts (Wetherell 2001). Women position themselves through their talk as strong and independent, or perhaps at times as lonely or needy, creating different subject positions (Davies and Harré 1990), or different identities, that become relevant for that moment in a conversation.

Conclusion

This review of models of identity in the empirical literature on singleness has sought to highlight some embedded assumptions concerning the subjectivity of the single woman. According to the different theoretical stances, the single woman is nagged, braced and cajoled to develop herself in particular ways. She is adjured to improve her negotiation of life stages and appropriate tasks for singleness. She is exhorted to deal with her conscious and unconscious feelings about growing up as her mother's daughter, her fears of dependency, loss and closeness. She is expected to learn and draw inspiration from the self-evident and untarnished 'truths' of other women's experience.

These models of a single woman's identity form an important aspect of the cultural context within which women pursue their personal identity projects, as I will demonstrate when I discuss my own data. My own description of the single woman is of someone who is capable of drawing on a wide range of common sense and more theoretical discussions on singleness in making sense of her situation. She is able to work with the contradictory cultural material that she is presented with and develop her own situated responses and interventions with which she constructs and fashions her identity. My task is to look at this process through examination of the identity work which takes place in the interviews with my research participants.

3

WORKING WITH A 'SINGLE' IDENTITY

And it's O dear me, how would it be,
If I die an old maid in a garret
(Traditional)

Introduction

Anne was visited at home by a colleague from work. The colleague paid some attention to a photograph on Anne's shelf. Who was the good-looking man pictured, and how come no one at work had heard about him? Anne explained that it was an important relationship and some of her reasons for wanting to keep it private. 'Anne, you should tell people about him!' exclaimed her colleague. 'Take that photo to work and put it on your desk and it will stop people getting the idea that you're some old maid who hides herself away.'

How do women on their own respond to and work with the typical constructions of their status available in the public arena? How do those typical constructions constrain and influence the ways in which women manage a 'single' identity? Media representations show single women as confident and pursuing successful careers, yet at the same time looking for the one true relationship. Bridget Jones (Fielding 1996) vividly conveys the dilemmas of looking while not appearing to be looking, and there is now a substantial genre of 'chick lit' adding to the range of typical constructions available.

Rosalind Gill and Elena Herdieckerhoff (2006), in their analysis of 'chick lit' of the era following Fielding's (1996) *Bridget Jones's Diary*, found an extraordinary tenacity of notions of heterosexual romance in spite of the backdrop of significant cultural change. They note that while women might be more sexually active and able to initiate sexual contact in this fictional genre, heroines are frequently 'revirginized' in the narrative in the progress of their sexual relations with the hero (Gill and Herdieckerhoff 2006: 494). By this they mean that they are constructed as more innocent, perhaps achieving true sexual fulfilment for the first time in this one special relationship.

I have found many examples of what Gill and Herdieckerhoff call revirginization: for instance, *Dead Sexy*, a romance by Kathy Lette (2003), follows the wooing of Shelly Green by Kit Kinkade, her husband (on paper only), after the two of them have won a computerized matchmaking competition and a very large amount of money if they go ahead with a marriage. Shelly is sexually aroused by Kit in a way she never has been before, but has been raised by her feminist single mother to hate all men, so has her own mistrust to overcome as well as Kit playing hard-to-get after his initially seductive moves. While this and others in this genre may provide a good story, linked (in a modern sort of way) to the traditions of romantic fiction, such representations of singleness may be not be helpful for ordinary women talking about their membership of this state.

Rather than being a natural fact, singleness varies over time and culture. Particular modes of representation of the single state dominate social organization at different moments. It is therefore important to explore the discursive context of singleness. By this, I mean that the ways of thinking about singleness provide a set of discursive resources that can be drawn on by single women and shaped to their own ends. My interest is in how women work up a single identity in their conversational practices. Discourse analysis provides some tools for exploring conversation.

Before looking at my exploration in detail in this and the next three chapters, I explain my approach to discourse analysis, and my use of interviews as discursive events.

Discourse analysis

Discourse research is the study of language in use and the study of human meaning-making (Wetherell *et al.* 2001). Discourse analysis provides a way of examining how important aspects of social life are carried out. An underpinning notion for all discourse analysts is that discourse *is* social action. Discourse does not simply provide a neutral picture of the object or events under discussion; rather it constructs and formulates them. Work is involved: speech is used to persuade, to present a particular version of affairs and it is oriented to other possible versions. The meaning of words is not fixed, but fluid, as meanings are socially constructed, vary according to context and are subject to continued modification negotiated in interaction (Speer 2005). Discourse is co-produced: meaning emerges because of a generally shared culture context within which distinctive associations are made, through more local uses in context by speakers, and through the co-operation of the participants who speak together (Wetherell 2001).

Traditions in discourse analysis

My approach to discourse analysis draws on several theoretical traditions, and follows the model developed by Margaret Wetherell and Jonathan Potter (Potter and Wetherell 1987; Wetherell and Potter 1988, 1992). The range of traditions of discourse research is diverse: two traditions prominent in the development of the field for social psychology are those that are influenced by the work of Foucault and those that draw on conversation analysis.

Discourse analysis that draws on Foucault's work has typically been concerned with the workings of power. The interest is in how language is organized in a culture so that particular ways of understanding are the ones that are taken for granted. For instance, Wendy Hollway (1984) theorizes the practices and meanings that reproduce gendered subjectivity. She explores, for example, why men choose to position themselves as subject to the discourse of male sexual drive, and why women continue to position themselves as its objects (Hollway 1984). In another example of Foucauldian research, Stuart Hall (1997a) addresses how representations of people seen as racially different are used to fix meanings and encapsulate a chain of associations that are demeaning to black people.

Conversation analysis (CA) is a sociological approach to discourse analysis which has developed from the work of Goffman on social interaction, Garfinkel's ethnomethodology and the work of Sacks and colleagues. It has emerged as an approach that uncovers the normative practices through which ordinary interaction is managed. Conversation analysts study the minutiae of naturally occurring conversations looking for the systematic properties of a particular phenomenon (Potter and Wetherell 1987). For instance, the sequential positioning of speakers' utterances; the range of possible responses; the overall structure of conversations; and the repair of difficulties in speaking, hearing and understanding talk are all areas that have been studied (Heritage 2001).

A more synthetic approach

In the synthesis of traditions that I follow, the aim is to blend the insights of conversation analysis with those of Foucault, giving attention to both the concern with participants' sense-making in social interactions and the use of broad cultural resources that are often taken for granted (Wetherell and Edley 1999). The approach examines what resources people use, or make relevant, in accounting for their actions. It assumes that people *do* things with their language and that the way people speak does much more than simply convey a picture of what they are describing. Critical discursive social psychology is concerned with the logic of accountability while also describing the collective and social patterning of background normative conceptions and their social and psychological consequences (Wetherell 1998).

Variability in people's talk can be problematic for researchers who are looking for broad themes that can be extracted from data. People often contradict themselves and this may be suppressed in some thematic research accounts which instead focus on the dominant view in a person's account,

45

and look for consistency in the person, rather than noting moments of hesitation or contradiction (Potter and Wetherell 1987). In this approach to discourse analysis, variability within accounts is an important area for analysis since it can reveal cultural contradictions in the resources that those talking are drawing upon.

There are some epistemological and methodological problems in combining approaches that have emerged from contrasting theoretical underpinnings, to which a debate between contributors to *Discourse & Society* has drawn attention (Billig 1999; Schegloff 1997b, 1998, 1999; Wetherell 1998). Writing from a CA perspective, Schegloff argues that, without more attention to participants' concerns in their analytic procedures, critical discourse analysts lose a close connection to their data and produce arguments that are merely ideological. Wetherell (1998) acknowledges the commonly accepted distinctions between analysis that is fine-grained and concerned with the action orientation of talk and that which is more focused on discourse, power and subjectification. She advocates, nonetheless, an eclectic approach that draws on both traditions as the most productive basis for discourse work in social psychology. I make use of both traditions in my own analysis, as I find it helpful to attend to the occasioned and contextualized nature of participants' talk as well as the social and political consequences of discursive patterning.

Interviews as discursive events

Unlike some conversation analytic research where the talk is the focus and the topic of conversation is unimportant, I had a dual focus both on topic and on how talk was organized. Jennifer Coates (1996) collected data on how women friends talk together through recording groups of friends: in the first place a group of her own friends. While I could have approached my study in a similar way, this would not necessarily have given me data that addressed singleness as a topic. On the other hand, I did not want simply to focus on talk 'about' singleness. I wanted to see women 'doing singleness' in action.

The approach I chose was to set up individual interviews as discursive events. It has been suggested that we live in an 'interview society' (Atkinson and Silverman 1997), and that the interview is a normatively organized device for revealing social structure that is itself worthy as a topic for investigation (Silverman 1973). Interviews are a particular kind of talk. People who take part in interviews are generally likely to have some idea of what is expected in an interview situation, based on previous experience either of taking part in them or from witnessing interviews presented through different media. The interview is a category of activity that participants can employ to recognize interactional situations and to guide their behaviour in them (Shakespeare 1998).

As participants, interviewer and interviewed draw on their cultural knowledge, including knowledge of interviews as a recognized form of social interaction, and, in the case of my own interviews, knowledge about how women alone routinely speak. Participants' accounts and responses are 'locally' organized as relevant to the context in which they are participating, in interviews as in other more casual conversations. In interviews, participants demonstrate how they assign sense and meaning to the category of 'singleness'. Interviews set up with the purpose of exploring singleness will also be showing something of how singleness is performed. I interviewed 26 women one-to-one, and did one group interview with 4 women. Appendix 1 gives details of my selection of participants, approach to interviews and transcription of interviews.

I identified myself as a single woman, and shared some features such as cultural and class background with many of the sample. I articulated this insider role (Adler and Adler 1987) in my initial information about the project, and in my approach to interviewing, where I sometimes used my own experience as an example of issues I wanted to explore. Through a degree of openness about my own situation I aimed to avoid reproducing a situation where women who define themselves as single are constantly put on the spot to explain their 'oddity'. While I generally refer to those interviewed as 'participants', I recognize that I was also a participant in the discussion and the resulting discourse was jointly constructed. My intention was to treat myself as one of the objects of study. I was drawing on and constructing a discourse together with the participants. This meant that at times I was more active in the conversation than might traditionally be expected of a social science researcher. I assumed that we were articulating some shared cultural beliefs, and that it might be possible to tease out more precisely what these were and how we made use of them through close analysis searching for patterns in our conversations. Where it seems important also to examine my own questions or responses I have included them in the extracts shown of interview transcripts. Reasons of space have prevented me from doing this in all extracts.

In the transcripts and my discussion of them I refer to my own speech as interviewer in the third person. I have found this to be an important first step in re-examining, as analyst, taken-for-granted activities and meanings. By this means I can examine speech turns from 'Jill' without assuming that I already know what the intentions of this speaker were. I can try to hear the turn and read it in transcription for how it might be 'hearable' or 'readable' by another.

Analytic concepts

Three linked concepts are key to the synthesis of different traditions of discourse analysis that I use in this chapter. Interpretative repertoires

47

(Potter and Wetherell 1987), ideological dilemmas (Billig *et al.* 1988) and subject positions (Davies and Harré 1990) are all tools for exploring data. These three concepts, although each stemming from different traditions, are coming to be seen as central to critical discursive psychology and there is a developing literature which works with all three concepts together as a package (Edley 2001; Wetherell 1998).

Interpretative repertoires

Wetherell and Potter (1992) argue for a focus on discourse as social practice and on the context of its use. This means that the sense of talk is from its situated use rather than any abstract meaning it might have, and that situated use involves analysing how discourses arise in everyday conversation or texts. The interpretative repertoire is a unit for more fine-grained analysis and this term is preferred by Wetherell and Potter to the more general term 'discourse' (see also Gilbert and Mulkay 1984). I use 'discourse' to refer to the overall set of interpretative resources, for instance as in a 'discourse of singleness'.

Interpretative repertoires are defined by Potter and Wetherell as a lexicon of terms and metaphors drawn upon for characterizing and evaluating actions and events (Potter and Wetherell 1987: 138). Interpretative repertoires are systematically related sets of terms (Potter 1996). They can be recognized in the familiar and well-worn images that 'everybody' knows and understands through shared cultural membership. Edley (2001) compares them to books on the shelves of a public library that are permanently available for borrowing, making the point that when people talk or think they invariably use terms already provided by history. Conversations can, of course, be original, but they are usually made up of a patchwork of 'quotations' from various interpretative repertoires (Edley 2001).

The use of interpretative repertoires as a tool for analysis is primarily as a way of understanding the content of discourse and how that content is organized: a focus on language use rather than concern with linguistic analysis as such (Wetherell and Potter 1992). Researchers have an interest in how people use various repertoires towards a certain function, and how they move in and out of them while constructing their accounts (Nikander 1995).

An example of an interpretative repertoire that was frequently drawn on by my participants is the notion that 'times are changing and things are getting better for women on their own'. For instance, the following comments came from three different interviews: 'the attitude certainly has changed and it has to be said that I'm asked less now whether I'm married', 'women on their own were to be pitied, they'd failed in some way; I don't think that applies now, or least it's not supposed to be, that's not politically correct', and 'I think that it's changing now; I think it's easier to be single and feel good about it.' The golden future is being conjured up here: things are so much better now and more progressive, so that the 'bad things' – images of spinsters and old maids – are all located in the past, in the bad old days.

What is being offered in these kinds of constructions is commonsensical: both participants in the interview are aware of the associations being made, within the context of the conversation. So a repertoire could appear as fragments or be alluded to in passing with the listener being able to supply the whole broader chain of association without elaboration being necessary (Wetherell 1998). Repertoires are customized in order to answer a question, for instance as an anecdote about the participant's childhood, or made part of a story about what other people might say to the single woman.

The four interpretative repertoires that I discuss in this chapter, because my participants drew them on with regularity, are different characterizations of singleness:

- singleness as personal deficit
- singleness as social exclusion
- singleness as independence and choice
- singleness as self-development and achievement.

Ideological dilemmas

The ideology referred to here is 'lived' ideology (Billig *et al.* 1988). In contrast to Marxist notions of ideologies as coherent and consistent chains of ideas that serve the interests of the ruling class in maintaining their domination, lived ideologies are composed of the beliefs, values and practices of a given society or culture. They are far from being coherent and integrated, instead they are characterized by inconsistency, fragmentation and contradiction (Edley 2001). The competing arguments and values which people draw on in making sense of their lives pose many dilemmas. People solve various kinds of everyday ideological dilemmas in their talk and use rhetoric to do it. Interpretative repertoires and ideological dilemmas are thus closely linked as speakers work with the inconsistency in the repertoires on which they draw and try to reconcile contradictory argumentative threads. I shall be discussing the ideological dilemmas that emerged for my participants as they drew on competing repertoires of singleness as a problematic state and singleness as a highly idealized and positive state.

Subject positions

Any speaker's identity is constructed by the different kinds of person, or 'subject positions' (Davies and Harré 1990), that are implied by particular ways of talking. The perspective on identity is that rather than being a fixed and immutable property of an individual, different identities are made available to a person through discursive practices and conjured up in conversational interactions. There is a connection here with the kind of subjects that Foucault argues 'personify' the discourse. I noted in Chapter 1 some familiar ones that are often applied to single women, such as 'the lonely spinster', the 'dangerous divorcee'. While these are rather crude stereotypes, which we might not expect single women to import wholesale into their conversation as positions for themselves, they nevertheless may emerge as subjects against which women position themselves in contrast. In other words, single women may demonstrate in their conversational moves that they are neither lonely spinsters nor dangerous divorcees.

In an article recalling her friendship with Bernice Rubens and comparing similarities in their lives, Beryl Bainbridge writes: 'As adults we had loved the men we married and they had walked away, crashing our hopes, after which we had gone in for gentlemen callers' (Bainbridge 2005). Several subject positions are implicit here: the loyal and loving wife, subsequently the abandoned and disappointed divorcee, and finally a more coquettish and mischievous person with an overlay of irony in the reference to times past and a demure positioning of men. These are familiar images to readers. Subject positions are widely shared cultural resources, readily understood by participants. Edley defines subject positions as locations within a conversation: the identities made relevant by specific ways of talking (Edley 2001).

The notion of positioning allows the self to be understood as dynamic and changing within encounters. Speakers position themselves and they position other participants in their conversations, by explicitly or implicitly addressing them as inhabiting a particular subject position. In different encounters or within one conversation, different positions may be taken up, as speakers avoid or 'ward off' unattractive identities in talk (Forbat 2005). In relation to conversational moves that produce contrasting subject positions, I make use in my analysis of the notion that subject positions can be 'troubled' (Wetherell 1998; Wetherell and Edley 1998).

Wetherell and Edley use the idea of trouble in relation to identity in two different ways (Taylor 2004). One meaning is that of a negatively valued identity, as when a young man talking of his sexual successes is positioned by another as 'on the moral low ground' (Wetherell 1998: 397–8). The other meaning relates to troubled identity work, when a speaker is inconsistent or implausible with regard to their identity (Taylor 2004). Speakers can be seen to do repair work in their conversation in order to explain inconsistencies:

> People are accountable to each other in interaction and thus departures from 'what everybody knows to be appropriate' require

explanation and create 'trouble' in the interaction which will need repair.

(Wetherell and Edley 1998: 161)

I draw on both of these meanings of trouble in my analysis.

These three tools, interpretative repertoires, ideological dilemmas and subject positions, are valuable in offering different ways of examining in detail the transcripts of talk from my participants, and identifying contrasting representations of singleness, moves to tackle apparent inconsistencies and dilemmatic alternatives, and ways in which participants position themselves in interaction. Analysing stretches of data for 'discourses' more generally has its limitations if there is no clear way to establish the presence of any particular discourse in any specific sequence of talk-in-interaction (Wooffitt 2005).

Analytic process

I worked with a corpus or data file derived from all the material produced in response to my request for self-description and for images of singleness that the speaker held or thought other people to hold. The extracts that I selected were quite lengthy. I looked first for patterns and regularities in participants' talk in general about singleness, and then for the identity management relating to these. The search for patterns was guided by the three analytic concepts discussed above.

Using data from my interviews, I examine the identities that women construct for themselves through their talk. What I found was that my participants drew on highly polarized constructions of singleness as a state that was both deeply problematic and at the same time full of rewards and potential. This had an important impact on the kind of identity work that they did to ward off the unacceptable face of singleness, and to deal with the apparent contradictions in their expressions of desire for intimacy.

Interpretative repertoires of singleness

Although participants referred to multi-faceted and contradictory images of singleness, there are some marked regularities in the repertoires which they drew on. The first two repertoires that I discuss here are strongly denigrated and the second two strongly idealized. These highly polarized repertoires present single women with a problematic ideological package, which has challenging consequences for their personal identity work. I first review the four major repertoires and some of the subject positions entailed in their presentation.

51

Singleness as personal deficit

This repertoire emerged in response to questions about images formed in early life, through descriptions of single women encountered when the participant was a child, or in imagining the views of others.

Extract 1

1	Jill	[. . .] I'm wondering if you have any
2		particular images about single women that
3		sort of going back, if you can
4		remember, to what you might have thought
5		as a child or a teenager or as a young
6		woman, coming up to the present really.
7		What it might have meant to you at
8		different times?
9	Rachel	Mm, mm. Well I think growing up as a
10		child, and as a teenager and as a young
11		woman, um, I think the image that I had of
12		single women was of women who were not
13		able to have a relationship or not able to
14		find a relationship or find a man. [. . .]

Extract 2

1	Jill	[. . .] I am interested in whether you've got
2		any kind of memories of your images of
3		singleness over time, what you might have
4		thought as a child or a young woman
5		growing up or at the point when you became
6		divorced and, perhaps how you see it now.
7	Jay	I think my images when I was growing up
8		were largely negative ones. Erm I've been
9		trying to remember whether I had any
10		spinster, maiden aunts or relatives in the
11		family and I don't think I had any. I
12		don't, so my images would have been the
13		ones that have sort of filtered down
14		through family perceptions and through,
15		obviously through, the media and erm ones
16		that come packaged for you rather than any
17		direct experience, but certainly, or
18		through literature I suppose, things like

19	Jane Eyre and you know them, erm the sort
20	of Victorian image of the spinster in the
21	family who had to be supported somehow by
22	the men in the family and who was erm, not
23	quite a whole person in some way. So I
24	suppose I grew up with those images, erm,
25	and with an expectation that it wasn't me,
26	it wasn't going to be me, I was
27	heterosexual I was erm at some stage going
28	to get married and have children which I
29	duly did.

The notion of singleness as signalling a particular kind of personal deficit is drawn on in Extract 1 and by many other participants as the 'canonical view', in other words as part of the familiar and well-understood stories of one's culture. In the personal deficit repertoire the focus is on the *personal characteristics* of the single woman, and a strong link is made between these characteristics and membership of the category. The characteristics of a woman who has failed to get a man and is in need of this missing support.

The single woman constructed here is pitiable and problematic as a character. She is one of the 'subjects' who personify the discourse in Foucault's terms, but this is not generally a subject position in the sense of one brought out in conversational moves that participants in my study take up and occupy for themselves. Phrases such as 'not chosen', 'not wanted', or 'on the shelf' dominated participants' accounts. As in both these extracts, participants were not necessarily referring to specific women they had known, but might bring out a composite picture of singleness and spinsterhood. Referring to her unmarried teachers in school, one person said 'there was this kind of stereotype that women who weren't married were less human'. It was also not unusual for participants to refer to having not anticipated a single life for themselves as a child, as in Extract 2.

The interpretative repertoire of singleness as personal deficit, as I shall demonstrate later in this chapter, powerfully shaped the management of participants' identities.

Singleness as social exclusion

An alternative, but still quite negative, repertoire involved a construction of singleness as social exclusion rather than personal deficit. Typically, this repertoire emerged in anecdotes and stories about other people's reactions to oneself involving reported speech and accounts of internal dialogue in response. It was developed most strongly in relation to questions about other people's images of singleness, and was presented through accounts of actual experiences rather than as the familiar story of culture, and was therefore more firmly 'owned'.

Extract 3

1	Lyn	[. . .] And I think that you don't get locked
2		into a sort of social network if you're
3		single, or I haven't, it hasn't been my
4		experience, and when I was in my thirties a
5		single friend said to me 'oh well couples
6		won't invite us because they're scared of
7		us; they think we're going to walk off
8		with their men' and I don't think of it
9		the same way now but I think there are,
10		there are, there is this sort of couple
11		network thing and they'll invite each
12		other round to dinner and you'll sort of
13		share it and swap it and make it equal and
14		as a single person I have never felt
15		included in that. [. . .]

Extract 4

1	Josie	[. . .] Well it's because I've been on my own
2		such a long time that, um, I remember
3		going to a birthday party a few months
4		ago, in a pub, and when I got there the
5		people were couples. The first people
6		that arrived were couples, and I launched
7		straight into this business about not
8		being in a couple myself and how I felt
9		odd and I clocked to myself, 'My goodness
10		me you're being very kind of up-front
11		about this'. And it's because, yes, I do,
12		in all honesty, sometimes I do feel
13		vulnerable, and sometimes even jealous.
14		For example my sister and her husband, and
15		my other sister and her husband, take my
16		mother on holiday; so they go off in these
17		sort of two blissful couples to take my
18		mother on holiday, you know? I sometimes
19		think that couples favour other couples
20		and it can make you feel left out and odd
21		[. . .]

In Extract 3, Lyn is responding to a question about what she finds it easy or difficult to do as a woman on her own. Josie, in Extract 4, is responding to a question about whether and how she lets people know that she is single.

The repertoire of social exclusion constructs a strong contrast between singleness and coupledom. Repeatedly women talked, as in Extract 3, of a different kind of social existence that they understand couples to have, dinner parties, return invitations and regular connections with others. In contrast, they spoke of their own experience of not being contacted by others and having to work hard to initiate all social activities themselves. A distinctive, but linked, theme is the notion that they may represent a threat to coupledom, as in lines 7 to 8 of Extract 3.

The implication in this repertoire is that the single woman is excluded from social events and coupledom as an ideal. The presentation is of singleness and coupledom as in effect two quite divergent, almost unconnected, social worlds or social spaces. The term 'Smug Married', coined by Fielding (1996: 39) through Bridget Jones, fits with this repertoire. In general, this sense of strong binary, a separated geography of two unrelated states, is a commonplace feature of the broader discourse of singleness. In this repertoire, typically, one of these spaces, coupledom, is constructed as privileged, and the other, singleness, as excluded, lacking and disadvantaged. In Extract 5, the sense of exclusion is such that it is described as difficult even to talk about being single.

Extract 5

1	*Marion*	[. . .] And also erm, you know, people don't
2		actually sort of talk about being single.
3		They always talk about the relationships
4		they're in, and therefore you're, even if
5		you, the one you've got is not terribly
6		wonderful or whatever, you are inclined to
7		sort of talk about it, and erm and also
8		even if you are not in a relationship at
9		all at the time it's always about what I
10		would like it to be or I was, rather than,
11		a poor pathetic creature really. (laughs)
12		[. . .]

The prevalent notion that relationships are the most important thing in life, and a sense of struggle with this, was repeated by others in my sample. As one commented: 'if that isn't the main business of your life it's very difficult, because you feel "well it ought to be the main business"'. A further common feature of this repertoire was for participants to talk of close friendships that ended when the friend found a partner, as in Extract 6.

Extract 6

1	Josie	I had three friends and they all had their
2		own homes and their own jobs, you know and
3		cars. They had everything except a
4		partner. They all wanted partners really
5		badly and they found them and in all three
6		cases the friendship finished after they
7		found partners. So I was no longer
8		required, you know? I was no longer, you
9		know, part of their social scene, you
10		know?

In employing this repertoire the emphasis is placed by participants on singleness being seen by others as an odd and not normal condition, with an impact that means that one cannot find positive ways of talking about one's status. The subject positions constructed in these extracts vary. The impotence derived from the overall construction of exclusion is mitigated in Extract 3 (lines 5 to 8) by the construction of an alternative source of power – the power of the single woman to take other women's men, and thus to be seen as a threat. Josie, in Extract 4, positions herself as direct and up-front (lines 9 to 11), but also as left out and ignored (lines 18 to 20). The speaker in Extract 5 is constructed as 'passing' in a world of relationships. She talks of using an unsatisfactory relationship, or talk of the relationship she would like, as her contribution to conversational exchanges (lines 6 to 10), rather than presenting herself as someone not involved in a relationship and therefore, as she suggests with irony, 'a poor pathetic creature' (line 11). The speaker in Extract 6 positions herself as dumped by her newly part-nered friends (lines 7 to 10).

There is some continuity in the repertoire of social exclusion with the more historic images of spinsters suggested in the personal deficit reper-toire. The notion that the extra, non-marrying and perhaps unmarriageable woman represents a problem is one that was common in the early and middle years of the twentieth century (see, for instance, Hillis 1936; Holden 2005). These first two repertoires of personal deficit and social exclusion are closely connected. A person talking of social exclusion describes her own engagement with combating or living with stereotypes and assumptions prevalent in the repertoire of personal deficit.

Singleness as independence and choice

In contrast to the first two repertoires this and the next repertoire present singleness as a highly positive condition. Singleness is idealized.

Extract 7

1	*Jill*	Are there other things you could pick out
2		that you enjoy or the things that you find
3		difficult?
4	*Annie*	Um well it's silly little things really. I
5		suppose like being able to decorate the
6		house exactly as you like there's no
7		compromise in anything, you can do
8		anything you want. I mean people can moan
9		and say that's stupid and say well there's
10		not a lot I wanted, you know, whereas when
11		I was married you are forever sort of um
12		toning down what you like, or what you
13		want. I know that's a very selfish
14		attitude but I do enjoy being able to have
15		exactly my own way. Bad things, I don't
16		think there's anything particularly bad
17		about it, it's hard put to find any down
18		side you know.

Extract 8

1	*Susie*	[. . .] And I think I'm really fortunate I
2		don't have to put up with all the negative
3		things about relationships and I think, I
4		think overall they're quite difficult
5		things; I don't think they're sort of
6		romantic, sharing of the burden things at
7		all. I think they are an additional burden
8		and I think most of the time I'm grateful
9		not to have to carry it. [. . .]

This repertoire of choice and independence constructs singleness as a positive decision, with stories and anecdotes celebrating one's independence. Participants regularly pointed to the freedom they had to make decisions in the way they wanted to, without needing to take others into account, not having to compromise, not having to clear up someone else's mess, not having to ask permission. The force of this repertoire depends a good deal on drawing out contrasts with remembered or assumed lack of freedom and choice for women who are married or in a marriage-like relationship. The two states of singleness and coupledom become differently marked. Now it is singleness that is the privileged and celebrated space. Women position themselves as grateful to belong to this free space of independence and choice. Indeed, as in Extract 7 (lines 13 to 14), privilege has to be carefully managed, to acknowledge the possible negative consequences that those who occupy privileged spaces might be held to account as 'selfish'.

Singleness as self-development and achievement

The final pattern that I wish to draw attention to in the data can be described as a repertoire of self-development and achievement. It is more diverse than the repertoires described above: four extracts give a flavour of the range. The first extract that illustrates this repertoire, is drawn from a group discussion.

Extract 9

1	Jennifer	I think also we have more time to think
2		than other people, to do what we want and
3		therefore we don't, we can actually take
4		time off to get off the wheel, and so we
5		have time to think about what we want to
6		do and therefore we can develop ourselves
7		more, maybe, sometimes.
8	Jane	We're like free spirits, we're not boxed
9		into some little cage.

The suggestion is that women on their own have the time to develop themselves. In Extract 10, Val is talking of a time when she was adapting to a new job abroad.

Extract 10

1	Val	I can remember thinking a lot of that time
2		when it was difficult 'I'm really pleased
3		I'm doing this on my own' because the
4		whole equation about because like I
5		say I had this conversation with myself
6		and this voice said, 'well just go home
7		you don't have to stay here, you can go
8		home now'; and this other voice would say,
9		'no, no'. So I really had to work out what
10		was really important for me; absolutely
11		for me and the terms on which I was there
12		and at which point I would decide to give
13		up and what difficulties I would decide
14		were worth sticking with and overcoming

```
15        and it was totally on my terms and if I'd
16        had to take someone else into account, and
17        weigh it all up with them and take their
18        feelings into account as well, I don't
19        think I could have done it. Well I know I
20        couldn't. [. . .]
```

As with the repertoire of choice and independence, freedom to make decisions without having to think about a partner is emphasized. There is a construction of challenge, and work on oneself in response to that challenge. Val constructs herself as achieving through adversity.

Extract 11

```
1  Claire   [. . .] I'm pleased to be the age I'm at. I'm
2           not sure, could I think how I think now at
3           the age of 25? Could my life have been
4           different? One of my pleasures since I've
5           been single, I've gradually become more
6           open myself to being more interested in
7           lots of different things. Does one become
8           more like that, more closed and rigid in a
9           partnership that's not fulfilling? [. . .]
```

Claire, at midlife, celebrates the way her life has unfolded and her sense that she has been more open to a range of interests since she became single.

Extract 12

```
1  Milly    [. . .] there are so many more professional
2           women who don't want to put their careers
3           aside while they have children and
4           marriage is largely about having children,
5           still, and so many women are choosing not
6           only not to have children but not to get
7           married, and so they are single because
8           they are career types and that to me is a
9           positive image. [. . .]
```

Milly, in her early thirties, relishes the subject position of the career women. This repertoire of self-development is also a repertoire of female ambition, formulated within both liberal feminist and humanistic psychological terms. There are close links with the previous repertoire. Singleness as self-actualization and achievement also gains force from contrast with marriage. Financial independence is a goal as well as other more diffuse aims of self-fulfilment, all of which may have been hard won. The notion is that there is so much more to life than getting married or looking after other people, and that without these distractions there is more opportunity to achieve desired goals. There are also traces of female solidarity in Extract 9: a positive feminist politics of singleness.

The repertoires in combination

These four interpretative repertoires are the prevalent patterns of sense-making that were present in my data in relation to the interview questions about images of singleness. They constitute a large part of the discursive resources participants used for talking about singleness. Most women drew on all four repertoires; a few drew only on the second two, none drew solely on the first two. These repertoires in part constrain or enable the kinds of conversations, dialogues and internal monologues that are possible around singleness. They offer certain ways of talking for single women. They form rhetorical point and counter-point and provide a discursive package creating a powerful set of ideological dilemmas without easy resolution. The ideal-ized third and fourth repertoires of independence and self-development, for example, can be a response and contrast to the first and second repertoires of personal deficit and social exclusion. The positive repertoires of choice and self-development were often undermined and shadowed by the first and second repertoires of personal deficit and exclusion. The subject positions offered to women across the repertoires vary widely from 'strong and independent' to 'pitiable and problematic' and from 'fulfilled' to 'attacked and excluded'.

As I have noted, the repertoires are highly polarized – two are strongly denigrated and two strongly idealized. The general impression is that single women are working out their identity in a context of a highly dilemmatic construction of singleness. Billig and colleagues (1988) have drawn atten-tion to the dilemmatic nature of many core ideological values, but there are particular challenges in inhabiting a social category with such polarized attributes. What are the consequences of this dilemmatic construction of singleness for the single woman's identity work?

It may be unusual to have to draw on a discursive and ideological space that is so polarized, where the ideological dilemmas raised by the contra-dictions between the repertoires are so closely linked to the possibilities for who one can be as a person. There are some contrasts with the repertoires drawn on by men and the positioning work they employ in relation to hegemonic masculinity. Rather than warding off implications of personal deficit, men are often negotiating their position in relation to something strongly valued. For instance, Wetherell and Edley show examples from their data of men keeping self-exaltation in check through modesty work and self-deprecation (Wetherell and Edley 1999).

Perhaps membership of other more marginalized social categories based on ethnicity, class, sexuality, older age and disability is more likely to involve managing both denigrated and idealized categorizations simultaneously. The development of some social conscientization over recent decades as well as new social movements that aim to counter denigration (Habermas 1981) may have given the members of these groups some new resources for their identity work. Single women, however, lack a feminist social movement or identity politics specifically related to singleness. There is an absence of any co-ordinated and collective efforts to deal with denigration for women alone. Possibly without this it is more difficult to unequivocally inhabit the positive, and distance oneself from the denigrated constructions.

As might be expected, the ways that participants dealt with the impact of these repertoires on their personal identity were more varied than the repertoires themselves. However, there were some regularities. In the remainder of my analysis I will focus first on two pervasive negative ways in which this pattern of repertoires seemed to shape the identity work of the women in my sample. From a feminist perspective, these modes of management suggest the need for a more positive and elaborated politics of singleness. I will then consider some examples of a more reflexive approach adopted by some participants, where they worked with the contradictions of the different repertoires to come up with a more integrated self-positioning.

Constructing the self as not a typical member

Rather than use the term 'single' and fully inhabit the category, participants often distanced themselves from the denigrated construction of singleness, and from the category of singleness defined in negative ways. There was delicate footwork over the ways in which one 'belongs' to the category and indeed how the category is defined in the first place. Consider Extract 13 below in which Val argues that although she belongs to the category 'woman living on her own' she does not fit within the category 'single', since she has a boyfriend.

Extract 13

1	Jill	Mm, yeah, absolutely fine. I think when we
2		spoke on the phone you didn't tend to
3		think of yourself as single and I didn't
4		hear you say that just then; just that
5		you're quite happy living on your own.

6	*Val*	Yes; I suppose when we were talking on the
7		phone I, um, I think what I said was 'I
8		think of myself firstly as financially
9		independent'. I don't think of myself as a
10		loner, as alone at all. I do have a
11		boyfriend, um, I don't think of him as a
12		partner, probably 'cos we don't live
13		together and our lives don't join up so
14		much that I have to take him into account
15		an awful lot. I've rarely not had a
16		boyfriend actually. In fact sometimes they
17		overlap, which can be difficult. So I've
18		never been short of a boyfriend and always
19		had, um, plenty of friends and two or
20		three close friends, women friends. So
21		'single' sounds awfully alone and I don't
22		think of myself as being alone, except
23		when I come back to this house I suppose,
24		but then again, yes, I think the first
25		thing is financial independence. I choose
26		how to spend my money and it's not really
27		a big issue until I see how other people
28		don't have that. I just take it for
29		granted.

Val draws strongly here on the personal deficit repertoire in constructing her reading of the category 'single'. 'Single' becomes constructed as a noxious identity. There is a lot of positioning work going on in this response. Val positions herself as

- financially independent
- not a loner or alone
- having a boyfriend whom she does not live with
- rarely short of a boyfriend
- having plenty of friends.

This is a lot of discursive work in response to Jill's suggestion that Val had previously said she did not think of herself as single. Val constructs herself as not single as in 'loner', but single as in 'financially independent'. Why does Val put so much into positioning herself in this way? She is doing this work without having been offered any negative meanings of singleness. She nonetheless anticipates and side-steps such meanings by portraying herself as financially independent, attractive to men and socially active. It is instructive to witness the kind of work which becomes necessary to manage the disavowal of inclusion in a troubled (cf. Wetherell 1998) category membership.

Could women avoid these problems altogether by defining the category 'single' entirely through the positive and idealized repertoires of choice and independence and self-development and achievement? It might not then be necessary to distance oneself from the category. Very few of the women interviewed followed this discursive strategy. The power of the characterization of singleness as personal deficit seems to be such that it is always 'around' as a potential reading of one's character. Its availability, and possible applicability to oneself, needs to be addressed in some way, and warded off. Women developed several ways of doing this. The next two extracts from Polly exemplify three common strategies. First, Polly finds another category outside 'single' that can hold the negative meanings of personal deficit, leaving 'single' to hold more positive connotations. Second, she reviews her own credentials to show why she does not herself qualify in the more negative personal deficit interpretation of the category. Finally, she contrasts herself positively with someone who does seem to have all the negative attributes.

Extract 14

1	Jill	Is it [single] a word that you would apply
2		to yourself generally and are there any
3		others that you might use instead?
4	Polly	No, I do say I'm single. I dislike
5		intensely the word 'spinster'. I mean
6		bachelor does not have a sinister,
7		pathetic or even unpleasant ring to it,
8		but spinster does have a very unpleasant
9		ring to it. Um, I would say from choice I
10		would like to have been married. Um, but
11		I'm not married and as I said I was
12		engaged three times; I had three options
13		of marriage, maybe that's a clearer
14		picture of myself; I had three options of
15		marriage and it was me that turned down
16		the engagements because I didn't love
17		enough, um, and I suppose I've always
18		looked for the ultimate love and maybe
19		that doesn't exist.

Polly does place herself within the category, but also tries to account for herself as a single person, rather than limiting her response to agreement that she would call herself single. She differentiates single from 'spinster' and contrasts the connotations of 'sinister' and 'pathetic' that it carries with the more trouble-free identity of 'bachelor'. Turning down three options of marriage is highlighted by her, and this is repeated in different ways three times. She constructs a picture of herself as having had a chance to become a non-member of the category 'single' by getting married, and therefore as someone to whom attributions of personal deficit are not relevant. In Extract 15 she does further work to distinguish herself from someone who she thinks does fit the category 'spinster'.

Extract 15

1	Polly	I think I've only got one friend that is a
2		spinster, as I am and I do think she is a
3		spinster with her trundle basket and I'm
4		afraid to say I was going to say her cat
5		as well, and she does fall into what I
6		feel is that spinster category; 'cos I
7		mean she's still in the same job I met her
8		in 30 years ago and she hasn't moved on.
9		She'll be there until retirement and she
10		hasn't moved on whereas, as I say, most of
11		my collection of friends are actors,
12		drunks, or Jewish, or Irish funnily
13		enough. I mean I have a sort of, I
14		suppose, an eccentric selection of
15		friends; I don't think any of my friends
16		would be categorized as the norm; and I've
17		got a lot of gay friends.

Here, while she includes herself in the category 'spinster', she is making a distinction between herself and the friend who 'does fall into what I feel is that spinster category'. Fitting the category is thus made more salient than the technical description which would include Polly herself. Marks of the 'typical spinster' include the trundle basket and the cat. Why does Polly apologize for being about to add 'cat' to the stereotypical image of the spinster with her trundle basket? She has a cat herself; by catching herself in an allusion to a 'spinster with cat' and reinforcing a stereotype, Polly is both adding to the picture of her friend as a typical spinster, yet still claiming that she is not herself typical. Polly then refers to the majority of her friends – eccentrics, not the norm (lines 14 to 16) – which has the effect of further distancing her from the category of spinster. Polly says that her friend 'hasn't moved on' (lines 9 to 10) and appears to contrast her other friends with this person by her use of 'whereas' (line 10). Yet this is a non sequitur, unless it is considered that actors, drunks and so on have by definition 'moved on'. The contrast to be made is more with Polly herself. By implication, in having friends who are unusual, Polly herself becomes unusual, and less like a spinster.

The last example of distancing oneself from the negative category (Extract 16) initially presented a puzzle.

Extract 16

1	Jill	Well, that's very good, thank you very
2		much, that gives me a very helpful
3		introduction.
4	Mary	I've got lots of friends, lots of friends
5		and supportive relatives, so my social
6		life is good.

This sequence comes after Mary has given a brief description of herself. Why does Mary go on to comment on her friends at this point? It appears as an afterthought to her introductory account of herself, in which she mentioned her divorce, another long-term relationship and discusses in more detail her career as a nurse. It is not a response to any question. It may be a response to the interviewer's comment that she has been given 'a very helpful introduction' – a conversational act that attempts to close off what has been said so far, preparatory to further exploration. If so, we can read Mary's response as an effort to fill out the portrait that she has given of herself, finding that it is incomplete in some important way. But there is a defensive quality to this interjection, as though she is warding off some unspoken accusation with this rhetorical work. The unspoken accusation, I suggest, arises from the negative repertoires of singleness. Single women in effect always stand accused. By her assertion 'my social life is good', Mary is positioning herself positively and countering association with the repertoires of personal deficit and social exclusion.

These are some examples of the ways in which participants claimed that they were not typical members of the category 'single'. Approaches to doing this varied, but the overall effect was the same: to distance the speaker from the negative connotations. There are affinities in this kind of positioning work with how speakers resist membership of other potentially relevant categories, for instance the work of Widdicombe and Wooffitt in relation to youth subcultures (Widdicombe 1993, 1998; Widdicombe and Wooffitt 1995). The authors show (1995) how their young respondents, selected for their unusual appearance, avoided ascription to a category such as goth or punk. When asked to describe themselves they might respond as though unclear what they were being asked, or equivocate in other ways. If they later acknowledged their membership of a specific subculture, this was often as merely one dimension of their identity, not the overriding one. Widdicombe and Wooffitt suggest that the respondents were resisting a way of being seen, and countering assumptions (no doubt routinely experienced) that it is possible to know just by looking at them what sort of person they are (Widdicombe and Wooffitt 1995).

However, Widdicombe and Wooffitt do not claim to be members of those youth subcultures that were of interest to them in their selection of interviewees. Their participants' cautious responses to how they might describe themselves or their style can be read as identity work to counter an interviewer's potentially uninformed or negative assumptions about the category being made salient by the interview. In the interviews with women alone, the interviewer was herself single, and I suggest that this makes the positioning work to avoid membership of the category 'single' the more remarkable. Some shared cultural assumptions between interviewer and interviewed might have been expected. It was possible for the category 'single' to be defined wholly in positive ways by participants in this sup-posedly 'safe' space. Nonetheless, such 'trouble-free' examples were rare in my data.

Troubled desire

The second prevalent area of trouble among participants arose in relation to the interview question concerning wishes about future relationships or future marriage. It was striking how often women appeared to be apolog-izing for acknowledging a desire for commitment with a partner.

Extract 17

1	Jill	[. . .] These are just some final things; um,
2		sort of summary things really, like, I
3		think you've partly answered this but, I
4		mean, let's just try you again. Do you
5		feel that you're actively looking now for
6		a long-term relationship, possibly?
7	Milly	Yes I think I am really. I've never been
8		the party animal type; I've never been the
9		one to want lots of dates. You know, I
10		tend to be a one-man woman I suppose and
11		while it was never a big issue when I was
12		younger, now I do appreciate the
13		companionship side of things; I value that
14		far more highly than perhaps I did before
15		and I want someone to belong to and
16		someone to belong to me, and I suppose, if

17   I'm honest, yes I'm looking for a husband.
18   Yes. I have to be specific. I don't think
19   I want to go into another one of these,
20   five or six year living together type
21   situations; I don't really want that. I
22   want to be married I suppose but,
23   you know, I'm not feverish about it! I'm just
24   hoping that it will happen in the near
25   future.

Milly presents an account of a pursuit of a long-term relationship in positive terms, so why does she frame the statement that she is looking for a husband with: 'if I'm honest' (lines 16 to 17)? This and similar phrases such as 'I must admit', 'I can't deny', 'in all honesty' occurred very frequently when women addressed the issue of future relationships. Often participants maintained that they were not actively looking for anyone. If it happened it would be nice, but it was not to be sought after. Where they did put a wish for a committed relationship more strongly this was usually framed as an admission. Research by Jamieson and colleagues (2002) with young people in their twenties found that women who presented themselves as open to a relationship said that they were not 'looking' for a relationship. The authors surmised that the women were only 'not looking' because they had a general rule against ever 'looking' (Jamieson *et al.* 2002: 9).

Why does this discursive pattern appear? What kind of work is being done when women confess to the desire for a relationship and present it as a truth? Specifically, a truth underneath what now becomes re-positioned as the rhetoric of desirable independence. In many ways this is surprising in the light of the pattern highlighted in the previous section, where I suggested that women have a difficult task in relation to being single. They have to acknowledge their membership of the social category, distance themselves from the imputation of personal deficit, and build a positive account of themselves. Superficially, one might imagine that the subject position of 'looking for a husband' (line 17) would help to ward off the position of personal deficit, and at times it did seem to be used in this way, as if to provide evidence that the speaker was doing her best. Yet it also appears to create trouble.

One aspect is that these extracts from interviews need to be understood in the context of the interactions that occasioned them. In some traditions of research the phrase 'if I'm honest' might be taken as a more true and faithful statement of the speaker's desire for marriage. Potter has drawn attention to the problems in assuming that cognitive descriptions, talk of thoughts and feelings, actually give access to an inner world that tells something factual about the speaker's mental state (Potter 1996: 103–4). He argues that cognitive descriptions should have no different status from an analytic point of view, than any other kind of statements. It is important to look at what participants are doing with their apparent admissions.

The phrase 'if I'm honest' might be construed as working to strengthen a claim, giving greater status to the veracity of the point about to be made. This is indeed one way in which the phrase is hearable (that is, can be understood) as being used on this occasion: as affiliative and a way of expressing the speaker's complete openness to the interviewer. However, I argue that in the context of Extract 17 it can also be heard as an apology. Jill has put the question on looking for a long-term relationship as 'let's just try you again' (line 4). This is hearable as testing Milly's commitment to earlier answers. Milly has been invited to re-appraise her wishes, and what she is saying now runs against the grain of some earlier discussion on the merits of independence. She builds up quite gradually her positioning of herself as someone who is ready for a long-term relationship before making this more concrete in line 17 as 'I'm looking for a husband'. To present this current response as a 'truth', and one that needs some accounting for, could be heard as acknowledgement of some contradiction with an account that generally stresses independence and freedom in being single.

Trouble may be arising from the highly idealized repertoires of singleness and the relative lack of discursive routes available to women to celebrate their single identity. If one avows a strongly positive view of singleness then this makes the desire to move out of the category troublesome to express. What seems difficult to hold together in the current western discursive climate – using commonly drawn upon discursive resources – is a positive construction of the category 'single' alongside the desire for a relationship. One seems to obviate the other. Women face an ideological dilemma here. The positive constructions of the idealized repertoires seem to render the desire for a relationship difficult to admit.

This lack of discursive routes has connections with the trajectory of singleness, and whether indeed it might be considered to have a trajectory. Rhetorical work by women to position themselves as having potential to enter a field of relationships – including marriage – can be seen as countering a more static conception of singleness as a fixed identity without a trajectory in relationship terms. As I noted in Chapter 2, a model of identity frequently used in literature on singleness is that of the life cycle. The ways in which this has been developed seem to assume that singleness as a state is permanent, and that what changes over time is the single person's attitude to their state, involving, for instance, grieving, acceptance, developing a positive notion of the self (see Lewis and Moon 1997). I discuss in Chapter 4 the dominant cultural storyline of marriage and family life, which is another kind of trajectory that my participants worked with, and at times against, in their own self-narratives. The notion of life stages, or ages, which imply particular kinds of relationship, connections to family, is a powerful one. It is visible in Milly's age-related account in lines 11 to 16 of Extract 17:

while it was never a big issue when I was younger, now I do appreciate the companionship side of things; I value that far more highly than perhaps I did before and I want someone to belong to and someone to belong to me,

Notions of companionship and belongingness are commonly represented as features that develop with an ageing, or maturing, process. Following on from this is a hard-to-define age or stage at which it becomes even more difficult for single women to talk of aspirations to marriage or companionship.

Milly disclaims any note of desperation: 'I'm not feverish about it' she states (line 23). Having admitted that she is 'looking for a husband' (line 17), she then does some rhetorical work to distance herself from an identity of a needy single woman. Not being 'desperate' was another frequently recurring subject position in my data. It has something of the status of what is 'sayable' (Hall 1997b) about singleness if one wishes to avoid the personal deficit repertoire. Given the ideological dilemmas generated by the available interpretative resources, the very best identity allowed to the single woman is to embrace independence, autonomy and self-development without remainder. The most shameful identity (as evidenced in what is warded off and avoided in the talk) is to express strong needs for others and to pitifully fail to have them met.

Some participants referred to an image of the single woman as 'predatory', which is the extreme case of this area of shame. This is a remarkably gendered image, which if applied to men does not conjure up the whole category of the single man in quite the same way as for women. Personal deficit for single women is marked by failure 'to get a man' or, as one participant noted, through the failure 'to be chosen by anyone'. Again there are traces of older discourses and continuities here with the notion that women are themselves to blame for their 'surplus' status. Such failures draw on the personal deficit and social exclusion repertoires, while single successes are constructed narrowly within the two idealized repertoires. So management of the personal identity is challenging indeed. One aspect of women's lives and experiences becomes mystified and pathologized. The next extract demonstrates this discursive and ideological tension being portrayed in psychological terms as splits and tensions within the self.

Extract 18

1	*Marion*	[. . .] You know, I think if, if I had a
2		choice, and you know I could have a
3		perfect person to be with, I'd much rather
4		have that than to be on my own. I can't

5   deny that (laughs). I was trying to, I was
6   trying to work out why I didn't want that
7   to happen but, because I know I want to
8   be, in my head I am perfectly happy and
9   content, but in my heart I am not really.

Marion in Extract 18 also frames her preference as an admission, 'I can't deny that' (lines 4 to 5). To deal with the dilemmas contained within the discourse of singleness she constructs a split or divided self, with head and heart going in different directions (lines 8 to 9). Splits within the available discursive resources become relocated as contradictions within women themselves. The subject position held is then one of ambivalence. The talk of a 'perfect person', however, does some complex work to sustain positive constructions of the single self. Marion effectively tempers her want as a serious choice by making it something potentially out of normal reach. It can feel dangerous to express a desire that may never be fulfilled and if it is portrayed as out of normal reach – perfection – then it is less undermining to claims to contentment with singleness.

Responses of apology for desire need to be seen as consequences of the extremely polarized interpretative resources of denigration and idealism that are available to women alone. This combination does not provide women with a position from which they can express both positive feelings about their current single state and desires for a relationship. In the context of the highly idealized view of singleness developed in reaction to the strongly denigrated account, such desires become unacceptable because they challenge the basis of the positive features expressed in the third and fourth repertoire.

Working reflexively with the contradictions

The third way that women in my sample worked with the highly polarized repertoires of singleness was to address the contradictions more directly in their discussion, and to explore the consequences for their personal identity. This was a less common approach than the two negative strategies I have discussed. Extracts 19 to 21 are examples.

Extract 19

1 *Rachel*   I think I have some real contradictions
2   about it because I like being independent;
3   I think that I have a lot of admiration
4   and respect for other women who are on
5   their own, and so my kind of political and

6	principled beliefs are as a woman you
7	don't need a partner and it's okay to be
8	on your own, and yet at an emotional level
9	it's I'm uncomfortable with that. I
10	think, well yes I can be jolly strong and
11	clear about, about it's <u>okay</u> to be on your
12	own, but that's actually not what I want.
13	Um, and I do feel that quite strongly, and
14	then feel a bit embarrassed about it, like
15	I'm letting the side down a bit. Or even
16	letting myself down a bit when I say,
17	'well you know things aren't complete
18	unless I've got a man', which goes back to
19	the kind of earlier thing about why have I
20	not been able to achieve that. And so
21	it's both wanting to be positive about
22	women on their own, including myself,
23	and yet having a yearning not to be.

In Extract 20 Jay is referring to a joke, which she says could be about any mother: 'How many Jewish mothers does it take to change a light bulb?' 'None, because it's all right dear, I'll just sit here in the dark.' She goes on, in lines 1 to 7, to explain how such passive stoicism features in her own way of presenting herself.

Extract 20

1	Jay	And I have got hell of a lot of that in me
2		and that has an awful lot to do with my
3		having spent, in retrospect quite a lot of
4		my life as a single person, because I
5		don't go out and get what I want. I don't
6		go out and get what I need, I sit and
7		suffer in silence. And I think that ties
8		up with being a bit unapproachable, and
9		not being the sort of person that people
10		would see as wanting to be in a
11		relationship. You know, you are generating
12		self-sufficiency and acting it and here I
13		am, I am self-sufficient, I am decisive, I
14		do this, I go here, I do that. So my image
15		is somebody who doesn't want to be any
16		different.

Extract 21

1	*Susie*	That core for me is, you know, marriage,
2		children, you know, ordinary family life
3		and so even though I've overlaid that with
4		layer upon layer of new stuff, which most
5		of the time is absolutely fine, at moments
6		of particular sort of pressure or
7		vulnerability then that's the bit that
8		comes back and says, you are therefore a
9		freak 'cos you're not in that situation
10		and totally loses sight of the fact that
11		I'm not made, or I have made myself now,
12		unsuitable for that and don't, really
13		don't need it. So, yes, lots of
14		contradictions, but I think along the
15		lines of wanting what you don't have.

The issue of an ideological dilemma over desire and independence remains. Indeed, at first glance Extract 19 seems to have little that distinguishes it from the extracts I have described as apologizing for desire. What is different in these speakers' strategies is their acknowledgement of the tension. Rachel, in Extract 19, for instance, raises the dilemmatic nature of both 'wanting to be positive about women on their own' (lines 21 to 22) and wanting a relationship. Like Marion, in Extract 18, all these speakers locate the tension in discursive resources as a contradiction within themselves. Rachel presents her wish for a partner as a 'truth' behind the more political position of 'it's okay to be on your own': saying that's 'actually not what I want' (line 12). Jay, in Extract 20, talks of 'not being the sort of person that people would see as wanting to be in a relationship' (lines 9 to 11) and 'generating self-sufficiency' (lines 11 to 12). Implicit in this self-critical and ironical description is the unstated possibility that Jay might want a relationship. Susie, in Extract 21, talks of the contradictions of feeling a 'freak' (line 9) for not having the 'core' (line 1) of ordinary family life, while she has made herself 'unsuitable for that' (line 12) and doesn't really need it.

The speakers leave the dilemmas unresolved. What they do is to recognize the difficulties of inhabiting this troubled category and how it is seen by others. They work with the contradictions. While they continue to draw on the strongly positive repertoires of singleness, the positioning of these speakers is less idealized, more reflexive.

Conclusion

Singleness is a troubled category – not one that many women wish to align themselves with. Yet paradoxically, the positive and idealized interpretative

72

resources that are available seem to make other aspects of single women's lives and expectations pathological. Women are faced with a difficult set of dilemmas. Either they can choose to construct singleness very positively through the repertoires of choice and independence and self-development and achievement, and then it becomes difficult to talk about any move out of the category. Or women can talk unashamedly about their desire for a relationship, and risk being constructed as deficient and 'desperate', and marked by their failure to already have a man. There seem to be few satisfactory ways out of these dilemmas given the contemporary politics of relationships. The only positive strategy used by a small number of women interviewed was to develop a reflexive account and talk about the dilemmas as such, rather than alternating between each side of them as experiential truths.

4

A NARRATIVE OF RELATIONSHIPS AND SINGLENESS

And I ain't gonna be the woman that you left behind
No I ain't gonna be the woman that you left behind
If we meet on the road, well that's just fine
But I ain't gonna be the woman that you left behind.
(Woehrle Blong 1974)

Introduction

The dominant cultural storyline for the lives of women is one of marriage and family relationships. Indeed, it has been argued that the narrative or storied nature of romance is one of the most compelling discourses by which western subjects are inscribed (Jackson 1995). Women who are on their own have to do rhetorical work that deals with this cultural storyline in presenting a positive account of a life and relationships. The previous chapter gave a number of examples of how women draw on common interpretative repertoires to work with their identity. This chapter focuses mainly on extracts from just one interview, in order to examine in more detail the kind of narrative and rhetorical work undertaken by a participant in explaining her life and relationships. The extracts form a 'self-narrative' (Gergen, K.J. 1994). Chapter 5 continues with a focus on the stories that my participants told, but features a wider range of narratives from different participants.

It's not unusual for couples to be asked how they got together, particularly when they are meeting with others early on in their relationship as a couple together. The story of 'how we met' can be fun for the teller and the audience, as well as a celebration of coupledom. In contrast, for a single woman to be asked 'how come you never married?' or 'why didn't you ever remarry?' can be stigmatizing as well as implying that it's never going to happen now (see also Adams 1976; Anderson and Stewart 1995). Try asking a couple 'how come you're still married?' to get the idea that it is neither a direct equivalent nor very usual as a conversational move.

Questions about a person's non-coupledness also seem less likely to elicit stories that the teller will be happy recounting. My own experience in my twenties and thirties was of regularly being asked whether I had met someone special yet, or (like Bridget Jones) receiving enquiries about my love-life (Fielding 1996: 40). In my forties and fifties all enquiries ceased. Both experiences were equally irritating – the first suggesting to me that only when I had met someone would I be interesting as a person – the second that I was no longer likely to have sexual or romantic relationships.

The narratives that people develop for their emotional lives are deeply connected with their sense of self (Lupton 1998). In talking of their lives, participants are nevertheless undertaking a form of psycho-discursive practice, taking their personal accounts from a cultural repertoire, and constructing their identity in the telling (Gergen, M. 1994). They present themselves as persons who are psychological, moral and competent. They demonstrate that they are *relational* persons, talking their relationships into being (Duck 1994). I want to look in detail at just how such narratives are told by single women, how individuals deal with the potential trouble attached to their category and use their narrative to perform their identity.

In this chapter and the next I am interested in the kind of identity work involved in giving a narrative account of relationships. In particular, how does a woman who is on her own explain how she got to where she is now? What cultural, discursive and story-telling resources does she draw on to describe her experiences and feelings?

Analytic concepts in narrative analysis

The field of narrative studies is very broad and includes a wide range of different disciplines, each with distinctive approaches to what is considered important for analysis (for overviews see Andrews *et al.* 2000; Elliott 2005). I discuss first a range of approaches that I find relevant before describing my own discursive approach to understanding narrative.

Relevant approaches

For the social sciences in general, narrative analysis has provided a way of returning to people's 'stories'. Within psychology, there is debate over how far a speaker's narrative gives access to a consistent identity and reflects the reality of lived experience (Crossley 2000) or allows for different identities to be performed according to the context of social interaction (Edley 2002; Riessman 2002; Taylor 2003b).

There has been considerable interest in the influence of narrative traditions on how people render their own life stories. Ricoeur (1992), writing of the connections between life and fiction, sees subjectivity as a narratively achieved identity that is done within the relevant cultural traditions. He argues that we keep reinterpreting the narrative identity that constitutes us, in the light of the narratives proposed to us by our own culture (1992: 32). This does not mean, for Ricoeur, that our lives are *told* by the stories already in existence. Instead we search for stories with which to understand our lives, and this includes potential stories, stories that have not yet been told.

From a social psychology perspective, Bruner suggests that the criteria for what makes a story worth telling are related both to the canonical (the well-understood and expected sequence of behaviour or events) and breaches of the canonical (which are also familiar, but often portray human plights such as the betrayed wife, the cuckolded husband). In a passage that I find very relevant to the story-telling tasks of single women reflecting on their lives, he remarks that while narrative is normative, it is not culturally terminal. Narratives deal with 'trouble' but do not have to resolve it: 'the "consoling plot" is not the comfort of a happy ending but the comprehension of plight that, by being made interpretable, becomes bearable' (Bruner 1991).

Some discussion on similar lines from Andrews and others (2002) has sought to bring together such 'counter-narratives' and the resistance that they offer to 'dominant cultural storylines' or 'master narratives' (which, while not fully defined, seem to be similar to Bruner's 'canonical narratives'). The argument is that members of outgroups tell stories to themselves and others that help to document and even validate a different, and 'counter' reality. While they may be experienced and articulated differently, they have some common meanings, and can subvert the strongly held prescriptions around, for instance, 'motherhood' (May 2003), what constitutes a 'family' (Throsby 2002) and 'proper' sexual behaviour for older women (Jones 2002).

Drawing on insights from conversation analysis, Schegloff (1997a) has cautioned against assuming that the interview context has no effect on a narrative produced by a speaker. He points out that a story must be considered within its interactional context, in order to see what functions it fulfils. Stories are not pre-packaged, and simply waiting to be solicited or elicited by the interviewer's approach to questioning. The story will be jointly produced or co-constructed between the interviewer and the narrator (Schegloff 1997a).

A number of narrative analysts have commented on the patterned consistency of the movement of certain types of stories through narrative time and space, and the potential for identifying narrative 'genres' (Bruner 1991; Jacobs 2000; Todorov 1990). Gergen argues that the structure of a good story requires it to reach a valued end-point, and be either progressive or regressive, with a stability theme being a third possibility (Gergen, K.J. 1994). According to Gergen, the progressive narrative charts the course temporally towards the valued end-point and shows how related events move steadily towards the accomplishment of this point. The regressive narrative has a negative state as the end-point, for instance death of a friend or other loss, and each event brings the protagonist closer to this end-point. A stability narrative might be a story of continuing success having achieved an earlier goal, although as Gergen and Gergen (1987) point out this has some difficulties as an option, furnishing a picture of stagnation and lacking dramatic force. Looking at the use of these genres in accounts of relationships, Gergen and Gergen (1987) note that married couples may have a shared story of 'how we got together'. They suggest that once stability has been reached there can be a temptation to engage in a regressive narrative 'I fear we are falling out of love' (Gergen and Gergen 1987).

A discursive approach to narrative

Gergen refers to 'self-narratives', and I have followed his definition in identifying narratives in my data for analysis:

> an individual's account of the relationship among several self-relevant events across time. In developing a self-narrative we establish coherent connections among life events.
>
> (Gergen, K.J. 1994: 187)

While there are undoubtedly links between literary construction and the ordinary construction of a person's self-narrative, there are limitations to how faithfully any self-narrative can be expected to conform to a literary genre. Within the context of an interview, or indeed in other kinds of conversation, I find that the self-narrative does not have a uni-directional form, as implied by Gergen (1994), that moves seamlessly without deviation from start point to valued end-point. The co-construction of narratives in conversation means that there is not one single story waiting to be brought forward by one speaker. The story can instead take different turns according to the construction of the conversation (see Bamberg 2004; Reynolds and Taylor 2005; Taylor 2003b). Rather than seeing 'progressive' or 'regressive' as identifiable genres by which the narratives of women alone can be typified, I look at the notions of progress or decline as resources which people may draw on but not necessarily use in a consistent way in telling their self-narrative.

My interest in narrative is as a discursive resource (Taylor 2006). I am interested in the patterns of meaning that are evident in participants' narratives, and the ways in which they construct an identity or identities. This does not mean that talk can never be reliably informative about events and circumstances, but that this is not the focus of my analysis (see also Taylor 2003a). I expect narratives and the structures employed in them to relate to how women constitute themselves within the interaction (Abell *et al.* 2000). Like Riessman (1993), I assume that narratives are essential meaning-making structures, and that researchers must respect respondents' ways of constructing meaning. When women who are alone are talking about their lives, they are dealing with something intensely personal and trying to make sense of their experiences. It is nonetheless important to analyse how that meaning-making is accomplished, and my interest is in this: in how stories are occasioned and told in the interview context (Stokoe and Edwards 2006), and what resources are drawn on in telling them, rather than the 'windows into lives' that Riessman also refers to (Riessman 2002: 707).

The process of living in the cultural 'slots' and identity possibilities for singleness constructed by social history, social practices and the surrounding ideological field is a personal identity project for individual single women (Reynolds 2006). In developing their self-narratives and making sense of their lives, people work up the available discursive resources as identity. The self-narrative provides participants with a way to manage their identity. Mishler (1999) brings a number of points together that I see as central to my analysis, in understanding personal narratives as socially situated actions, identity performances and combinations of form and content. People do not simply relay information about themselves, they present events in recognized forms that correspond to story-telling, and draw on culturally available resources to perform their identity, in ways that will vary according to context and purpose. We can expect that women will tell their self-narratives within their cultural tradition, drawing on shared ideas of what makes a good story, what kind of stories it is appropriate to tell about oneself, and attending to the dominant cultural storylines of women as wives and mothers.

As discussed above, I have not found it helpful to make a simple division of my participants' self-narratives as either progressive or regressive towards a valued end-point. Instead, I draw on Goffman's (1974) concept of 'frame' as a tool for analysis that I have adapted in my own way to more fully account for the variability that I found in my data.

Goffman is interested in the multiple worlds and multiple realities to which people can attend in their talk: for instance, the world of 'everyday life' coexisting with worlds of make-believe, the theatre and dreams. His perspective is situational, meaning a concern for what one individual can be attending to at any given moment. He suggests that in taking part in any interaction, the individuals involved face the question: 'What is it that's going on here?' (Goffman 1974: 8). Goffman uses 'frame' as a concept for identifying how participants may have dealt with this question. By frame, he refers to moment-to-moment changes in how participants define their encounters. He assumes that whatever an individual takes to be going on may turn out to be mistaken, and that constant re-readings of the situation will be required, so that many frames will be employed in any encounter.

My use of 'frame' is more broad-brush than Goffman's. I use it to refer to some over-arching structures that my participants employed in their narratives. However, in common with Goffman, my use of the word allows for recognition of the situated nature of their accounts, and the context in which they were given. These structures also served as a frame for the encounter between interviewer and interviewed as participants, women of similar relationship status and sometimes similar and sometimes contrasting ages. The frames are co-constructed between us as participants. They can, in addition, be thought of as frames for the more invisible encounter that participants have in a research interview with an assumed research audience or readership.

Examining self-narratives, and in this chapter focusing in particular on one participant's account, is an opportunity to take a different lens to my material, and for different insights to emerge. I continue to refer to the concepts I used in Chapter 3, of the dominant interpretative repertoires drawn on by participants, and the ideological dilemmas and subject positions that open up in their self-narratives. The concept of subject position is particularly apposite to an exploration of identity as performed in self-narrative, since it is the concept that connects wider notions of discourses and dominant cultural storylines to the social construction of particular selves (Edley 2001). Edley (2001) quotes Hall's claim that identity is formed 'at the unstable point where the "unspeakable" stories of subjectivity meet the narratives of a culture' (Hall 1988: 44). The speaker's identity is constructed by the different kinds of person, or subject positions, that are implied by particular ways of telling one's self-narrative. On similar lines, Harré and van Langenhove describe a position in a conversation as 'a metaphorical concept through reference to which a person's "moral" and personal attributes as a speaker are compendiously collected' (Harré and van Langenhove 1991: 395).

Analytic process

I analysed data for stretches of text that were in the form of a narrative about past relationships, and a separate data file was created of all such examples. My criteria for recognizing a self-narrative were very broad; unlike some analysts I did not require talk to be organized around a beginning, middle and end, or introduced and closed with entrance and exit talk (Riessman 1993). Gergen's definition of a self-narrative given above (Gergen, K.J. 1994) provides a good description of what I searched for: passages that had some sequencing and movement from one event or relationship to another. I looked for accounts that seemed to connect up with earlier or later references and that were explanatory rather than simply descriptive. Participants sometimes moved back and forth temporally in talking of past relationships so examples were not always neatly sequenced.

The main question in my interviews that in particular sought to elicit a narrative was one about important relationships in the participant's life and her understanding of how she had got to where she was now. The exact form of my question varied according to what the participant had already said. One fairly typical request was: 'I'm asking people about sort of relationships, intimate relationships over the course of the life and obviously that could be a huge area; I'm not asking for detailed accounts but just to get a sense of how you make sense, really, of the course your life's taken and where you find yourself now.' Additionally, in the first stage of the interview, in response to an invitation from me to 'just say a few things to introduce yourself, say who you are and what you do', participants sometimes opened their self-descriptions by talking about past relationships or marriages. My later question would acknowledge this; for instance, one person was asked: 'You've said quite a bit really about important relationships, but there might be others that you'd want to say have been important in the course of your life, and I suppose what I'm interested in is what, well, how you understand the kind of shape that your life's taken, that you haven't remarried, or found someone that you would elevate to position of partner. How do you make sense of that?'

Most of the data compiled in this file related to the questions referred to above, and it all came from the 26 individual interviews, since I did not ask the women in the group interview about their lives to date. I grouped together lengthy extracts (including interviewer questions and comments) from individual interviews that I identified as contributing to a participant's self-narrative (or narratives) across the interview as a whole. Questions, and their responses, that did not invoke a relationship history, for instance questions on images of singleness or future expectations, were not included in this data file.

In some cases participants spoke of episodes or gave an overview of their relationships within one turn of talk, and at times I refer to these shorter, more boundaried accounts as 'stories'. I have looked for commonalities in the ways that participants told their self-narratives, and done a more fine-grained analysis of the subject positions that are opened up through the jointly constructed narratives and stories.

Frames in a narrative

A striking pattern in participants' self-narratives was the use of three frames that at different points dominated the way in which they spoke. In one extended turn of talk Sarah demonstrates all three: most other participants employed only one or two. I call these frames *life cycle*, *life events* and *life as progress*. Although for purposes of analysis I consider each of these here separately, it will also be evident that these frames are linked. They are used in overlapping ways within Sarah's narrative account.

Life cycle

Sarah is a 50-year-old woman who has remained single.

Extract 1: Twenties

```
 1  Jill    Okay. Um I'd like if you can to say
 2          something about, it's a sort of sketch
 3          rather than a sort of detailed history
 4          (laughs) that I'm looking for, and really
 5          around the sort of point that women
 6          sometimes find it difficult to say wh-
 7          I mean, I think you said you have made
 8          choices, so what sort of choices have you
 9          made, what people have there been in the
10          course of your life that you've been close
11          to and that, how do you explain it to
12          yourself?
13  Sarah   I have to tell you that, and it's fine to
14          tell you the detail, but I think this is
15          what sort of explains it for me. I
16          actually lost my brother when I was 21 so
17          er, somewhat tragically, so that was a
18          major influence for me in terms of my,
19          certainly all of my twenties. So the men
20          that I went out with, I mean I went a bit
21          mad really I think, in retrospect, but I
22          went travelling, I went out with loads of
23          guys, was not interested in long-term
24          relationships; there was no way I was ever
25          going to be close to anyone, so I think,
26          you know, that's, that was very
27          influential and has been, I think, in
28          many respects um, ongoingly.
```

The stages that Sarah refers to in this and later extracts are ones of which she says: 'I can see it in decades almost'. First, she refers to the 'twenties' in Extract 1. Youth is often depicted as a time of trying out different relationships and of fickleness in romantic attachments. However, Sarah's story is inflected with the early loss of her brother and she draws on a psychodynamic model of identity to explain a continuing influence from this loss. Sarah responds to the request to sketch out what choices she has made, what people in the course of her life she has been close to and how she explains it to herself. Jill's question is complex and hedged about with qualifications. Although she does not ask 'how come you never married?' Sarah nevertheless responds to this unasked question with an abstract (Labov 1972) that pinpoints the death of her brother as a major influence.

No individuals are picked out by Sarah in this period of her twenties. She parcels up this period as one in which she adopted the same attitude to all the men she went out with. While the notion of relationships that do not go very deep is not an uncommon way to talk of youth, this is not a story of carefree times. Sarah combines a strong sense of the reaction to the loss of her brother with a sense of her own agency in opting for 'loads of guys' and not 'going to be close to anyone'. In positioning herself as active and in control in her relationships with men, Sarah is also dealing with the interpretative repertoire of singleness as personal deficit: that a woman who has remained single has not been chosen by a man. She avoids one troubled subject position, but the link she makes with the influence of her brother's loss takes her to another kind of trouble, that of a woman who does not want to get close to a man.

Sarah also reflects some gendered assumptions about the nature of intimate relationships for women. At the time when Sarah was in her twenties it was becoming more common for western women to have sex before marriage with a range of men, but the sexual double standard operated to make women's active sexuality a more negative attribute than it was for men. Positioning oneself as young, not looking for long-term relationships and trying things out is a way of avoiding labels of 'wicked woman' (Holland *et al.* 1996) or 'slag' (Lees 1993; Jackson and Cram 2003). In the 1980s and 1990s women were occasionally seen wearing t-shirts that proclaimed 'So many men, so little time' (also lines in a popular song). This may be intended as a straightforward representation of women as actively sexual: it also can be read as an ironic and humorous resistance of the sexual double standard through its contradiction of ordinary assumptions. Imagine Tennyson's Lady of Shalott weaving this slogan into her tapestry as a way of countering being positioned as grief struck (no love of her own and only the shadows of coupledom in view) (Tennyson [1833/1842] 1998). However, it seems that in more recent times there continue to be challenges for young women in resisting the sexual double standard in ways that go beyond individual and muted responses that subvert traditional expectations (Jackson and Cram 2003).

In the next extract I want to discuss, Sarah has moved on to her 'thirties' (the intervening lines between Extract 1 and Extract 2 are shown as Extract 7).

Extract 2: Thirties

37 Sarah   [. . .]   So, and then
38   in my thirt- I mean I can see it in

39	decades almost really, in, in my thirties
40	I started going out with people for longer
41	and um I suppose it's timing really. I
42	mean that's how I would see that, you
43	know, there were some people I wasn't
44	ready for and some people who weren't
45	ready for me really in terms of what you
46	wanted out of your life; whether you
47	wanted to have kids, set- you know, live
48	with somebody etc. and, um I certainly
49	think of my thirties there was one person
50	I met in my thirties who probably the only
51	person I would have actually married; I
52	mean marriage has never been particularly
53	an issue but he is somebody that probably
54	I, I would have married but, you know, it
55	didn't work out; we were in different
56	places really.

In her account of her thirties Sarah addresses more directly the normative life cycle of marriage and child-rearing. This decade provides the moment where she identifies a person she would have married but 'it didn't work out'. 'Timing' is offered as an explanation – other people were at different places with their life courses unrolling at a different pace to Sarah's. No blame for unfortunate timing attaches either to herself or to the people she went out with 'for longer'. Sarah positions herself as 'reasonable' here and throughout her life and relationships narrative.

Although she says marriage as such has 'never been particularly an issue' Sarah nonetheless conveys through her reference to marriage both the importance of the relationship that didn't work out and the possibility of an alternative life cycle stage that she did not take. She moves momentarily from her first person narrative to the more impersonal 'you' in lines 46 and 47 in talking of 'what you wanted out of your life; whether you wanted to have kids' and repairs what seems to be the start of a reference to 'settle down', in line 47, substituting instead 'live with somebody'. The repair conveys a rather more impermanent potential future. Sarah distances herself from ownership of hopes and dreams of having kids and settling down (using the universal 'you' instead of 'I') in contrast with what she describes as actually taking place.

Sarah is dealing with an ideological dilemma here (Billig *et al.* 1988). Women who have not seen marriage as their goal have not necessarily rejected a wish for long-term partnership. Do they use the language of marriage, commitment and children, or do they attempt to define relationships in other ways? Sarah responds to the implicit request to account for her single status, and gives evidence of a relationship that had potential as a marital type relationship, while maintaining that marriage was not an issue for her. Even then it is not clear that she is against marriage as such: in lines 53 and 54 she says he is someone that probably she would have married. Is she using 'would have' in the hypothetical sense of she would have lived with him in what would have been a marriage had she been the marrying kind, but might have instead been a committed and long-term relationship? Or is she saying that she would have married him if that had been what he wanted and he had pressed her enough? The meaning is ambiguous, allowing both possibilities to remain open. Bauman identifies in the modern 'liquid love' the possibility for people to 'follow simultaneously the drive for freedom and the craving for belonging' (Bauman 2003: 34), and Sarah seems to be playing out these contradictory drives in her narrative.

The next extract relates to the 'forties'.

Extract 3: Forties

```
56  Sarah   [. . .]              Um, and it's got
57           better each decade actually. My forties
58           were, I was much more together, um and
59           made, I suppose that's when I made the
60           sort of most together choices of leaving a
61           relationship I'd been in for a while
62           because, I just felt that wasn't right for
63           me really and that felt like a major step
64           for me, to not just be batting around, you
65           know, letting things happen to me really.
```

Just one action is chosen to stand as representative of this decade. Rather than discuss more directly a relationship that she had 'been in for a while' (line 61), Sarah highlights her choice to leave. She presents this decision as strongly positive: 'most together' (line 60). Sarah continues to give a balanced and non-blaming account, the relationship 'wasn't right for me really' (lines 62 to 63). However, by presenting this as a 'major step' with herself more active and in control, she re-positions herself in the earlier stages as having less agency, 'batting around' and 'letting things happen to me' (lines 64 to 65).

Sarah's 'stages' account conveys an overall impression of 'naturalness'. One stage follows another. In her story relationships are presented as fitting with maturational processes, rather than as full of struggle and difficulty. 'Timing' is one kind of explanation she offers: the different life cycle imperatives of individuals not always meshing.

Timing often has a special resonance for women, in relation to the biologically and socially limited time frame for childbearing. The next extract is from an interview with Patsy. The extract follows Patsy's response to a question on whether having children was important to her. Patsy replies that while she was in her last relationship, she would have wanted children, but that her partner was younger than her and did not want them at that time. She says that now she is 43 it is not an issue for her. Following a discussion from Patsy about how often women who have had children have said to her: 'Don't you regret not having had children?', the exchange in Extract 4 takes place.

Extract 4

1	Jill	For some women it obviously is very
2		important and that's the drive that's more
3		important than finding the right man to be
4		with.
5	Patsy	Yes.
6	Jill	It's the person to have children with.
7	Patsy	Yes, which has never really been, that's
8		never been at the front of my mind, I've
9		always wanted that soul-mate to be with,
10		you know rather than the children that
11		come from, you know from that relationship
12		really. But I've had a lot of people, a
13		lot of women say to me, and I suppose to a
14		certain extent that I agree with them,
15		that, that I spent you know, that 'the
16		best years', or the kind of final years,
17		of my possible child-bearing time with
18		[name] and that he, you know he wasn't
19		fair to me in those times. And I never
20		really looked at it like that, but I
21		suppose I look back now and think oh yes I
22		s'pose he did. But a lot of women say
23		that, a lot of women say how selfish he
24		was.
25	Jill	Mm. About your relationship?
26	Patsy	About, yeah, and the fact that I was you
27		know, I met him when I was, how old would
28		I have been, 30, how old am I now, I met
29		him ten years ago so I'd have been about
30		32, 33 when I first met him. And then I
31		was about 36 when we got, 37 probably when
32		we got into a relationship. Um so he knew,
33		you know.

34	*Jill*	It was a crucial time in terms of, if you
35		had
36	*Patsy*	Yes, that's right.

Patsy in lines 7 to 24 treats Jill's comment as inviting further explanation of her own views, and both participants construct together a story that examines the potential place of childbearing in Patsy's long-term relationship that has now ended. The voices are invoked of other women who accused Patsy's partner of not being 'fair' and 'selfish'. People often use the authoritative voice of others as a rhetorical resource to support their own views or as something to argue against (Bakhtin 1981; Maybin 2001). The attribution of views to unnamed others rather than being presented as Patsy's own view gives the point additional force. These accusations position Patsy as a wronged woman, but one who is herself reasonable about this wrong (lines 19 to 20). She herself never looked at it this way, and only with hindsight does she see that she could agree with it. As with Sarah's reflections on marriage and children, Patsy's expressed feelings about whether her partner was unfair and selfish, and whether she minds, are fluid and ambiguous. The socially and culturally defined working up of an emotion (Lupton 1998) appears to be in evidence here. If others see us as unfairly treated, we can come to see ourselves in this way too.

Patsy refers to her age at different points of their acquaintance and subsequent relationship, and moves without further explanation to her evaluation: 'so he knew, you know'. That her meaning is accepted by Jill is shown by the incomplete response: 'It was a crucial time in terms of, if you had' (lines 34 to 35). Both women are invoking the dominant cultural storyline (Andrews 2002) of the right time for having children, and tacitly suggesting that women's lives are structured around the potential for this activity whether or not it is an option they wish to take up.

Analysts of narratives comment on their chronological structure and sequencing (Labov and Waletzky 1967), and the expectation from interviewers of temporally sequenced plots (Riessman 1993). The classic identity model of a 'life cycle' portrays individuals negotiating universal aspects of development that present the need to adapt and change at key transitional points. As I discussed in Chapter 2, these transitional points or stages are usually designated as courtship, early marriage, birth of children, family with adolescents, children leaving home, retirement and old age (Carter and McGoldrick 1980). Despite the cultural prevalence of the belief that there is a clearly defined developmental series of stages that contribute to the achievement of identity, the developmental approach has been widely criticized by narrative analysts (Josselson 1996; Mishler 1999).

It may seem rather banal to note that Sarah divided her account into stages, and appear to lend support to a developmental model for the life cycle, which is not my intention. The depiction of a life cycle made up of stages or transitions provides a frame for narrating the relationships over the course of life. It is also a map to which some women may feel obliged to refer in explaining the route they have taken. I point to the parallels in my data with a life cycle perspective not to support its universality as a developmental framework, but to suggest that it is a resource that people use in trying to make sense of their own lives (see also Plummer 2001: 191–193).

The life cycle offers a familiar frame and trajectory for telling a self-narrative, and an apparently natural way of ordering and conceptualizing choices and decisions. It divides time up into discrete and boundaried stages in a tidy way, while allowing for some change from one stage to the next. A life cycle frame does not have to consist of prescribed stages; women can characterize and define their own preferred conception of stages that make sense to them. At the same time, by reference to the culturally established life cycle model, single women can tackle, directly or indirectly, the issue of discussing the opportunities that they have had for establishing family and partnership relationships. In this sense it is both a resource that single women can use actively and shape to their own ends, and a dominant cultural storyline that single women may want to position themselves against.

Life events

If there is a dominant life cycle storyline that forms part of expectations of how a life should be, another familiar narrative form is of events that change the life cycle. From the perspective of narrative analysis, life events such as chronic illness have been theorized as creating 'biographical disruption' with implications for the disruption of social relationships and the ability to mobilize material resources (Bury 1982). A link has been noted in narratives between discontinuities in career paths and other events that might otherwise seem relatively independent of them: divorce, depression or a move to another city, for instance (Mishler 1999).

In an analysis that combines a life course with a life events perspective, Allen describes the process of not getting married (for single women born in 1910) as made up of 'a series of events and transitions in childhood and young adulthood that cut across several life course careers' (Allen 1989: 77). The image of the spinster who failed to marry because of an early disappointment is a familiar one in novels, Miss Havisham in *Great Expectations* being a prime example (Dickens 1920, first published in serial form in 1860–61). The First World War famously left a generation of women whose lives were considered to be disrupted by the loss of their boyfriends or fiancés (Holden 2005).

Serious events have an impact on people's lives and I do not question this. My focus is not in investigating the reality of claims that lives have been changed by unpleasant events, but in exploring how past events are used as explanatory frames by single women talking of their lives and relationships. A life events frame, the notion that unpleasant events can throw a life off its planned course, can be considered as another resource upon which my participants drew in making meaning of and describing the shape of their lives to date. The events that participants referred to as life-changing and affecting their subsequent relationships included the death of a brother, the ending of an important relationship, an early sterilization, going to boarding school, and acquiring a mental illness label.

Sarah recounted in Extract 1 the influence of the early death of her brother on her subsequent relationships. Extract 5 forms the coda (Labov 1972) to what she has said: at the end of her extended response to Jill's initial question (Extract 1) she returns to her brother's early death as providing an overall explanation (see Extract 8 for the lines immediately preceding this coda).

Extract 5

84	*Jill*	Right.
85	*Sarah*	But I do think my brother's death actually
86		has had a major influence in me not
87		actually 'settling', for want of a better
88		word, with somebody.

Sarah does not attempt to justify how the influence of her brother's death explains her attitude to long-term relationships, and Jill does not query the connection being made. This influence could be seen as an explanation competing with 'timing' as the reason for Sarah's not settling with someone. The two are interwoven throughout her story but are, however, also inter-linked. A psychological journey has been route-marked by Sarah. Short-term relationships are seen as the outcome of her distress at the loss, and also as the result of her part in the wrong timing, when she was not ready for a close relationship.

Attributing strong and continuing influence to a major life event could position a speaker as a passive victim. It could also provide an excuse for the subsequent pattern of events, letting the speaker off the hook in a way that could be seen as 'bad faith' and a failure to grapple with personal responsibility for choices made (Craib 2000). Sarah intertwines the twin themes of loss and timing. This makes it hard to discern what functions each of these fulfils in her narrative. It appears that timing, as an expla-nation, has a stronger effect of distancing Sarah from any sense of agency than the reflection on her loss does. However, since Sarah accounts for her difficulties in matching timing through the driving motif of loss, it could be argued that it is functioning to absolve her of some responsibility. Sarah does not position herself in these extracts as a victim, rather as a person working with grief, developing and growing in the course of dealing with it. I return to discussion of this in relation to a frame of life as progress.

Metaphors of journeys and paths abound in the talk of interviewer and those interviewed. Jill asks Rachel, in another interview: 'Can you say something about important relationships over your life, and I'm looking really for the kind of sketch that's saying how you make sense, if you do, as to why you're now on your own really and what kind of path you've taken through life in terms of close relationships?' Jill's introduction of the term 'path' does some work to shape Rachel's response. Rachel plays with the metaphor of the path, and explains that when she was younger, her contemporaries were getting married and having families. She says she felt odd or different by choosing not to, but found no one with whom she wanted to follow the same path, and felt that she was sticking to a principle of being on her own rather than in a relationship she didn't want. After the ending of one intense and important relationship in her twenties she built up her life in other ways around work and friends and still felt she was holding out for something very special. When she met the person who became her partner for many years, they had what she thinks was a very good relationship: 'that clearly suited me extraordinarily well, both in terms of intimacy and freedom; and nurturing and a whole load of things'. But the partnership ended when he went off with someone else and 'in terms of the path then I suppose I'm now on the sort of path of, you know, being on my own, but now clearer that's not how I want to be'. Rachel queries whether she has made sense or said enough about a 'path' in her responses so far, and in Extract 6 she describes how she sees this.

Extract 6

1	Rachel	I think I'm rather, sort of, startled at
2		the ending of the path I was on with
3		[name], (laughs) actually. And I think
4		that really, really threw me, both
5		emotionally, obviously, and my sense of
6		self-esteem and blah blah blah; all of
7		that, but also my sense of a path because
8		the path, you know, we were staying
9		together and we were going to grow old
10		together and we were going to go round the
11		world in a camper van when we were 90,
12		and, and that's the surest I've ever been
13		of a path; I've never been that sure of a
14		path and it was a bit of a blow, and so

89

15	I'm having to sort of re-create paths, a
16	path, now because that was the one I was
17	on and I was really happy with it; I liked
18	that path.

The event of Rachel's partner leaving is depicted as putting an end to the path they were jointly following. Rachel does not minimize her reaction, she moves from 'startled' (line 1) to 'really, really threw me' (line 4), intensifying the impact. At the same time there is an ironic note to how she tells this story, with the more throwaway 'blah blah blah' (line 6) as a shorthand for the many effects of the relationship's termination, the understatement in line 14 'bit of a blow' and the use of rhythmical, poetic language to describe the plans now not to be realized.

The repetition of 'we were' and 'we were going' in each of lines 8 to 10 is followed by a repetition of 'path' in lines 13 to 18. The image of a path through life came from Jill's question, but Rachel has appropriated it and worked with it. Again the story is potentially one of a victim, but Rachel resists this position while at the same time asserting her commitment and faithfulness to the projected future that is now not to be. This is quite an unusual accomplishment. In talking of relationships that had ended some time previously, participants often denigrated their importance, or reflected chiefly on what was problematic. Rachel holds on to her story of the rightness of her last partnership, while recognizing that she has to 're-create paths'.

By exploring Sarah's and Rachel's use of life events as a frame I do not want to undermine the meaning of events for participants. However, a narrative of real or potential relationships disrupted and influenced by an earlier life event is also an explanatory frame that provides single women with an easily recognizable justification for their current state. That recognition owes something to psychological and lay storylines of loss and change. The life events frame introduces a wider canvas to narratives than a focus on the dynamics of intimate relationships.

It could be argued that the use of a life events frame and talk of paths and journeys in narration fits within a more classic narrative genre, the tragic or regressive narrative. Bury quotes Robinson (building on the ideas of Gergen and Gergen 1987) as characterizing regressive narratives as having 'a continual and increasing discrepancy between "valued personal goals" and the possibility of their attainment' (Bury 2001; Robinson 1990). However, as I shall show in discussion of my final frame, 'life as progress', unpleasant life events and the unfolding history that is narrated can also be combined with a progressive narrative. As Bury (2001) has pointed out, many accounts move from one narrative form to another, and the degree of consistency achieved will depend on the context in which the narrative is constructed and presented.

Life as progress

As with most people reflecting on the past, Sarah presents the past from the perspective of present realities and values (Riessman 2002). She speaks from a different place from that of the wild 20-year-old who 'went a bit mad really' (lines 20 to 21 in Extract 1). Sarah's references, in Extract 3, to being 'much more together' in her forties (lines 57 to 58) and 'a major step' (line 63) illustrate the third frame for structuring her narrative: as progressive. The two frames already identified link in Sarah's story with a frame of life as progress to provide a narrative that overall achieves a sense of progression.

In contrast to the progression of a coupledom narrative with changes in status such as those associated with marriage or parenthood, in my participants' accounts progression was often depicted as a story of inner growth and change (Reynolds and Taylor 2005). Frequently participants avoided a troubled subject position of having failed at relationships and family life by bringing forward the ways in which they were succeeding at other goals, or more generally improving psychologically and emotionally. These accounts do not simply provide a progressive structure for the speaker's life story. The framing of progress also does rhetorical work against any assumption that singleness is a fixed or static state outside the progression expected in any normal life trajectory (Reynolds and Taylor 2005). Above all, it positions the speaker, rather than any other observer, as the authority on the success of her own life.

This frame is more easily seen by considering Sarah's extended account overall. Much of it has been already presented. A further extract from Sarah's talk occurred between her description of her 'twenties' and her 'thirties'.

Extract 7

28	Sarah	[. . .] I mean, I
29		think that, you know, probably it's more
30		in its place now than it's ever been
31		which is why I feel probably better now
32		emotionally than I've ever been, but, um,
33		so I think that, that in terms of people I
34		chose to have as partners and
35		relationships then were short-term, you
36		know, no threat people really; great time
37		but nothing else.

In lines 28 to 37 Sarah gives an evaluative (Labov 1972) reflection on her depiction of her twenties and the causal relationship she traces between her brother's death and her behaviour when she 'went a bit mad really'. She

91

distances herself from the influence that she has just claimed her brother's death had on her in an ongoing way by saying 'it's more in its place now than it's ever been' (lines 29 to 30), and links this to feeling 'better now emotionally than I've ever been' (lines 31 to 32). This is a very rapid and immediate contrast with the troubled subject position in Extract 1 of not being able to be close to anyone because of grief from her loss. She then, in lines 35 to 36, in apparent response to Jill's opening question about choices and people, characterizes her choices in this stage as short-term relationships and 'no threat people'. Having made a claim of serious and lasting consequences from her loss, Sarah is able to redress the balance by pointing to psychological repair. She makes it clear that this is not to be heard as a story that gets worse over time. This also goes some way to defuse the potential for construing her subsequent discussion of her thirties (shown in Extract 2) as a time of disappointment and failure to settle down.

In lines 56 and 57, shown in Extract 3, Sarah adds another comment that may persuade the listener or reader to hear her narrative overall as progressive: 'it's got better each decade actually'. As I have already noted, she presents the ending of a relationship in her forties as a positive choice. The extract shown below rounds off Sarah's account (which ends with the evaluative coda already discussed as Extract 5).

Extract 8

66	*Sarah*	Um, and, I've only just become 50 so for
67		fifties, who knows? But um, certainly this
68		relationship I'm in now is very different
69		and I think I'm um more balanced in it
70		really in terms of I feel quite calm
71		about what's going, I feel much more
72		centred in myself I suppose is what it's
73		about and he's very different than a lot
74		of people I've been out with. So, so I
75		do, I do see it in these blocks (laughs)
76		of, sort of, time, of me, no, meeting some
77		nice people but timing being, you know, me
78		wanting at certain points to be living
79		with somebody and having kids when they
80		weren't ready for that and, and also times
81		when I've, you know, I've not been ready
82		for it and I've met people that wanted it.
83		So, yeah, timing.

Sarah reflects on her current state and what she expects from this decade. The relationship, the person she has chosen and her inner state (more centred), lines 67 to 74, are all very different. In response to an earlier question in the interview, when Jill enquired whether Sarah had someone she would call a partner, Sarah described this person as 'somebody very much in my life that I see regularly and that I sleep with and that, you know, I share things with but I don't know that I'd call him a partner'. However, the reference to a relationship that is different, which by implication carries more potential than previous ones, continues to build the story here as one that has a positive outcome.

Finally Sarah returns to the twin themes of timing and her brother's death as the explanation for not having settled with somebody (Extracts 8 and 5, lines 83 to 88). There is still some continuity with her previous experience and identity, despite progress and improvement in her life. Her introduction of the stage of her fifties with 'who knows' (line 67) and her reference back to the period of her youth and 'not actually "settling" . . . with somebody' (Extract 5, lines 85 to 88) could be heard as making it clear that the new relationship does not signal a change of state.

Many of the events referred to by different participants, as in the extracts from Sarah, had taken place when the speaker was much younger, and typically speakers would position this earlier self as an innocent young girl, more victim than active agent. Later, the young girl might give way to a more mature woman, with agency and the ability to make choices about relationships.

In Extract 9 Lyn ends a story of important relationships which has also been presented in stages characterized by different kinds of relationship at different points in her life course. The story included feeling devastated when her first man left her 'overnight' – an event to which she attributes some continuing impact.

Extract 9

1	Lyn	And then recently, just before I was 50, I
2		had a very short affair with somebody,
3		and it felt good because it (laughing)
4		made me realize it was still possible! And
5		that felt very positive. I also realized
6		this time that when the man was not
7		willing to negotiate with me about what
8		our relationship was going to be, and how
9		it was going to be, then I was able to
10		say, 'In that case I don't want this
11		relationship' and that was the first
12		time that I had the strength to say, 'I'm
13		worth more than this and if you're not
14		willing to negotiate with me and to agree

15   to certain things, then I'm not willing
16   just to be here for you when you feel like
17   it.' So it took until I was 49 for me to
18   have the strength to say that and that
19   feels very positive. At the same time it
20   enabled me to realize what I was missing,
21   and that was very painful.
22   So I suppose I see, theoretically, in the
23   future, that I might have a relationship,
24   and that I hope I will, and that I hope it
25   will be as good as some aspects of the
26   last relationship and I know that if I do
27   have a relationship with a man it will be
28   much more aware than any of the ones I had
29   in the past and that I won't stand for any
30   nonsense (laughing), or if I do it will be
31   because we've negotiated it.

In this extract Lyn is telling about the ending of a relationship: potentially a regressive account. However, like Sarah in lines 60 to 65 (Extract 3), Lyn presents the positive aspect of making a decision to end a relationship that was unsatisfactory. While Sarah refers to putting an end to 'batting around' and 'letting things happen to me', Lyn reports herself as saying 'I'm not willing just to be here for you when you feel like it' (lines 15 to 17). Both women draw on and rebut an interpretative repertoire of women as passive and waiting for men to make the moves. In its place they employ a repertoire of women seizing power, albeit negative power. Lyn's use of reported speech and repetition that the man was 'not willing to negotiate' gives her a subject position of 'strong and forthright' in this instance, even if it took until she was 49. Her comment in lines 19 to 21 that it was painful to recognize what she was missing can appear to be a digression, but it works to position her as appreciative of the potential of a good relationship, and thus emphasizes her femininity. It also acts as a bridge to her coda summing up where she is now (lines 26 to 31) – someone ready for a more mature relationship with a man.

Commentators suggest that women and men search for the right way to live in a society which focuses on the growth of the individual. Love is elusive, but remains idealized and invested with hopes for a better future (Beck and Beck-Gernsheim 1995; Giddens 1992). Sarah's story exemplifies the ideological dilemma of giving a positive account, for a person not currently involved in a committed partnership. My participants were often drawing on idealized interpretative repertoires of singleness as involving independence and achievement. They also recognized, and worked to counter, more denigrated repertoires of singleness as personal deficit and as social exclusion. Employing a frame of life as progress involved presenting a story that drew on psychological self-improvement, while admitting, and perhaps opening up, the possibility for better relationships in the future. Margaret Gullette has pointed to what she finds encouraging narratives of midlife women in 'progress novels' that can combat cultural stereotypes of midlife as inevitable decline (Gullette 1988, 1997). In the same way, depicting one's life as a story of progress offers a resource to women, allowing them to find a valued end-point of their own choosing that does not have to be the story of a happy-ever-after relationship.

Conclusion

Through looking at an extended extract from one interview, I have argued that women who are on their own have to do rhetorical work in presenting their self-narrative in order to deal with a dominant cultural storyline of marital and family relationships that leads progressively to a valued end-point. The extract I have used brings together a use of three frames that were also drawn on either separately or together by other participants. These frames worked well together and separately and could lead to a narrative that was progressive in its overall structure.

The use of a life cycle frame naturalizes the account in a way that has an apparent logic to it. It provides some distance and perspective for the speaker so that emotional experiences can be presented relatively dispassionately in the retelling. It draws on a dominant cultural storyline which participants may want to position themselves against; this also provides a resource that participants can shape to their own ends. A life events frame offers a justification for speakers for their deviations from the dominant narrative. Framing life as progress through a psychological story of self-improvement allows women on their own to avoid negative subject positions of powerlessness in relationships and of failure to establish a central and continuing intimate relationship. These frames may not appear to offer strong resistance to dominant assumptions about marriage, partnership and family life. Yet the identification of such variations in framing can encourage the listener or reader to 'begin to question dominant frames' (Harris *et al.* 2001), and allow for the possibility of other stories to be told.

5

CHOICE AND CHANCE IN RELATIONSHIPS: NEGOTIATING AGENCY

[. . .] and when the single woman becomes consciously aware of her position she is able to draw upon many justifications or rationalizations. She may tell society that she had to care for an invalid father; that she wanted a career rather than marriage; that she had to give up the man she really loved because of this or that, usually on religious grounds, or even that she preferred sexual freedom outside marriage; or that her mother had such a terrible time in marriage that she decided never to marry; or that she was never able to be sufficiently forward to hunt men, or – the commonest one – 'The right man never came along'; and so on endlessly.

(Smith 1952: 115)

Introduction

I have argued that in spite of changes in contemporary relationships there is still an emphasis on coupledom as part of 'normal' adult life. This suggests a dilemma for a woman who is not in a couple relationship of how to feel good about herself and have an empowered self-image. How does she manage this in her talk of relationships? In this chapter I continue to focus on the narratives told by my participants, exploring here some discursive strategies within their stories. In particular I look at how my participants depict agency and choice in their relationships, and the impact this has on the ways in which relationships between women and men are constructed in participants' self-narratives.

The quotation at the start of the chapter indicates some of the justifications used by women in the 1950s to account for their single state. My data suggest that women are still called upon to account for singleness, as well as held responsible for problems in their relationships. 'Oh Helen, not again!' was the response from a friend's sister-in-law, when she heard that Helen had been dumped by her current man friend, as though it was clearly through some failing of Helen's that this sort of thing kept happening to

96

her. There is an unequal marketplace of intimate relationships. Not everyone has one important and committed relationship that lasts for a significant period of time. Berke (2006) argues that there is little appreciation of uncoupled lives and that encountering the stories of these lives could teach something about the practice of intensive coupling. So how do single women tell the story of their relationships and deal with issues of their self-image within this unequal context?

Chapter 3 shows how the highly polarized constructions of singleness drawn on by participants had an impact on the kind of identity work that they did to ward off the unacceptable aspects of singleness and to deal with the apparent contradictions in their expressions of desire for intimacy. The detailed work in this chapter adds to this analysis: looking at different interpretative repertoires used by participants in giving a self-narrative of intimate relationships.

A question that empirical literature has attempted to explore is whether women choose to be single. I approach 'choice' not as a factual issue – did she choose singleness or not? – but as part of the discursive resources available to single women (Reynolds *et al.* 2007). In this chapter I look at the implications of such resources for identity work as a single woman.

Single by choice?

Whether or not women have chosen to be single is an important theme in literature on singleness. Although lifelong singleness has been a significant alternative to marriage throughout history (Allen 1989), a focus on representations of women as actively choosing singleness, and enquiry into whether or not singleness has been chosen is relatively contemporary. This focus seems to be linked with the increase in numbers of women who remain single, or divorce or separate after marriage or cohabitation (see, for instance, Adams 1976; Anderson and Stewart 1995; Clements 1998; Gordon 1994; Peterson 1981; Reilly 1996; Stein 1976). There is an interest in literature on singleness in whether remaining or returning to being single can be a preferred option rather than a problem to be endured. Choice is generally approached as a factual issue in this literature, with an assumption that it is possible to determine whether or not women have chosen to be single. Some more polemical texts promote, in particular, stories of independence and freedom (Anderson and Stewart 1995; Clements 1998; Reilly 1996).

One line of discussion based on empirical research has been of singleness as a category containing the binaries of stable versus temporary on the one hand and of voluntary versus involuntary on the other (Gordon 1994; Stein 1981). Such discussions see singleness as a clearly discernible entity, with valid and unchanging distinctions between how people come to be members. My own data suggest much more fluidity around membership of the category, and variability within individual responses to such membership.

Another line of discussion is of choices not to accept offers of marriage (Peterson 1981) with the implication that women have to wait to be asked, and have very limited agency in these matters. Instead of focusing on whether women have 'really' made choices about singleness, and what kinds of singleness they have chosen, I look at 'choice' as a flexible resource that my participants used and worked with to position themselves in different ways according to the context of our discussion. Representations of women as having to wait to be chosen by a man are part of the commonly understood personal deficit repertoire of singleness, which continued to be drawn on, and at times countered, in participants' self-narratives.

A recent focus of analysis has been ambivalence among single women over their state (Gordon 1994; Lewis 2000; Lewis and Moon 1997). In Lewis and Moon's study (1997), responses to a question 'Are you single by choice?' were fairly evenly divided between 'yes' and 'no'. However, almost identical comments from women on their questionnaires amplified these different responses: '"Yes, I am single by choice because I have not met anyone I want to marry." "No, I am not single by choice because I have not yet met anyone I want to marry"' (Lewis and Moon 1997: 125).

Lewis and Moon are concerned with the need for therapists to be sensitive to ambivalence in single women and to help in its resolution. In contrast, my interest is in how these contradictory explanations provide a useful insight into how women can work with the different meanings of 'choice'. Ambivalence is embedded in cultural representations of singleness, and it is at this level that it needs consideration. Rather than think about choosing to be single as some internal process, a fact to be discovered about the self, I consider choosing or not choosing, and thereby taking responsibility or not for a choice as an *act* (see Harré 1995). It is an act that we might expect to be performed in people's accounts and narratives, where they may position themselves in contrasting ways according to the situational context.

The dance of choice and chance

The analytic concepts and process undertaken have already been explained in Chapter 4; in detecting self-narratives I looked for passages that had some sequencing and linking with earlier references and were explanatory rather than descriptive. Within these self-narratives, a number of interpretative repertoires for thinking about intimate relationships were drawn upon with some regularity by participants, and I look at four of these and show how they appeared in the data. 'Choice' was used as a very flexible resource in these repertoires, which enabled participants to position themselves in different ways. The other resource that recurred quite frequently was the notion of 'chance'. Either of these offered ways of dealing with the dilemma of presenting oneself as having some agency. Each repertoire solved some problems for the speaker in the context of the immediate discussion, yet

presented her with other quandaries. The patterned nature of these repertoires, as well as the variability with which they were used (sometimes in
contradictory ways), leads me to identify them as interpretative repertoires
rather than simply common themes. Speakers moved between different
subject positions implied by the repertoires they drew upon. The movement
resembled a kind of dance as they alighted on a different position to avoid
the trouble thrown up by the last one occupied.

'I want to feel chosen'

The personal deficit repertoire of singleness that I discussed in Chapter 3,
and characterized as a personal failure to get or hold on to a man, was
more usually evoked as one of the images of singleness that relates to
others, rather than the speaker. However, there are examples in my data
where participants made links with the personal deficit repertoire to talk
about themselves and choice. In Extract 1, Lyn, in her early fifties and
unmarried, talks of an assumption that the man has to choose her.

Extract 1

1	Lyn	[. . .] I think I'd lost my faith and another
2		assumption that I grew up with, and that I
3		found really hard to shake is the idea
4		that the man has to choose me and I can't
5		choose him; he has to tell me that I'm the
6		one he wants and then I can say yes or no
7		to that. And I think I'm still influenced
8		by that idea; I don't have the confidence
9		to think – oh if that's the man I want I
10		can go and get him. I've never had the
11		confidence and I'm aware that some women
12		do have it. But it was very much the idea
13		of a one-way pursuit and that the man
14		somehow had to observe in me something
15		which he wanted and then I was either
16		available or not available. [. . .]

In Extract 2 Milly, who is in her early thirties and also unmarried, talks of
marriage and being chosen.

Extract 2

1	Milly	Yes, I'm the sort of woman who, you know,
2		if there was a man I liked and I knew he

3		was free, I wouldn't hesitate to ask him
4		out for a drink, you know, if we were
5		getting on really well and I thought it
6		might be a good idea; I wouldn't just wait
7		for him to ask me. But when it comes to
8		marriage, I don't know, there's something
9		ritualistic about it.
10	Jill	Oh right.
11	Milly	You have to wait to be chosen.
12	Jill	Yes, because there are a number of steps
13		aren't there, between going out for a
14		drink and thinking of marriage?
15	Milly	Oh yes.
16	Jill	But you think even when a lot of those
17		have been gone through and it was pretty
18		obvious to both of you that this was
19		something pretty solid, you don't think
20		you'd be the one to say, what about it?
21	Milly	Yeah, I would still wait for him because I
22		want to feel chosen. Yeah, it's
23		definitely that.

In Extract 1, Lyn's notion of the man doing the choosing restricts her own choice to accepting or rejecting him. She recognizes that this is a traditional idea that she is holding on to (line 3 'found really hard to shake'), and that there may be other women who would be more active ('I can go and get him', lines 9 to 10). She positions herself as dependent on male approbation.

Milly combines different positionings of herself in this extract. First, she depicts herself as an active modern woman, someone direct and outgoing, able to take the initiative in getting to know a man. But in relation to marriage, she says 'you have to wait to be chosen'. The position taken here is passive, the woman becomes a 'Cinderella' passively awaiting the man's choice to marry her. She develops this theme to apply more to herself and her own desires and comes to a firmer statement in lines 21 to 22, that she herself *wants* to feel chosen. This young woman, who earlier in the interview describes herself as a feminist, is drawing on the interpretative repertoire of singleness as personal deficit. At first glance she appears to be using it in the classic way – women have to wait to be chosen by a man. Only this will validate them as women who have succeeded in the relationships business. However, Milly's choice of 'want' in line 22 gives a different twist to this repertoire. By framing her statement that she *wants* to feel chosen, she becomes less passive. To 'want' conveys that this itself is a choice she has made, emphasizing her own version of femininity in a positive way.

In both these extracts, the speakers are orienting to a dominant hetero-normative cultural storyline, or narrative, of men as the ones who choose, and women as those who wait to be chosen. I use narrative here in the sense of the canonical narratives referred to by Bruner (1991), as an established understanding of sequence or consequence and a potential life trajectory which becomes a resource for speakers to draw on (Taylor 2006). The participants also both recognize that women 'can go and get' the man in the first place, Milly positioning herself as capable while Lyn positions herself as incapable of such initiatives. The storyline of women waiting to be chosen has a long tradition, while that of women who 'go and get' in a direct way is more recent. Nevertheless, the positions taken up by both these speakers seem to leave them with very little agency over forming lasting relationships with men.

Drawing on this repertoire of singleness places speakers in a troubled position. They have little control over their prospects of marriage, and possibly even partnership more generally. There are few ways out. If it's the men who do the choosing in marriage, and perhaps in all relationships, then to be unmarried and without a key relationship links a woman with 'singleness as personal deficit'. Not surprisingly, speakers also drew on alternative repertoires that countered this positioning.

'I haven't felt the need'

If a woman has remained single or returned to singleness, one way of countering an anticipated disappointment with her lot is to say that marriage, or even partnership, was not what she really wanted. Extracts 3 and 4 are examples of this.

Extract 3

1	Jill	Well in the context of that, women often
2		find it quite hard to say whether they
3		think they've chosen to be single and
4		perhaps most don't think they have and yet
5		when it comes down to it there are, I
6		mean, do you see choices in what you've
7		just been describing?
8	Milly	Yes, I mean when I think about it, if I
9		had really, really wanted to get married
10		then I would have done I'm sure. I think
11		it's just been that I haven't wanted to
12		that much. You know, I've been happy
13		living with someone or being on my own. I

14   haven't felt the need and part of that is

15   driven I suspect because I don't, I'm not

16   desperate to have children. I mean I'm

17   not ruling out the possibility that I

18   might one day have a child but, you know,

19   I haven't got that much time left and when

20   you sort of get to 33 and you've had no

21   overwhelming maternal instincts, I'm just

22   not that bothered! I think quite often

23   it's wanting children that makes a woman

24   look for marriage and, you know, that

25   hasn't been a driving factor for me at

26   all. So, you know, I've not been that

27   bothered about it really. I'm sure though

28   that if I really, really wanted to, then I

29   could and I would have done by now.

In Extract 4 Lucy, married and divorced in her twenties, and now in her late forties, also responds to a question about the extent to which she has made choices.

Extract 4

1 *Lucy*   I think I have, I'm not always the sort of

2   person perhaps, rightly or wrongly I don't

3   always think things through consciously,

4   um, but I do believe that if I'd wanted to

5   be married, if I'd wanted to remarry I

6   would have done. You know, I don't think

7   there's anything about me that would make

8   that, impossible (ha).

In this repertoire of not needing marriage the speakers draw on 'choice' differently. Instead of being the man's choice, for which they might still be waiting, it becomes a choice that they have already made, because if they had *really* wanted to be married they would have done so by now.

In Extract 3, Milly represents herself as having made a choice, and capable of having chosen otherwise had she wished. Jill's question draws attention to the possibility of agency, suggesting that Milly might see that she has made some choices. Milly is swift to take up the position of active agent that she has been offered. She uses 'when I think about it', in line 8, as a bridge to cross the contradiction of the passive position she had previously inhabited, wanting to be chosen for marriage, and her positioning here as someone who *could* have chosen to get married. While 'I

102

want to feel chosen' is a recognizable and acceptable state for a young woman, 'not having been chosen' and without agency in the matter seems to be a troubled subject position. Lucy, in Extract 4, positions herself as marriageable and potentially lovable. Both speakers frame their choice as a 'virtual' choice, one that they apparently did not make knowingly at the time; almost a discovery about the self. Milly prefaces her account by interrogating her possible motivations (lines 8 to 12) and Lucy hers by 'I don't always think things through consciously' (lines 2 to 3). The data suggest it is more comfortable to assign oneself some responsibility in having chosen not to get married.

In explaining her choice, Milly draws on another membership category, as a woman who has not had a child. Marriage is seen as distinctive in having a purpose mainly for those who want to have children. The alternatives to marriage, presented in line 13 are 'living with someone or being on my own', and referring to both experiences does important work for Milly in positioning her as someone with options, both of which she finds fulfilling, rather than as someone who has been overlooked by potential marriage partners. With some rhetorical work in regard to having children, Milly defends herself from a potentially troubled position by saying she is 'not desperate' (line 16) and 'not that bothered' (lines 22 and 27). However, drawing on this repertoire may create a differently troubled position.

Accounting for not marrying through a story of indifference to the enterprise might appear to be work that only heterosexual women feel required to do. However, Extracts 5 and 6 suggest that women who identify as lesbian or who have had relationships with other women can also draw on a repertoire of 'I haven't felt the need', although in these extracts it is inflected differently.

Extract 5

1	*Maggie*	[. . .] I don't think I've had a very strong
2		urge to go into a very close, you know
3		emotional and sexual partnership with
4		another person, the drive to do that
5		doesn't seem to be very strong in me,
6		while there's things that being in a
7		partnership I would really like, and would
8		love the companionship and to have
9		somebody who thought I was okay no matter
10		what, so to have some kind of family
11		background, and not sort of have to work
12		at defining everything all the time, a lot
13		of those things are not necessarily things

103

14		that are provided by having a live-in one-
15		to-one relationship they're all things
16		that can be got from something else, so I
17		don't know about that really.

Extract 6

1	Sue	I see myself as always having lived my
2		life alone with romantic attachments along
3		the way and I've never, I mean I've never,
4		um, bought a house with anybody or, um,
5		yeah, I've never become that kind of
6		knitted in with somebody really.
7	Jill	Yes. And so how do you make sense of
8		that? Do you feel that's a choice that
9		you've made or do you think?
10	Sue	Um, well I suppose I feel as if I've
11		had a slow start because of, um, I
12		feel I've had a slow start in a way
13		because of my sexual orientation and my
14		sort of, um difficulties I suppose in
15		coming to terms with that really, or, yeah
16		yes. And also I feel that, um, it's
17		taken me until I don't know how to put
18		it really cos it's taken me a long time to
19		sort of even have a sense of, a <u>positive</u>
20		sense of being with somebody and how that
21		could be good and how I want to
22		communicate and how I want to be and
23		to sort of enjoy intimacy in a sort of
24		wider sense of the word and I'm not
25		actually sure that you have to be in, I
26		mean I don't think you have to be
27		necessarily in a partnership to experience
28		that really either.

In these extracts the speakers are accounting not for *never having married*, but for *not having a partner*. As well as drawing on a repertoire of 'I haven't felt the need', the speakers are also using the notion that intimacy does not have to be with just one other person (see also Jamieson 1998; Reilly 1996). A contrast is set up between living together in one-to-one partnerships and other kinds of relationships. These speakers position themselves as independent: not looking to one primary relationship to provide their sense of identity. Support, companionship and even intimacy, 'in the wider sense of the word', can be got by other means. As with Extracts 3 and 4 there is a sense of discovery about needs or the lack of them. Maggie in Extract 5 says 'the drive to do that doesn't seem to be very strong in me' (lines 4 and 5), and Sue in Extract 6 refers to the time it has taken her to have a positive sense of being with somebody (lines 18 to 20). There is some struggle to articulate this counter-proposal to the powerful cultural storyline that being in a committed partnership is the ideal that all aim for.

Becky Rosa argues that a strong link between sex and love emerged from writings of sexologists in the first half of the twentieth century:

> Women were not just forced into compulsory *heterosexuality*, but also into compulsory *sexuality*. Women are expected to be in, or to want to be in, a sexual relationship. This pressure exists inside and outside of the lesbian community.
>
> (Rosa 1994: 110)

She advocates that lesbians are well placed to break down the false boundaries between love, sex and friendship and challenge the rules for conducting relationships, such as the expectation of monogamy.

Assertions of 'I haven't felt the need' work to defend the speaker from appearing unsuccessful at a commonly shared goal. However, the very degree to which this particular goal is shared makes this a hard position to maintain consistently. The speaker may find that through her use of this repertoire she has effectively excluded herself from expressing ordinary wants and desires. These are implications that were hinted at in the discussion in Chapter 3 as to why participants might find it necessary to frame their desire for a relationship as an admission. Too strong a reliance on a repertoire of 'I haven't felt the need' can place the speaker in a more troubled subject position, for instance as asexual spinster. Alternatively, she may not be believed and have to face accusations that she is just rationalizing and 'making the best of a bad job' (Adams 1976: 57).

The repertoire of 'I haven't felt the need' does some useful work for women in defending them from apparent failure at marriage or the relationships game, since they can argue that they have chosen not to pursue these goals. However, holding on to a position of lack of interest in a partnership may bring other dilemmas. In the main, participants moved quite quickly to draw on contradictory repertoires and different positionings.

'I want to be in a relationship'

The repertoire 'I want to be in a relationship' was almost always taken up in contradiction to a previous positioning, or in amplification of what had been said earlier. Sometimes it followed an assertion of 'I haven't felt the need'. As I noted in Chapter 3, it was difficult for participants to present the desire for a relationship in a straightforward way. Extracts 7 and 8 illuminate this further by showing how participants moved between other positions and this one, in a dance-like movement (Extract 8 begins at line 4 as it is part of the longer Extract 17 shown in Chapter 3).

Extract 7

1	*Rachel*	[. . .] Somebody said to me the other day when
2		I was moaning on about being on my own,
3		they said 'you're good at relationships';
4		um, and I think, I think I probably am. I
5		think I'm good at them and I like them and
6		when they're going well of course, and
7		I think, yeah, it's something that I hope
8		for much more than saying I hope for
9		becoming more comfortable with being
10		single, which would be another way, you
11		know, I could be saying well I, you know,
12		hope I get my act together on that and
13		just stop whining about it; and I don't
14		think I whine particularly, um, but, no, I
15		still seem to be, still seem to have slid
16		back into this image of what I want is a
17		close, intimate relationship.

Extract 8

4	*Jill*	[. . .] Do you feel that you're actively
5		looking now for a long-term relationship,
6		possibly?
7	*Milly*	Yes I think I am really. I've never been
8		the party animal type; I've never been the
9		one to want lots of dates. You know, I
10		tend to be a one-man woman I suppose and
11		while it was never a big issue when I was
12		younger, now I do appreciate the
13		companionship side of things; I value that
14		far more highly than perhaps I did before
15		and I want someone to belong to and
16		someone to belong to me, and I suppose, if
17		I'm honest, yes I'm looking for a husband.

Rachel, in Extract 7, is responding to a question from Jill about her hopes for the future. Her tone is apologetic. She sets up a contrast between her hopes for a relationship and the possibility of becoming more comfortable with being single. In lines 15 and 16 she depicts her move as having 'slid back into this image' of wanting a close, intimate relationship. Extract 8 is a shorter reproduction of one discussed in Chapter 3 (Extract 17). In an apparent contradiction of her other self-positionings shown earlier in this chapter (Extracts 2 and 3), Milly here presents her search for a husband and hope to get married as a 'confession', a 'truth' that lies behind the rhetoric of choice and independence. The apologetic tone of both speakers may be occasioned by the context of the interview with Jill, as well as contradiction with their own previous subject positions of an independent woman. Rachel, and to a lesser extent Milly, appear to be positioning Jill as some-one who believes in the repertoires of independence and achievement for single women. It is not an unreasonable assumption to expect a person who is doing research on women alone to be interested in a positive image for singleness.

With respect to a dilemma of feeling good about oneself in an unequal marketplace of intimate relationships, this repertoire of wanting does not work that well. Rachel struggles with the notion that she should be com-fortable with being single. Both speakers are dealing with some contra-diction with their own previously achieved subject positions as independent women. This is also why the repertoire is drawn on apologetically. The apologetic tone is warding off emerging trouble. The trouble, or ideological dilemma, is in maintaining some credibility in relation to inconsistent identities (see Wetherell and Edley 1998).

The repertoire of wanting to be in a relationship can make use of the resource of choice. On one level the speaker performs choice by stating her wish for a relationship. However, just wanting is not a key to making sure that it happens, and the more agency a person assigns herself, the more she is at risk of failure. Wanting a relationship was usually presented as a current desire, and therefore there could be as yet no outcome. When participants spoke of earlier points in their lives and their disappointed hopes and expectations of meeting someone for a lasting relationship they were more likely to emphasize the part played by the other major resource they used, that of 'chance'.

'It just hasn't happened'

The repertoire that 'it just hasn't happened' was used as a more measured piece of accounting that emphasizes chance and contingency rather than choice in relation to the shape of the self-narrative and relationships to date. Extracts 9 and 10 are examples.

Extract 9

1	Jill	Yes. Have you found any answers that you
2		feel good about when people say 'how come
3		you're not married?'
4	Sarah	Um I think I feel much more
5		comfortable about it now. Um I mean
6		what I tend to say if it does happen now,
7		I just say 'well some things just don't
8		happen really. It's a bit like having
9		kids' I suppose I would say that about
10		more than anything because probably if I
11		have a sadness it's to do with not having
12		children so I feel quite comfy these days
13		about saying, well you know that's
14		something I would have liked but it
15		doesn't happen, and the compensations for
16		not having them. [. . .]
29	Jill	So you'd say it along the same sort of
30		lines would you about – it just hasn't
31		happened – in terms of a partner? A
32		committed long-term one?
33	Sarah	Yes, I mean I think in terms of, you know,
34		for one reason or another it just hasn't
35		happened and, er, I feel quite comfy with
36		that really, because that for me says I
37		have made choices. You know it hasn't
38		just been that I've been a victim to other
39		people's decisions. Yeah.

Extract 10

1	Jill	Someone else I was talking to was saying
2		how she felt about, I forget quite how she
3		said it but it was about 'not being
4		chosen' and that even though she would see
5		herself as a feminist, independent, and so
6		on, that something about marriage is about
7		the man choosing the woman still. Is that
8		what people mean when they say 'how come
9		you're not married?'
10	Polly	I think so. You see I would definitely

11	not say I was a feminist and I'd hate to
12	be put into that category. I mean
13	occasionally if I'm asked why I'm not
14	married I say 'it's lack of co-ordination;
15	that either I loved or I was loved but I
16	never managed to co-ordinate the two', and
17	I think that would be the ultimate
18	honesty; that I've never managed to get it
19	quite right; either I've been adored or
20	I've adored.

In Extract 9 Jill's initial question clearly requires a positive response. Sarah is given an opportunity to present an untroubled identity, and it is hard to imagine how she could decline it. The proper thing to do when asked to suggest 'answers that you feel good about' is to present a positive example. The approach in drawing on this repertoire 'It just didn't happen' is to present chance and contingency as driving events. The desire for marriage or a long-term relationship is not played down, but there is a resigned and stoical acceptance that this has not taken place.

Sarah is also able to draw on a sense of agency in Extract 9. She rehearses projected future speech events, adding that it 'says I have made choices' (lines 36 and 37). It is not clear quite how she makes this connection. She may be referring to earlier parts of her self-narrative when she described ending an unsatisfactory relationship. Alternatively, she may be seeing the neutral tone of 'it just hasn't happened' as the reverse of having been rejected by others. If this is the argument, then in the process of it not happening, she depicts herself as having made choices not to marry unsuitable partners, rather in the manner of Lewis and Moon's (1997) respondents (who said that they were single by choice because they had not met anyone they wanted to marry).

In Extract 10 Polly also assigns herself some agency; having described a more neutral 'lack of co-ordination' (line 14), she goes on to say that she 'never managed' to co-ordinate and to 'get it quite right' (lines 18 and 19). These later phrases imply the taking of responsibility for a degree of personal failure. If you don't manage something the notion is left hanging that 'managing' was what you were supposed to do.

The matter of agency is a key quandary in relation to this repertoire. In general, if things just don't happen, there should be no blame to deal with. Things not happening cannot be your fault. Yet things not happening can also leave the speaker a victim of circumstance, carried along by fate. This is a less positive position to take up which may explain why in both extracts the speakers claim some agency. Portraying questions of partnership and marriage as matters of chance allows a person to provide a measured account of decisions and events. It can also make them appear less powerful, less in control of their lives than they might wish. Potentially they continue to be personally accountable through some failure of the self for why it did not happen to them.

Changing positions in the dance of choice and chance

Participants drew on older discourses of women waiting for a man, while also working with newer resources. These different repertoires offer a variety of possibilities for dealing with the dilemma of presenting oneself as having some agency, power and control. Participants represented themselves as having made a *choice* – the one relationship hadn't been their goal, so they hadn't failed to achieve it, it just wasn't that important. There were a number of ways of downgrading the importance of a loving partnership or marriage as the central focus of life. In contrast, when participants represented themselves as 'wanting a relationship' they had to deal with the risk of failure as well as how this want might be construed as in some way not being independent enough to be happy and content to be single. So some kind of apology was often offered alongside the goal of a close relationship.

How should the apparently contradictory statements from Milly in Extracts 2, 3 and 8 be understood? According to some approaches to analysis such statements demonstrate Milly's ambivalence (Lewis and Moon 1997). She has represented herself in turn as capable of asking a man out, as wanting to wait for a man to make the choice in relation to marriage, as already having chosen not to marry, and ultimately as wanting to marry. Each contradictory positioning has been taken up with the appearance of conviction. However, rather than understanding this as ambivalence on the part of the individual, we need to consider the social context for singleness, and the ideological dilemmas with which women are faced. As I have argued in Chapter 3, the polarized repertoires of singleness as denigration and independence make it difficult for women to express a wish for a committed relationship while at the same time expressing satisfaction with their single state. The notion of 'choice' in relation to enduring relationships or marriage offers single women a very flexible resource in their situated and ongoing conversational acts, which can include the act of taking responsibility as well as a more passive, negative set of choices, and can still allow for other desires.

When participants drew on resources that emphasized *chance* they attributed far less agency to themselves or to others in their lives. It was just the way that things fell out, simply bad timing, not meeting the right person at the time when they were ready for each other. While this resource could absolve her of responsibility for not having found a partner, it did not allow the speaker to give an account that portrayed her as strong and in charge of the direction of her life. Each of the repertoires solves some problems for participants in offering an account of how they come to be single – however, given the prevailing ideological climate, they also bring other quandaries, which is why participants move between different approaches. Dealing with the dilemma of representing oneself as a powerful woman with agency and control in her intimate relationships involved participants in a complicated dance as they drew on different repertoires and took up contrasting positions to help them with this task.

In the next section I look at how these issues of choice and chance were woven into participants' more detailed stories of relationships with men, as well as the constructions of men that emerge. References from participants to their intimate relationships with women were less often in a narrative form and for that reason are not included in the analysis presented here.

Patterns in the telling of intimate relationships

There were some interesting patterns in participants' detailed narratives of past relationships.

'Got it wrong'

These extracts give examples of narratives of past relationships where participants constructed some men as disappointing, or at times, dangerous. However, the dominant pattern in all these narratives was that the speaker herself had 'got it wrong'.

Extract 11

1	Pauline	So after that I had three important, no I
2		had two important male relationships after
3		that, shortly after that I began living
4		with a West Indian man, about three and a
5		half years that went on but that ended,
6		when he became violent, he tried to kill
7		me one night so he had to go. And then
8		after that I took up with a bloke a white
9		man who had just come back from the West
10		Indies so he had that West Indian culture
11		in common, and that lasted about a year
12		and then he, I mean it's so classic, I
13		mean these things are so classic it's
14		almost embarrassing to say it, that we
15		tried to have an equal relationship and

111

16		this is now the mid 70s where men should
17		do the housework blah blah blah but it's all
18		new, it wasn't accepted, I see accepted
19		now in the world around me. If I'd said
20		'would you hoover the floor?' he'd say yes
21		but he would never notice it needed
22		hoovering in his own time so the classic
23		thing was it was his turn to cook, I came
24		home from work and he'd gone. A note on
25		the kitchen table job, planned it for
26		weeks, couldn't find out where he went,
27		took me a couple of weeks to find out
28		where he'd gone to, so once again my
29		judgement had been questioned, I should
30		have recognized that he couldn't, that he
31		was spineless I should have recognized
32		that the first one was violent, my self-
33		confidence absolutely got flattened and I
34		think it took me a long time to recover
35		from that. Or maybe you don't recover you
36		just assimilate, don't you?

Extract 12

1	*Jill*	Yes, so would you say that's something
2		you're actively seeking or working
3		towards? The notion that you might, with
4		this chap or with another, be able to
5		establish an intimate relationship?
6	*Val*	Well, no, it's not that I'm actively
7		seeking that; I think at the moment, after
8		the last one ended, with the guy, this was
9		when I came back from [place]; we finally
10		got round to living together and within 8
11		weeks he'd tried to kill me. I mean he
12		was a psychopath; it was truly awful.
13		Since then, which completely threw me, I
14		thought, you know, my choices, how am I
15		ever going to trust my feelings again,
16		ever? This was absolutely terrible. I
17		always thought I was in charge of my
18		feelings, you know? Got it completely
19		wrong, completely, in a very dangerous way

20	and so after that, since then, and I think
21	I'm still reeling from that really,
22	although that was two years ago, I'm still
23	healing from that; at the moment I don't
24	feel, I don't, it would be nice to think
25	there would be some time in the future
26	when I could look at someone and say 'yes
27	I really love you, I want to live with you
28	forever' but at the moment I don't feel
29	capable of saying that because I've said
30	it before and it was the wrong, it was
31	wrong. And I don't know what was driving
32	me to say that at the time and that's what
33	I'm learning at the moment. So if the
34	chance arises, maybe with this guy or
35	maybe with somebody else, it would be nice
36	to think that I could honestly say yes.
37	But that's a bit different from actively
38	seeking it. If the opportunity doesn't
39	arise then, um, then I'm quite happy like
40	this.

In these extracts men are found wanting in a number of ways. These men don't play an equal part in housework, they are spineless, violent, danger-ous and may even try to kill you. What is striking is that these are not presented as relationships that went wrong somewhere along the way, they are representations of men as deep down faulty and potentially dangerous. Although these two are the only examples where participants spoke of threats to their own life, a portrayal of a man as exceptionally disappoint-ing was more common. What such accounts have in common is the speaker's representation of herself as having failed to recognize the signs. But why does each speaker end her story by blaming *herself* for lacking judgement, rather than by expressing feelings about the *man's* failure or betrayal?

Edwards has pointed to the social acts that are performed in the ways emotions are talked of, for instance the use of metaphors, or how particular ways of describing events can work up behaviour as blameworthy, a tem-porary state or a continuing disposition, positioning the speaker as more reasonable or justified than others in their narrative (Edwards 1999). However, in these extracts the 'emotion discourse' is focused more on the speaker's reaction to her own lack of judgement, than on her reaction to the man's behaviour. So, in Extract 12 'This was absolutely terrible' (line 16) refers to the speaker's lack of control of and inability to trust in her

113

feelings. In Extract 11 'my self-confidence absolutely got flattened' (lines 32 to 33) refers to her inability to recognize the man who was 'spineless' and the one who was 'violent'.

The work that talk of emotions is doing in these extracts is to represent the speaker as swept off her feet by emotion and as a result unable to use her own judgement. There is acknowledgement from Pauline in Extract 11 that the inequities in housework are a 'classic' story of the times (see also Jamieson 1998). Yet principally participants are telling their own stories, rather than reflecting on men as a category. They focus on the effect on them of men whom they portray as difficult. Participants position themselves as reasonable, as not really contributing to a problematic dynamic, and as a reasonable and sound person they need to account for their own connection to such clearly faulty individuals.

There is a problem in producing a positive account of the self when talking of relationships that have gone wrong, and perhaps this is heightened when it is the other person whose actions have ended the relationship, as appears to be the case in these extracts. Insofar as a participant was representing herself as having agency for events in her life then she was likely to assign herself a high level of self-blame over things that had gone wrong. Participants were also often drawing on a 'life as progress' frame that assumes better judgement in maturity and they may have felt required to account for an apparent lapse in their self-improvement and control.

Lewis and Moon found that single women in their study both internalized and externalized the reasons for their singleness. Women interviewed in focus groups often discussed the mismatch between women who were looking for more emotional responsiveness in men and the men they encountered, who were looking for women 'to take care of them' (Lewis and Moon 1997: 124). However, the same speakers would then switch back to identifying what was wrong with themselves as the reasons that men were not interested in them. The women's own explanation of this contradiction was that if they could identify a problem within themselves they had a goal. They could fix the problem (lose weight, work on intimacy) and then be able to find a partner.

Lewis (2000) refers to her therapy work with single women and the tendency she has found for self-confident women to make use of a language of self-blame and revert to the old message that relationship problems are their fault. Loewenstein (1983) attributes the tendency of women towards self-blame as stemming from a popular belief that the mainspring of our actions is within ourselves. She suggests that this gives women a sense of agency and control over their lives (Loewenstein 1983).

Finding the causes for disappointments in life within oneself may make some sense as part of a self-narrative that is concerned with making coherent connections between events. Representing oneself as having choices and agency over how relationships pan out can do important work in positioning a woman as in control of her life and not someone to be pitied. However, it leaves women with more accountability for things going wrong. The emotion discourse of self-blame does not provide speakers with a strong feminist politics of singleness.

Relationships with unavailable men

Another interesting but problematic way in which participants spoke of men in their lives was as not wholly available to them. Extracts 13 and 14 are examples of this.

Extract 13

1	Lyn	[. . .] and then into my forties I had very few
2		relationships and two of the most
3		important relationships that I had in my
4		forties were with men who were married to
5		other people and that felt very safe
6		because I didn't want them to leave their
7		wives or anything like that, I simply
8		wanted someone to be looking after me,
9		which they were able to do, and they
10		probably felt free because I wasn't making
11		any demands on them, and I felt I was
12		getting a little of what I deserved, which
13		was to be cared about, and it was safe
14		because they and I didn't have to make any
15		decisions about whether we were going to
16		live together, because we knew we weren't.
17		So that was one experience which I
18		wouldn't, I wouldn't do that again now
19		because I can see it as harmful but at the
20		time it felt to me that it wasn't harmful
21		to anyone and it was positive for me. Um,
22		I never felt that I was doing anything
23		wrong and I still don't see it in that
24		light, even though I wouldn't make the
25		decision to do that same thing again now.
26		I think my reasons would be now if a man
27		wanted a relationship with me then I would
28		want that man to take responsibility for
29		whatever other relationships he already
30		had and to make some responsible

31   decisions, whereas in that time in my life
32   I didn't require that of the men I was
33   with.

Extract 14

1   Jill   So at the moment, would, would you
2   describe yourself as having a partner at
3   the moment, or?
4   Lucy   I haven't got a partner at the moment, but
5   I'm having an affair at the moment. Which
6   erm, it's been going on for about three
7   years but it's. It is actually the, by far
8   the most, the best relationship I've had
9   with a man but unfortunately we don't live
10   anywhere near each other. So we only
11   actually get together, we probably manage.
12   We manage to get together five or six
13   times a year, but never for more than a
14   couple of days but erm. We build the
15   relationship through letters. We write
16   every fort, every two weeks or so. And
17   also we do a lot of work, a lot of
18   academic work together. And we exchange
19   novels, and we exchange music, so we do
20   have an ongoing strong relationship, but,
21   it's er, unfortunately, well I'm not quite
22   sure how unfortunate it is, but we can't
23   get together very much. In some ways it's
24   difficult, at times, erm, but I must
25   admit, that when we do get together, and
26   have a couple of days together, and it's
27   very good, it's a bit sad to leave, but
28   that's a kind of fairly superficial
29   feeling, and really I'm quite happy to, to
30   get back to my single existence again,
31   till next time we meet. (laughs) I think
32   if I was going to, you know if I was sort
33   of given the option, or, not at all sure
34   that I would want to change.

In Extract 13 married men are represented as 'safe', because the speaker did not want them to leave their wives and no decisions had to be made about whether to live together. The representation of men in this talk is that there is a need to avoid making too many demands of them, and close relationships with men can be more trouble than they are worth. They gave the speaker 'a little of what I deserved'. The speaker distances herself from the subject position of 'the other woman' doing wrong, by placing the events firmly in the past (lines 17 to 21). She asserts a position more on moral high ground for any potential future relationships by arguing that a man with other relationships who wants a relationship with her should take responsibility for his decisions (lines 26 to 31). Interestingly, she does not envisage a scenario where she might be the one who initiated a relationship, or needed to consider the effects of her actions on others.

In Extract 14 the speaker separates out from her 'single existence', the relationship she calls an 'affair': pursued through letters and intellectual exchange and occasional short periods together, this is depicted as strong. However, she repairs her initial portrayal of their distance from each other as unfortunate in lines 21 and 22, and puts a more positive framing on the impossibility of getting together much, referring to her sadness on leaving as 'a kind of fairly superficial feeling' (lines 28 to 29). Her reference to if she was 'given the option', in expressing uncertainty on whether she would want to change this arrangement, suggests that it may not be entirely in her power to make changes. Indeed, she depicts herself, and to a lesser extent the man involved, as having remarkably little agency in how the relationship is carried on. They 'don't live anywhere near each other' (lines 9 and 10), but there are no apparent thoughts of change so that they can get together more frequently. The subject position is of passive enjoyment of a relationship that does not require her to take action.

A depiction of married men as 'safe' seems to be a reversal of ordinary understandings of relationships. It might be expected that commitment would be seen as desirable in relationships, and associated with feeling safe and secure. For Lyn, however, in Extract 13, safety consisted of not having to make decisions about commitment. In her study of 65 single women involved with married men, Richardson (1988) found that because such relationships were defined as temporary, they were seen by the women concerned as safe. Not one of the women she interviewed had an expectation in the beginning stage of a long-term or permanent relationship with her lover. Richardson considers that this expectation of temporariness led to feelings of freedom and safety for the women concerned. She suggests that this and the secrecy of the relationship, required by the man's marital status, led in time to greater emotional intimacy (Richardson 1988). However, Richardson argues that such liaisons proved particularly safe for the men involved, while the secrecy, which meant that the women lacked public acknowledgement of their status, increased women's dependence on the married man's attentions.

Richardson's (1988) analysis pays close attention to the importance of secrecy, which she regards as linked with a power imbalance, reinforced by the man's marital status, gender and, often, higher socioeconomic status. She concludes that secrecy protects the interests of the powerful. My participants were not always referring to married men when they talked of relationships with men who were not fully available. What I find to be a common feature of their narratives is the portrayal of the speaker as gaining some control and autonomy in a relationship that is limited through the man's physical distance, emotional availability or personal commitments elsewhere. These are accounts of choice rather than chance. However, since it appears to be in all cases the man who is withholding availability, these positive accounts, like those of participants in Richardson's study, point at the same time to a power relationship in which it is the man who sets the terms.

A 'five-year term of office'

This pattern of telling introduces what might be termed a 'new realism' about relationships, with which the analyses of changing features of relationships in late modernity have some resonance (Bauman 2003; Beck and Beck-Gernsheim 2001; Giddens 1992). Relationships with men are depicted as lasting for a period and then no longer meeting needs and so finished. Extracts 15 and 16 are examples.

Extract 15

1	Josie	[. . .] So those two, [name] and [name], are
2		probably two of the most important
3		relationships, and of course, their
4		fathers because you know I had these five-
5		year relationships with them, and then
6		when [name] was 9 I met a really nice
7		bloke called [name] and we lived together
8		for five years, another five-year term of
9		office, and um, that worked well for a
10		while until I got bored and fed up with it
11		and since then I've been on my own.

Extract 16

1	Ruth	[. . .] I think it became um a situation where
2		it was hard to see where the next ten
3		years were going to go and um I don't
4		really see relationships to be for life,
5		that's not my view, I think you just, I
6		think relationships are there for as long

7	as you both want to be in them and then
8	when one of you doesn't want to be in it
9	then there's a problem.

In Extract 15, Josie speaks of her important relationships with her sons (lines 1 to 3) and in doing so makes reference to their fathers and one further relationship. Each of these relationships lasted five years. The last one worked well until she was bored with it. Ruth, in Extract 16 talks of her partnership and justifies its ending through the idea of relationships as not for life but 'as long as you both want to be in them' (lines 6 and 7).

In this pattern choice and chance could both be drawn on in explaining the ending of a relationship. This could be represented as a decision, as in Extract 15 when Josie describes herself as bored, or as more the chance unrolling of events, as in Extract 16 where it was 'hard to see where the next ten years were going' (lines 2 and 3). As with the repertoire 'It just didn't happen' there is a resigned acceptance that the relationships ended, and a more neutral tone to the narrative. This is not to argue that the relationships themselves were necessarily less emotional in comparison with any others, simply to note that the pattern of descriptions was to unfold changes in the relationship without invoking the emotions in the telling.

Stories of relationships that finished when no longer meeting needs are not the tales of mourning a lost relationship and complaints of the man's failure to provide emotional intimacy or sense of betrayal from his infidelity that Riessman identified in her research with divorcing women (Riessman 1990). 'A five-year term of office' is a more contemporary theme. The relationships constructed here were valued for a period of time but then become irrelevant and no longer needed. There is some resonance in these stories with Giddens's argument that the 'pure relationship', continued only for as long as it is thought to deliver enough satisfaction for each individual to remain within it, has replaced a concept of 'romantic love' (Giddens 1992). Bauman's notion of revocable relationships is similarly applicable (Bauman 2003). There appear to be a different set of expectations of relationships in these stories from notions of commitment or the 'have/hold' discourse of monogamy, partnership and family life (Hollway 1984).

I suggest that the notion of some transience in intimate relationships offers a new discursive resource to women in constructing a self-narrative. I hold in abeyance questions of whether the nature of intimate relationships has *really* changed to a more impermanent and easily disposable arrangement, as this is not my focus. What is of interest to me is what this resource allows the speaker to accomplish in her self-narrative. In telling of relationships that are right for a time, the importance of a relationship is not detracted from. It can last for considerable periods of time and can work well. This appears to be a peculiarly contemporary way of describing the ending of a relationship. This pattern of telling is ambiguous in its depiction of agency – if relationships end because of boredom or because relationships do not have to be for life the speaker can retain some agency without assigning final responsibility for the ending of the relationship to either party. For Giddens the pure relationship condition of relating to others in an egalitarian way means autonomy. Yet these stories are inflected with acceptance rather than success. Like the other two patterns I have identified here, they are not entirely happy stories, and the narrators often went on to speak of their longing for closeness, their disappointment at not finding 'the other'.

Conclusion

The self-narratives discussed in this chapter and the previous one have in common an orientation to a dominant cultural storyline and trajectory of happy-ever-after marriage and the advent of children. The challenge for a woman who is on her own is to find positive resources that help her to account for why she has deviated from this storyline, while maintaining an image of self-worth.

Alongside an understanding of women as lacking agency, needing to wait for men to make the first move, I found participants responding to the dilemma through rhetorical work drawing on repertoires of 'choice' and 'chance' as explanations in their stories of intimate relationships. However, participants rarely stayed with just one kind of resource in their self-narratives. At times the speaker would appear to be dancing in and around different repertoires, alighting on the subject positions that these afforded her. Each repertoire produced a different quandary for her narrative. The dance-like movement, occasioned by the changing context of the interview talk, would take the speaker away from one quandary, only to draw on a different interpretative repertoire which landed her with a new kind of trouble.

A particular issue for the woman in seeking to represent herself as self-determining and making her own choices with regard to men is in accounting for relationships that have gone seriously wrong. In the self-narratives from my participants there was a strong pattern of work on the self rather than 'the other' following disappointment, dishonesty or even violence from a man. As well as constructions of men as deeply faulty, where participants blamed themselves for their poor judgement and flawed choice, there were other interesting variations in how relationships with men were constructed in the narratives. Men who were in some way unavailable were often portrayed in a positive light, for instance providing a little bit of caring or intellectual companionship which did not disturb the stability and self-determination of the participant's independent life. A further construction of relationships with men was as variable over time: right for a period but dispensable when their time was up.

120

The empirical literature on singleness has pointed to ambivalence among single women regarding whether they have chosen to be single. In my view, rather than understanding contradictory statements as ambivalence on the part of speakers, they should be considered in relation to the social context for singleness. In a society that holds strongly to a dominant cultural storyline for women's lives, the individual who is not able to fit her self-narrative into that storyline has relatively few resources with which to produce a consistent account. Repertoires that stress 'choice' or 'chance' offer some flexible ways that a woman on her own can present herself as having at times some agency in the events of her life or alternatively as swept along by fate or contingency.

6

THE EVERYDAY POLITICS OF
SINGLENESS

In the first place, we are all very much influenced by public
opinion, and public opinion treats a spinster with a kind of
mild disapproval, almost as if she had no right to deface the
world with her presence. This is due partly to the fact that she
is considered a failure. Despite her achievements in other
spheres, she failed to attract or entrap a man into marriage.

(Smith 1952: 28)

Feminists may weep, but we must face facts: from the age of
about eight onwards [. . .] the race is on to get a boyfriend.
  [. . .] once past the age of 25, most women feel a tiny pulse
start to beat at the back of their minds telling them that it is
time to stop having a laugh and settle down. [. . .] I'm the most
self-sufficient, misanthropic person I know and even I was
found sobbing in the kitchen on my 27th birthday because
another sodding wedding invitation had come through the
door, which, if I held it up to the light, actually had the words,
'There will be a special chair for you at the Desiccated Hags
table' engraved on it.

(Mangan 2007: 28–32)

Introduction

My analysis of data has argued that the range of interpretative resources
for women alone involves them in trouble of various kinds. In my approach
to data for this chapter, I examine in detail some patterns of troubled
interaction in the interview itself, and consider the relationship of interactions in the interview to broader issues of stigma and social exclusion. It
seems that the privileging of marriage and coupledom over singleness puts
pressure on those who are single to account for their status. DePaulo and
Morris argue that single adults in the USA are targets of stereotyping,
prejudice and discrimination. They call the process 'singlism' and view it as

based on uncontested beliefs constituting an ideology of marriage and family (DePaulo 2006; DePaulo and Morris 2005a).

How do we talk about partners or lack of them? Finding out whether someone is attached or unattached, or has children or not, often appears to be a circumlocutory process, moving from the known to the unknown ('what does your partner do?', 'how old are your children?'), or requiring some kind of relevance to the topic in hand. A direct question can be experienced as intrusive. I have been known to duck and weave when asked whether I have a family: referring to my brother and his children, or to when my mother died, in order to avoid feeling obliged to account with more than a 'no' response as to whether I have a partner or children.

A 'reality' television series shown in the UK (ITV 2007), features Holly and Fearne searching varied venues for someone they can put forward as a 'match' for the interests and requirements of a man or woman focused on as looking for a partner ('one of love's losers' as the programme notes describe them). They approach likely looking individuals at rock festivals, larger-size fashion shows or sporting events, for instance, and open proceedings with 'Are you single, by chance?' A positive response is followed up with 'What do you think the reason is?' or 'Why do you think you are single?' The exchanges highlight normative assumptions that unproblematic, attractive people will have a partner, as the person searches for an explanation, for instance that they are a bit fussy, or they had a racy sex life when they were a teenager. The relationship history of the person seeking a partner is regularly explored in the shows: ex-partners may be interviewed for their appraisal of whether that person is now 'ready for a relationship'; the potential barrier to a relationship that may be presented by a 40-year-old living with his or her parents is considered and dissected. A possible candidate for the trial date is referred to in an aside: 'There was nothing actually wrong with her was there?' Singleness, meaning no current partner in this version of reality, is presented here as a problematic state that must be accounted for by mistakes made or unusual behaviour, rather than viewed as a possible preferred choice.

Single women face a range of economic and status disadvantages (Choi 1996). Chasteen (1994) has noted that single women are located outside traditional expectations of what a woman's place should be: as well as the economic disadvantages and social subjugation of being a woman, they also face the social and economic drawbacks of being single in a couple-oriented society.

There are many reminders for women who are alone that they are not living a normative lifestyle. The 'courtesy' title of 'Mrs' is often applied to women engaging in health care and commercial encounters without regard to their legal marital status or their preferred form of address. Social conversations about children or partners may be experienced as excluding by those who have neither. A strong and widespread expectation that marriage is the main place for giving companionship, support and sexual pleasure has been said to render relationships outside marriage thinner and less meaningful (Barrett and McIntosh 1982; Chandler 1991; Rosa 1994). A survey of young single people found that the majority of both men and women saw loneliness and lack of companionship as major disadvantages for the single, while more women than men picked financial insecurity as an important issue (Jamieson *et al.* 2002). A single woman eating in a restaurant or at a function mainly attended by couples can feel she stands out in some way or is seen as deviant by others (Chasteen 1994). Supermarket portions are often packaged for two people. Hotel accommodation booked on a holiday package is frequently subject to payment of a 'single supplement'. Travelling alone at home or abroad presents women with additional risks.

This chapter uses a detailed analysis of interaction in interviews and considers whether these interactions also indicate something of the workings in everyday experience of broader issues of social exclusion.

Analytic concepts for exploring social interaction

I have explained (in Chapter 3) that the approach to discourse analysis that I use draws on and synthesizes different traditions from Foucauldian research and conversation analysis. This chapter draws further on insights from conversation analysis. Goffman, Garfinkel and Sacks are central figures in the development of conversation analysis (Heritage 2001). All had an interest in the detailed scrutiny of social interaction. Goffman established that social interaction is a form of organization in its own right. Although he did not test his theories by applying them to data, he contributed the recognition, later developed by conversation analysts, that talk-in-interaction is a fundamental social domain that is worthy of study. From Garfinkel came the notion that there are shared practices and procedures through which people produce and recognize talk, and that these practices can be identified and studied. With his colleagues, Schegloff and Jefferson, Sacks absorbed these two perspectives into the new methodology of conversation analysis (CA) (Heritage 2001).

An important assumption made by conversation analysts (and also receiving widespread recognition in discursive psychology; see, for instance, Edwards and Potter 1992) is that the practices of conversation can be understood independent of any reference to motivational, psychological or sociological characteristics of individuals. While people may have intentions, motives or interests, CA does not treat their interaction as providing a key to what these may be (Wooffitt 2001). It is not assumed that what people say reveals what they think. Explanation in terms of agency, intention, prior planning and other mental states is therefore deliberately avoided. The interest is in 'how' conversation practices are accomplished (Sacks 1992).

A further aim is to avoid approaching data with questions led by theory. Participants bring their own endogenous (within the exchange) interpretation to their interactions, and this is revealed in how they respond to their understanding of other participants' contributions. It is important to investigate participants' interpretations rather than impose a set of assumptions as analyst (Wooffitt 2001).

A contribution from Sacks to issues of identity and social organization involves consideration of the ways in which people manage their description of events. People use categories to store knowledge about society (Sacks 1992). According to which category a person is assigned by herself or others, there is a rich store of expectations, understandings and links with particular kinds of behaviour. So in the child's story which Sacks (1992 Volume I: 236) describes as starting: 'The baby cried. The mommy picked it up', the 'mommy' will be understood by most people to be the mother of the baby, without any need for further explanation of how she comes to be there (Sacks 1992 Volume I: 236). Each identity is heard as a category from a set, which Sacks calls a membership categorization device (MCD). 'Mommy' is heard as a category from the set 'family'.

Choosing one category from a set excludes someone being identified with some other category from the same set (Silverman 1997). Within each set there is a category which can classify any member of the population. However, any one person will have a range of different sets by which they may be classified, so someone who is a mother is also a woman, from the set gender, and might be, for instance, a doctor, from a set concerning occupations. The kind of activities that persons from a particular category are expected to undertake are often 'category bound': crying is 'bound' to baby, in the example of the baby and the mother (Sacks 1992 Volume I: 236). On the introduction of the category 'baby', people start looking around for the mother and understand 'the mommy' who picks up the baby as that baby's mother. There is nothing there that needs further explanation: she is just doing what mothers are supposed to do.

The sequential aspects of interaction are a central focus in CA (Heritage 2001). The approach of sequential analysis looks at how one utterance 'fits' with a prior utterance, and what kind of implications it holds for what should come next (Wooffitt 2001). One of the observations made by conversation analysts is that there are 'first parts' and 'second parts' to what are termed 'adjacency pairs'. Questions, for instance, are paired with answers, or a reason why an answer cannot be given. Invitations are paired with responses. A view, or assessment, of a situation from one speaker is paired with one or more views from subsequent speakers. Speakers show, by the production of the next action, their understanding of a prior action at a multiplicity of levels. For instance, in giving an 'acceptance', they show their understanding that the prior turn was possibly complete, that it was addressed to them and that it was an action of a particular type (an invitation) (Heritage 2001). However, the ranges of possible 'second parts' are produced in different ways, which are not equivalent.

Conversation analysts use the term 'preference turn shape' to discuss this feature of sequential question and answer structures. The preference turn shape, or preference organization, does not refer to the personal preferences of the questioner or the other participant. Instead it characterizes conversational events in which alternative but non-equivalent courses of action are available to participants (Atkinson and Heritage 1984a: 53). Particular kinds of turns from one speaker, such as invitations or assessments, have been noted to have alternatives of preferred and dispreferred turns following from a second speaker.

The preferred turn is, generally speaking, the kind of response that the question expects or invites. Invitations are normatively accepted rather than rejected (Drew 1984), agreement with some prior speaker's assessment or view on a subject or event is normatively preferred to disagreement, except when the original assessment involved self-deprecation (Pomerantz 1984). Preferred and dispreferred alternatives are routinely performed in different ways. The preferred activities are normally performed directly and with little delay, while dispreferred activities are usually performed with delay between turns, delays within turns and may be softened or made indirect (Atkinson and Heritage 1984a).

Although the explanations above have concentrated on how talk is organized, this is not the defining focus of CA. Instead the objective is to illuminate how meaningful conduct is organized by people in society: how actions are produced and how people make sense of the world about them (Pomerantz and Fehr 1997). So, the detailed analysis of data undertaken for this chapter aims to look at what conversational exchanges can contribute to an understanding of singleness as an identity. The point is not to treat participants as direct informants and reporters on the experience of singleness, but to explore how the identity of singleness is used in talk, the talk in question being the interview itself. How do the categories 'single woman' or 'woman alone' work in conversation, what activities are they bound to, and what activities require explanation and accounting work? What kind of preference organization is evident?

Analytic process

My attention was first drawn to awkwardness over interaction in the interview relating to questions on 'do you have a partner?' I collected a file of the whole corpus that included this question and discussion on this topic and started to look more closely at the similarities and differences. A more detailed transcription of these exchanges was needed in order to capture nuances of the locally organized and collaboratively produced interaction, for instance, delays in responses, interrupted and overlapping speech, or speed in following on a turn (see Appendix 2 for a list of the additional transcription conventions used in this chapter). The result was a lengthier set of data that I could examine for hesitant or instantaneous speech and note similarities and differences in the ways that the question was asked and responded to.

The interview as a context for talk-in-interaction

The data that I examine are from my interviews. Conversation analysts focus on 'talk-in-interaction' as the object of their enquiry (Schegloff 1997b). Some primacy is given in CA to 'casual talk', as the primordial kind of talk from which all other kinds of talk-in-interaction, such as interviews, derive or deviate (Edwards 1997). Casual talk contains no obviously asymmetrical or pre-assigned turns at talking, and participants are free to choose and change topic. An analytic focus on casual talk can provide the researcher with what is often referred to as 'naturally occurring data'. That is, data recorded without a special event being set up (although there is scope for debate on how far the very act of recording for research purposes may affect the data collected).

An interview clearly contains some asymmetry and prior determination of topic weighted towards the interviewer. However, as discussed in Chapter 3, it is nonetheless a form of social interaction and in many respects appears like a conversation. Like other more institutional forms of talk, research interviews also draw on everyday understandings of how social interaction is expected to proceed. Widdicombe and Wooffitt remark that it seems highly unlikely that people use a special set of communicative competencies just for interviews, and that if they do orient to talk as 'interview talk' then this should be apparent in the data (Widdicombe and Wooffitt 1995). The talk-in-interaction of interviews can be expected to show something of everyday practices and understandings of interviews as well as everyday practices more generally.

An interview may, of course, contain casual talk as well as more structured questions and responses. Indeed, it is not easy to distinguish 'casual talk' and 'conversation' from other kinds of talk. Nor is there consensus about what 'other kinds of talk', sometimes called 'institutional talk', might be, and whether analysis of such talk is also the province of CA (Billig 1999). Billig has pointed to a lack of sharp definition from conversation analysts as to what constitutes a conversation. He argues that the use of this word turns on the rhetoric of 'ordinariness'. He suggests that the vagueness of the term risks building in an assumed distinction between the public and the private world, or the institutional and the domestic, in ways which feminists have sought to criticize (Billig 1999). If 'conversation' is treated as meaning 'that which deals with the domestic' there may be more asymmetry in everyday conversations (for instance along gender lines, or other perceived differences in power) than the method allows for. Schegloff responds to this criticism with denial that conversation analysts believe that ordinary conversation is egalitarian in nature. He argues that an understanding of the organization of turn-taking provides a resource for recognizing and inspecting asymmetrical interactions to see how disadvantages are reproduced in conversation (Schegloff 1999).

CA is described by Schegloff as a flexible resource that provides a 'canvas on which the practices end up having painted a picture of inequality, or exclusion, or oppression, or asymmetry without a sense of oppression' (Schegloff 1999: 564). This argues its usefulness for analysis of my interview data. My approach to interviews in this project was to treat myself as a participant to a conversation about experiences of singleness and give more of my own views than might normally be expected from a research interviewer. In effect, the interviews were set up as women-only spaces where different aspects of singleness could be explored in a sympathetic context, with an interviewer who was herself single. Although I treated the interview as a conversation, I do not assume that it was a symmetrical conversation or that both participants were equally free to choose the next topic of conversation.

Identity work and questions about a partner

In this section I show some extracts of exchanges that involved questions about a partner, and examine and discuss the patterns suggested.

A direct request for information

Extract 1

1	Jill	Um uh at the moment do d- is there anyone
2		that you would describe as a partner?
3	Polly	=No not at all not recently no

Extract 2

1	Jill	Mm (2.5) okay (2.0) and um you said you've
2		got lots of of friends. W- would you
3		describe yourself as having a partner at
4		the moment or (0.5) no?
5	Mary	=No I haven't had a partner for years

Extract 3

| 1 | Jill | [. . .] Anyway (0.5) .hh okay and (0.5) at the |
| 2 | | moment would you describe yourself as as |

3		having a partner?
4	Thari	No
5		(1.0)
6	Jill	°Oka:y° (1.0) [and]
7	Thari	[But] you wouldn't be
8		interviewing me otherwise hh then would
9		you? huh huh

Extract 4

1	Josie	So I always put single (1.5) but
2		unattached free yeah independent all of
3		those things I think are a lot more
4		positive
5	Jill	Mm (1.0) [yeah]
6	Josie	[than] just sort of (0.5) ticking
7		yourself as divorced
8	Jill	Mm (2.0) okay um would you describe
9		yourself as having a partner at the
10		moment?
11	Josie	N:o no I wouldn't

Extract 5

1	Milly	I was never quite sure how to describe
2		myself really [clears throat]
3	Jill	[Yes wo-would] you have
4		described yourself then as having a
5		partner?
6	Milly	(1.0) Mm
7	Jill	And you might describe him as your
8		partner?
9	Milly	=yes
10	Jill	mm and- and you wouldn't say that at the
11		moment?
12	Milly	(0.5) N:o oh no (0.5) no I mean I haven't
13		(0.5) he hasn't been my partner since the
14		New Year (0.5) um and in the last few
15		weeks I've I've been (0.5) going out with
16		a (0.5) chap who lives in [place] but I
17		certainly wouldn't call him a partner
18		either he's (0.5) you know he's a
19		boyfriend (0.5)

20	Jill	[mm]
21	Milly	[He's] you know someone I (0.5)
22		go out with huh huh huh huh so it's a
23		(0.5) yeah there seem to be subtle (0.5)
24		differences.
25	Jill	°Right [right°]
26	Milly	[yeah]

Extract 6

1	Jill	So at the moment (0.5) would (0.5) would
2		you describe yourself as having a partner
3		at the moment or (0.5) °or no°?
4	Lucy	I haven't got a partner at the moment but
5		I'm having an affair at the moment. (0.5)
6		Which erm (0.5) it's been going on for
7		about three years
8	Jill	Mm
9	Lucy	but it's:s (1.0) it is actually the:e by
10		far the (1.0) the most uh the best
11		relationship I've had with a man
12	Jill	Mm
13	Lucy	but hhh unfortunately we don't live
14		anywhere near each other
15	Jill	[Mm]
16	Lucy	[So] we only actually (0.5) get together
17		we prob- we manage to get together (0.5)
18		five or six times a year
19	Jill	mm hm
20	Lucy	but not never for more than (1.0) a couple
21		of days
22	Jill	Mm

Extract 7

1	Alix	I suppose I might describe myself as
2		looking for (1.5) or (2.0) that there's
3		space in my life for a partner I think I
4		don't know
5	Jill	Well we can come back to those things
6		anyway (2.0) um (1.5) oh yeah I suppose
7		that covers what I was going to .hhh ask
8		you next huh huh huh I was going to say

130

9		would you describe yourself as having a
10		partner at the moment?
11	Alix	Well that's a ve:ry moot point huh
12	Jill	[huh huh huh]
13	Alix	[if we'd had this interview in erm] end of
14		January I'd have said no oh well no I
15		don't know actually (2.0) then I'd have
16		said no not a partner but I was in I was
17		having a 'fling' with somebody (1.0) erm
18		but no way could that be called a
19		partnership um and now I don't know
20		whether I've got a partner or not it'll
21		have to wait and see till he comes back
22		from [place] hhh huh
23	Jill	Right
24	Alix	umm I sort of feel like I have (2.0) in
25		that I'm not looking I'm certainly not
26		looking for anyone else I'm not open to
27		suggestion (1.0) um (1.0) but it doesn't
28		feel umm I'm not entirely (1.0) con-
29		confident that
30	Jill	Yeah
31	Alix	it is going to turn into a partnership
32	Jill	yeah
33	Alix	because of the history of well (0.5) .hh
34		what's happened in the past
35	Jill	mm
36	Alix	But I certainly feel that there's more
37		prospect of that happening than any time
38		in the last three years
39	Jill	Mm
40	Alix	And that's what I'd like to see happen
41	Jill	Mm
42	Alix	Yeah

Extract 8

1	Jill	Yeah so so you are single and you (0.5)
2		always have been (1.0) and and would you
3		describe yourself as having a partner?
4	Grace	Ye:s yes I- I have a partner (0.5) but
5		it's it's a distance (0.5) relationship as
6		you know (0.5) and so erm (1.0) [name]
7		lives in [place] and works in [place] and

```
8          I live and work in [different place] (0.5)
9          and erm we have a weekend and holiday
10         (0.5) relationship I suppose. Well I mean
11         other people don't like singleness, they
12         they want to to make people into couples
```

Although answering a question about whether one has a partner is of a somewhat different order to accepting an invitation, or disagreeing with another speaker's views, there is some value in thinking about these inter-actions in preference organization terms. If the way to recognize a preferred turn shape is that it is performed with little delay, while the dispreferred turn shape shows silences, and delays within and between turns, there is some evidence for the answer 'no' as a preferred response in these extracts. The first four extracts show no hesitation in giving the answer 'no', with some additional confirmation or explanation in the first two and the fourth. However, in the context of interviews with women who are 'alone', and therefore potential members of the category 'single' and there to reflect on such membership the question is an odd thing to ask, and the participant in Extract 3 points this out with her laughed-through 'but you wouldn't be interviewing me otherwise'. Although I have listed the whole set of extracts as being 'a direct request for information', the design of the question in Extracts 2 and 6 ends with 'or no?' which may effectively be leading the response to a 'no'.

The responses given in the next four extracts display more of a dispre-ferred turn shape. There are only two responses that are a 'yes' as such, one of which refers to an earlier relationship in Extract 5, and the other in Extract 8. However, Extracts 5, 6 and 7 contain strongly qualified 'no' responses and all three of these interactions show more detailed accounts with more delays and hesitations than in the first three extracts. This suggests that to answer yes or an equivocal 'no' is a dispreferred turn. The speakers seem to have felt required to give a fuller account and do some alignment work to bring the potentially conflicting categories of 'woman alone' and of 'woman in a relationship' together.

To consider this analysis in more detail, in the first four extracts the participants being interviewed give a clear negative answer to Jill's question. The first two of these involve quite rapid responses following closely on from the end of the question, known as 'contiguous' speech. The question from Jill takes a fairly direct form in these extracts, yet there is some perturbation in her opening to the question, 'do d-', 'W- would' in the first two extracts respectively. There is hesitant speech from Jill in all of extracts 1 to 6, which may signal that a 'delicate' matter is about to be broached (Silverman 1997), or perhaps the redundancy of the question. Jill prefaces or tags her question with 'at the moment', indicating that it is current rather than past partnerships that are being queried. An exception to this is in

Extract 5 where the local context of Milly's description of what she used to say when she was living with a man is followed by a question about how she would have described herself then (lines 3 to 5). A further question follows about her current situation, again using 'at the moment' (lines 10 to 11). The notion of 'at the moment' takes in the possibility that partners come and go and that having a partner may be a changeable state. Jill uses the word 'describe' in all versions of her question. In the Extract 1 version it is the hypothetical person whom the participant might 'describe as a partner', which is also used in relation to Milly's former partner in Extract 5, while in all the other versions here the query is about the participant's self-description, 'would you describe yourself as having a partner?'

Although the context of the interview as being about singleness and with people who identify themselves as 'women alone' might suggest that 'no' is the expected answer to the question, there is some additional qualification or explanation, albeit limited, in most of these extracts. 'No' is not left to stand on its own as a sufficient answer. In Extract 1, it is both intensified and qualified as 'not at all not recently', and in Extract 2 intensified to 'I haven't had a partner for years'. These brief statements also function as identity work for the speakers, indicating that absence of a person who fits the category 'partner' goes in the first extract as far back as 'recently' and in the second extends to 'for years'. The question may be heard as checking whether the participant fits the category of 'woman alone', and therefore the criteria for being interviewed. If so these answers may be firm demonstrations that the speaker does indeed fit the category and has a track record of 'aloneness'.

Extract 3 seems not to show identity work accompanying the answer 'no': the 'no' is unqualified. However, it is followed up by a statement that again places the speaker firmly in the category of 'woman alone' and performs her identity: 'you wouldn't be interviewing me otherwise then would you?'. In Extract 4 the 'no' is a stretched out word, which seems to express some reluctance in the answer, but is not accompanied by identity work. However, the speaker has already done such work in her comments in lines 1 to 4 and lines 6 to 7, giving positive descriptors for single in contrast to ticking the 'divorced' box when completing a questionnaire.

In Extracts 5 to 8 there are contrasts with the first four extracts in that they involve lengthier and more equivocal responses, which display more detailed accounting. In Extract 5 the speaker has several different questions to answer, all of which are treated in different ways. To the question 'would you have described yourself then as having a partner?' (lines 3 to 5) she gives a slightly hesitant 'mm' and a more confident 'yes' that follows as contiguous speech Jill's question 'you might describe him as your partner?'. In response to the question (which invites the answer 'no') 'you wouldn't say that at the moment?' (lines 10 to 11) she gives a hesitant and stretched out 'no' which is then followed by accounting work to explain that the

133

person just referred to is no longer her partner and that currently she has a boyfriend rather than someone she would call a partner (lines 12 to 19).

In Extract 6 (transcribed more simply in Chapter 5 as Extract 14) the speaker gives a negative to having a partner but offers instead 'an affair', which she goes on to describe. It is not clear why 'affair' has been selected as a more suitable description than that of 'partner' or what the distinctive aspects of each are. What category of person might one be expected to have an affair with? An affair seems to be an out-of-the-ordinary matter, perhaps seen as a light-hearted and temporary relationship; perhaps there is a sug-gestion that it is something illicit. Lucy repeats Jill's use of 'at the moment' in her response in relation to both 'partner' and 'affair', so the duration of the relationship does not seem to be a defining criterion for distinguishing partnerships and affairs. The immediate information that it has been 'going on for about three years' lends some support to this supposition. The assertion that it is 'the best relationship I've had with a man' suggests that the distinction is not about quality or lack of seriousness either. The distance of the parties and consequent difficulty in getting together, which they manage 'five or six times a year, but never for more than a couple of days' seems to be proffered as an account of why this is described as an affair.

There is identity work in this account. On the one hand, the speaker is having an affair with a man. This is a category-bound activity which constructs her as heterosexual, although the descriptor that it is 'the best relationship I've had with a man' allows for the possibility that she has had other kinds of relationships with women. On the other hand, she does not live near him, or even see him that often, and she does not consider that he is a partner, all of which does work to suggest that she fits the category 'single'.

In Extract 7 Alix has some hesitation in choosing a form of words that she might use to introduce herself. She repairs a possibility of 'looking for' to a less active, more neutral 'there's space in my life for a partner'. Jill (lines 5 to 10) introduces the idea of an orderly and planned set of questions underlying the exchange, first by saying 'we can come back to those things' and then by her laughter because 'I was going to say would you describe yourself as having a partner at the moment?'. Alix treats this second obser-vation as though Jill has asked the question, and produces several possible responses. She relegates one relationship of a few months earlier to the category 'fling' rather than 'partnership'. Now she does not know whether she has a partner. In contradiction to her earlier repaired suggestion that she might be 'looking for' (line 2) she says 'I sort of feel like I have in that I'm not looking I'm certainly not looking for anyone else', emphasizing this with the intensifier 'certainly' and the repetition of 'not looking'. The issue is whether this unnamed relationship will 'turn into a partnership', which raises some questions of unspecified criteria for partnership. These may include duration of time. The man is elsewhere, and Alix will have to 'wait and see till he comes back'. It is not clear what will have to happen for it to 'turn into a partnership'. There is an implication that 'partner' is not a category that can be bestowed instantly on someone entering a new or changed relationship.

In Extract 8 Jill summarizes earlier self-descriptions from Grace, 'single and you always have been', and offers her a potential identity conflict in following this with the question about having a partner. Grace draws out her 'yes' and hesitates in providing a justificatory account of how she can have a partner at a distance and still call herself single. Grace qualifies her initial claim to have a partner. She downgrades it to a 'weekend and holiday relationship', and suggests in lines 10 to 12 that it is others who treat them as a couple.

Participants demonstrated accounting work when they did not give a straightforward 'no' to a relatively direct request for information as to whether they had a partner. This leads me to suggest that, within the context of the interview, 'no' is the preferred turn shape in response to this question. I do not assume that this is the preferred response in other situations, and would expect that in the ordinary way 'no' would be dis-preferred, with 'yes' followed by a brief description the preferred turn shape. As I have shown, there is a degree of identity and accounting work in all of these extracts. This is more extensive in the last four extracts where speakers are accounting for someone who might be thought to fit the category 'partner'.

The next set of extracts give some more evidence of preference organization and show other interesting features.

An odd question in the context of the interview

Extract 9

1	Jill	Yeah okay an:d (0.5) because people
2		obviously can be in a range of situations
3		I'm asking everyone whether they would
4		describe themselves as (0.5) having a
5		partner at the moment
6	Sue	Right I don't have a partner no
7	Jill	Okay (1.0) Um (0.5) s:o th- the first sort
8		of things that I want to talk about are
9		kind of images of singleness (1.0) and the
10		ones that we ourselves carry and [the]
11	Sue	[mm]
12	Jill	ones that we think other people do

Extract 10

1	Jill	Um (1.5) would you at the moment would you
2		describe yourself as having a partner? I'm
3		sort of [asking that because]
4	Patsy	[No (0.5) I don't]
5	Jill	people are in a [whole sort of range
6		of situations]
7	Patsy	[Yes yes] yeah no no I
8		haven't at all

Extract 11

1	Jill	Um (0.5) I'm asking just to check
2		really because people can be in a range of
3		situations but most people say that
4		they haven't got anyone they think of as a
5		partner at the moment do do you?
6	Lyn	=I don't have [anyone I think of as a
7		partner no]
8	Jill	[°Not at the moment right°]
9		(0.5) It just seems important because it
10		sort of shifts a bit the way people might
11		respond and [what I] might ask them I
12		suppose
13	Lyn	[Yes]

Extract 12

1	Jill	°Oka:y° (0.5) I I'm asking people (0.5) um
2		sort of almost not in the expectation that
3		they would say 'yes' but because I've
4		(0.5) realized that (0.5) just because
5		people live alone and might think of
6		themselves as single (1.0) doesn't
7		necessarily mean they don't have someone
8		who they think of as a partner
9	Susie	[mm]
10	Jill	[um] that obviously changes a bit in some
11		of the ways people are thinking about some
12		of the questions I ask
13	Susie	mm
14	Jill	would you say there is anyone you think of
15		in that way?

136

```
16  Susie    Um (2.0) °hm° there is someone um (1.5)
17           there is someone who's hugely important
18           who cannot be called a partner because
19           he's someone else's partner
20  Jill     Mm
21  Susie    um which does complicate things somewhat
22           .hhh um but no I wouldn't I would never
23           call him 'my partner'
```

Extract 13

```
 1  Jill     Most people .hh who I'm talking to
 2           obviously because they've come (0.5) or
 3           I've heard of them or they've volunteered
 4           as as fitting the 'woman on their own'
 5           don't have a partner but sometimes they
 6           say they do and is there anyone that you
 7           think of as a partner?
 8           (1.5)
 9  Rachel   Isn't that a contradiction in te:rms? hhhh
10  Jill     Mm
11  Rachel   Um (1.5) no I don't think of (1.0) myself
12           as having a partner (2.0) but I: no I
13           don't I don't I think of myself as (0.5) a
14           single woman on my own um hhhhh with a
15           possible relationship or friendship that
16           may becom:e more important (1.0) but I
17           certainly don't think of myself (0.5) as
18           having a partner and if I did I wouldn't
19           think of myself as single (1.0) I
20           wouldn't be talking to you now
```

These extracts are primarily distinctive in that Jill's question is more convoluted. Extracts 9 to 11 all show relatively straightforward negative responses to the 'partner' question. In Extract 9, Sue opens with a response to a comment from Jill about difficulties other women have encountered in using 'Ms'. Jill follows up with an account of the question she is 'asking everyone', explaining it as 'because people obviously can be in a range of situations'. Here the hesitation and form of the question appear to be less because of the potential delicacy of the question and more clearly an explanation of why a question that might appear odd in the context of an interview on singleness is being asked. Sue understands the question as being put to her even though she has not actually been asked for her own situation. Sue's response (line 6) is a straightforward 'Right I don't have a partner no' and does not include further accounting. It may be that the shift in the shape of the question that has been indirectly put makes it less of a personal accounting issue: the person to whom it is addressed is simply an example of 'everyone' rather than an individual dealing with a delicate question.

In Extract 10 there is overlapping speech as Patsy answers the question that has been put while Jill continues accounting for asking such a question. Again this is a straightforward 'no', although Patsy's overlapping acknowledgement 'yes, yes, yeah' in line 7 with Jill's explanation makes the speech more complicated. Patsy repeats her negative response and adds an interesting reinforcement: 'I haven't at all'. This may be in relation to Jill's suggestion that there is a 'whole sort of range of situations', which has constructed partnership as potentially a complex matter for interpretation or detection. As in Extract 9, the accounting from Jill appears to be more in relation to the oddness of the question in this context, rather than any general delicacy.

Extract 11 shows accounting from Jill before she asks the question, and a strong indication that a 'no' answer is expected: 'most people say that they haven't got anyone they think of as a partner'. There are some slight pauses in Jill's assertion that the request is 'just to check really' (lines 1 and 2). The meaning of checking in this context is not clear, one possible meaning is as a reference to the authority of the record and the orderly process of the interview which requires that all questions be asked whether or not they are necessary (as in a survey interview). Another possible meaning is that she might be expected to know already whether or not Lyn has a partner. Lyn's negative answer follows on immediately without any accounting and Jill chimes in with quiet and overlapping speech; 'not at the moment right', and then gives further explanation of why the answer to the question is important information.

Why does Jill interject this overlapping modification to Lyn's response? Jointly constructed utterances involving simultaneous speech are usually observed to involve shared knowledge of local events (Coates 1996: 122) or to imply that the first utterance was incomplete (Sacks 1992 Volume I: 654). Lyn has not finished her response, and rather than predicting what she might be about to say, Jill's comment seems to be suggesting more an improvement or a softening of her statement. I suggested earlier that the function of the regular appearance of 'at the moment' linked to the questions about a partner was to indicate an interest in the current, as well as a recognition that having a partner may be a changeable state. However, the use of the phrase here highlights another possibility. Not having a partner 'at the moment' offers some flexibility to the category of 'woman alone', which can also be seen as a transitory category which does not have to fix the incumbent for all time. The overlapping speech here indicates some effort from Jill to mitigate the impact of a delicate question and a potential difficulty in giving a negative response.

As well as interactional rights and obligations linked to more constant aspects of personal identity and larger social institutions, Goffman recognized a complex set of expectations with regard to 'face' (Heritage 2001: 48). For Goffman, 'face' is the positive social value that a person claims within a particular interaction, as understood by the 'line that others involved assume' that person to be taking during a particular contact (Goffman 1955: 213). He observes that members will go to some lengths to save the feelings and face of others. He suggests that tact is often reliant on a tacit agreement to use unofficial communication where the sender acts as if she has not officially conveyed the message she has hinted at, while the recipient has the right to act as if she has not officially received the message contained in the hint. Jill's quiet interjection, which is not followed up or acknowledged further by either herself or Lyn, appears to be an example of such face-work.

Extracts 12 and 13 have some contrasting forms of response, to questions that like the others in this set involve some equivocation from Jill about why she is asking the question. Susie in Extract 12 does not give a straightforward negative to the question of whether there is anyone she thinks of as a partner. She hesitates, says 'um', then 'hm' for which she lowers the volume of her speech, and does some accounting work. She cannot assign the category 'partner' to the 'someone who's hugely important', since he belongs to a different category: 'someone else's partner'. This is an interesting assumption of partnership as a category-bound activity involving serial monogamy. Having only one partner is presented as the normative state.

While 'husband' is a category that can only fit a person who does not have another wife, it would seem possible to consider 'partner' to be a more flexible category. If Susie had referred to the important person as her partner, this would have involved either ignoring the claim of someone else upon him as a partner or explaining that Susie is not the only partner of the person concerned. Instead she apparently attributes a stronger claim to the third person. As with Extract 7 there are questions of what gives someone the right to claim that a person is a partner, and in Extract 12 the issue appears to be over the possessive pronoun which Susie gives emphasis: 'I would never call him my partner'. There is an implication (left unstated) that the man would fit the category 'partner', but for the stronger claim of another to such a relationship.

The question put in Extract 13 takes a somewhat different form, in that it sets up two kinds of participants, one kind being 'most people' who fit the 'woman on their own' category who obviously don't have a partner, and the other kind who seem to be rarer ('sometimes') and say that they do. Effectively Rachel is being offered the opportunity to join either kind of participant, but one has a consistent identity while the other does not. She hesitates and then points to the contradiction and inconsistency and Jill gives a response token without attempting to explain or justify further.

Rapley (2001: 316) argues that while silence or response tokens from inter-viewers may work to 'produce' the interviewer as facilitative and neutral, such interviewers may not in fact be 'being neutral' in that they continue to control the trajectory of the talk. Jill's relative silence here has the effect of encouraging Rachel to say something in answer to the question. Like Thari in Extract 3, Rachel asserts her identity as a single woman on her own, and differentiates a 'possible relationship or friendship that may become more important' (lines 15 to 16) from thinking of herself as 'having a partner', which would be incompatible with the claim to be single.

The notion of a preference turn shape to the question 'do you have a partner' stands out more clearly in this set of extracts. Extracts 9 to 11 look like preferred 'no' responses. The speakers respond immediately to the question, and do virtually no accounting work for their answer. In Extracts 12 and 13 responses are delayed, involve hesitation and the speakers are drawn into accounting for their much more equivocal 'no' which is more of a 'maybe', suggesting a dispreferred turn.

A puzzle, however, remains when the lens of preference organization is used in analysis. If 'no' is the preferred response, why does Jill interrupt in Extract 11 with some face-work ('not at the moment right') that implies that it might have been a better answer if Lyn had been able to say 'yes'? According to Goffman (1955), face-work takes place when a person presents an image that is inconsistent. Not to have a partner would seem to be consistent with an identity as a single woman, so where is the trouble coming from? Goffman also observes that 'face' is 'an image of self delineated in terms of approved social attributes' (Goffman 1955: 213). The approved social attributes would seem to be the source of the difficulty. While in the context of the interview it is very much in keeping for a single woman not to have a partner, in the wider context of everyday social interaction, not having a partner is not an approved social attribute. It is possible that Jill is attempting to ward off such trouble by her softening of Lyn's statement.

Shifts in the burden of accounting

Goffman's (1955) observations on face-work are also helpful in making sense of the different kinds of interaction that take place according to how participants are asked the question about whether they would describe themselves as having a partner. In discussing co-operation in face-work, Goffman suggests that lack of effort from one person induces compen-satory effort on the part of others, while a contribution from one person relieves others of the task. In the first six extracts shown above, Jill's question was asked with little preamble. In each of these the other parti-cipant did some additional explanation or accounting work in giving their response. This was significantly less in the responses in Extracts 1 to 3 that gave the preferred 'no', where the turns that answer the question follow on almost immediately the question has been put. In Extracts 4 to 6 more accounting was given for a dispreferred response of a relationship that was respectively either not a partnership, not definitely a partnership yet, or partnership as a distance relationship that still allowed the speaker to consider herself as single.

In Extracts 9 to 13 Jill takes on some of the accounting burden by giving explanations – at times quite laborious – as to why she is asking the question, either as a preamble or a follow-up to asking the question. Effectively this accounting from Jill covers the kind of justifications made by participants who were asked the question without preamble. This may have had an impact on the extent of accounting work the person being interviewed then did. In Extracts 9 to 11 where the preferred 'no' is given, I suggest this appears a more unequivocal 'no' response than in the first set of extracts, and again shows no delays or hesitations. In Extracts 12 and 13 where a more uncertain response is given an account follows and there is the more hesitant and delayed speech that might be expected in the dispreferred turn shape.

Overall there seems to be a slight shift in who carries the burden of dealing with what I suggest is a troubled interaction. Where Jill asks the question directly, the other participant does some accounting work or explanatory work, more when a dispreferred response is being given. When Jill equivocates and explains why she is asking the question, again varying according to the unequal alternative courses of action taken by the other participant, they give a more straightforward response. What I do not have is any examples of where this question was both asked and answered in a way that was free from accounting work. As I have argued throughout this book, I suggest that there is trouble surrounding the inferences commonly associated with the category 'single', and this sharing of the burden of accounting is another indication of it.

Identity work in talk-in-interaction

Another interesting feature of these extracts is the identity work that is done through the use of different categories. Being a woman alone does not give a clear and straightforward identity as single and partnership also seems problematic to explain and categorize. 'Do you have a partner?' appears to be a closed question that simply invites a yes/no answer, and the preference organization in the context of these interviews seems to be for a 'no'. Yet it still appears difficult for anyone to say 'no' without someone in the interaction doing some accounting work. The extracts shown here suggest that this is work to indicate what kind of a 'no' it is. There may have been a partner at some time, even if not recently, and even if not for years. A total and uncompromising 'no' seems difficult to give, and difficult to receive, perhaps reflecting on the identity of the speaker as someone without an important social attribute of a central adult relationship.

Explaining a relationship that does not fit the category 'partner' involves another kind of work. Speakers draw on different aspects, including their own attitude, as in Extract 7 'not looking for anyone else', 'what I'd like to see happen'; the other person's behaviour, 'have to wait and see till he comes back'; the claims of others, 'someone else's partner' (Extract 12); and the attitudes of others, 'other people don't like singleness, they want to make people into couples' (Extract 8). What counts as a partner, as well as what counts as single, is defined differently by the speakers. For some it is clear that the definition of being single does not allow for partnership, for others the boundaries are more fluid.

Speakers do different kinds of work to build up a positive identity that can include a central relationship, or allow for satisfaction without one. Alix, for instance, in Extract 7, evokes an identity of a woman who is independent but open (not looking for a partner but might have space for one, lines 1 to 3), receptive to a new possibility (not looking for anyone else, lines 25 to 26), while discriminating over what the future holds (have to wait and see, line 21). Her corrections and repairs help to work up this positive identity.

In these extracts it is apparent that speakers do identity work as discussed by Antaki and colleagues (1996) and Wetherell (1998). They invoke identities, negotiate their features and begin to accumulate a record of identities that can be drawn on in later conversational interactions (Antaki et al. 1996). As I discussed in Chapter 1 the definition of singleness is not clear-cut, and the data discussed here suggest that partnership is also not easily defined or instantly recognizable. Singleness emerges here as a contested identity.

The interview context

It could be argued that the kind of troubled interaction displayed in this set of interviews is a result of the interview context. Perhaps the 'trouble' belongs to the interviewer in asking questions that appear redundant in the context of the interview. Features of interviewing undoubtedly affected the interaction and the 'interview-ness' of the context produces something that does not always look like ordinary conversation.

There is a debate in social science on how far interviews can act as a resource that also tells something about the world and social reality, and how far they can only be used as a topic in themselves, reflecting a reality jointly constructed by the interviewee and the interviewer (Suchman and Jordan 1990; Seale 1998; Rapley 2001; Lee and Roth 2004). In the main I have focused on interviews as a topic in itself worthy of investigation rather than as directly informative about the reality of participants' lives. I nonetheless wish to argue that the jointly constructed trouble that I focus on in this chapter does provide some evidence of what I have called the everyday politics of singleness. As Zimmerman (1998) proposes, participants' orientation to their own or others' identities is a crucial link between interaction on particular occasions and the wider social structure.

The corpus of data relating to discussion of partnership shows that some such question as 'Would you describe yourself as having a partner?' was asked of the majority of participants in individual interviews, although the question was only posed in exactly that form to a small number. In a few interviews there was discussion on partnership but the question as such was not asked. In these interviews, discussion was usually related to a participant's mention of a person that she saw regularly, and, as in Extract 4, might include a query from Jill as to whether the participant considered this person to be a partner.

In the 16 interviews where a participant was asked *whether* she had a partner, the two different forms in which the question was put are divided evenly along the lines shown in the two sets of extracts presented above. One form for asking the question was a fairly direct request for information, an example being: 'would you describe yourself as having a partner at the moment?' The other distinctive form in which the question was asked involved considerable equivocation from Jill to account for the question, an example being: 'I'm just asking also for the record really and also because I suppose it tends to shape what we talk about a bit, as to whether you would describe yourself as having a partner at the moment?'

It is not clear why the question was posed in these contrasting forms. The direct question could be expected to bring forth a simple yes/no answer without further elaboration. If the aim is just to establish whether all participants fit the category 'woman alone' as understood by the criteria for participation then this kind of answer might be satisfactory. There are times when it does appear as though this is why the question is being asked. For instance, in Extract 7, lines 8 to 10, Jill says 'I was going to say would you describe yourself as having a partner at the moment?' appearing to make a reference to a schedule or mental plan of an order to the interview. In Extract 11, lines 1 and 2, she says, 'I'm asking just to check really' and in the example I gave in the previous paragraph, she says, 'for the record really'. All perform similar functions of giving the impression that there is some order to the structure of the interview and some externality to the 'record' that needs to be kept of it. Procedures are being followed, whether or not the question seems relevant to the conversation that is also in process.

Suggestions of a 'check' and a 'record' give the question some legitimacy, and frame the interview, and the audio recording of it as a resource that will be referred to for accuracy and provide some neutral measure through which interview data can be compared (Suchman and Jordan 1990).

However, this approach of ticking of the correct box is not the way that the interview was generally portrayed. Comments from Jill at the outset of interviews suggest a more informal sort of exchange, for instance: 'I suppose the whole thrust is about kind of making sense and what we make of our situation' and 'I'm interested in what people's ideas are'. References to checks and records may be an example of how cultural knowledge (in this case the interviewer's) of interviews as a recognized form of social interaction leaks into even interviews designed as a comfortable, stigma-free space for discussion.

There is a shift in the interview process from initial talk about preferred terms for self-introduction, and the general ways in which the participant might refer to herself, to this more direct and quite personal question. Questions about partners can be asked in survey-type interviews where boxes require completion by ticks or crosses. Casual enquiry on such matters is more difficult to bring off, and this is another aspect of the trouble surrounding this area of questioning. Alongside phrases which serve to introduce this area of questioning almost under the guise of completion of a schedule of pre-planned questions, bridging phrases from Jill can also be seen that work on making the question a more natural next thing to say. For instance, in Extract 8, lines 1 and 2 make a bridge summarizing what Grace has already said about herself 'so you are single and you always have been' and moving on to ask her about a partner. In Extract 2, a similar connection is made with Mary: 'you said you've got lots of friends, would you describe yourself as having a partner at the moment or no?' (lines 1 to 4).

Questions about partners – in particular questions on whether or not they exist – do not fit easily into casual talk. Generally, personal questions require some kind of relevance to the conversation, or to prior knowledge about co-participants. So ordinarily, an enquiry might be made about a known partner: 'How is X?' Knowledge about others is often sought gradually, building on what is already known, and Jill's bridging introduction to the topic works, somewhat uncomfortably, on these lines.

Sacks points to a rule of conversation, that if you ask a question you have a chance to talk again afterwards (Sacks 1992 Volume I: 51–6). The person who asks a question has control of the conversation, according to Sacks, and can 'perform an operation' on the answers to draw some kind of conclusion (1992: 54). We can see the rule of the chance to talk again in the extracts shown in this section, but there is no clearly identifiable 'operation' being done or conclusion being drawn from the answers about a partner.

Where the preferred 'no' has been given, there is usually an 'okay' response from Jill, often in a lowered voice level, followed by a pause before the next area of questioning. It seems there is little to be said about the inability of someone to describe herself as having a partner. This can be seen in Extract 3, and I reproduce this extract here, and show more of the ensuing interaction.

Extract 14

```
 1  Jill    [. . .] Anyway (0.5) .hh okay and (0.5) at the
 2          moment would you describe yourself as as
 3          having a partner?
 4  Thari   No
 5          (1.0)
 6  Jill    °Oka:y° (1.0) [and]
 7  Thari               [But] you wouldn't be
 8          interviewing me otherwise hh then would
 9          you? [huh] huh
10  Jill        [huh] it's surprising what people
11          sa:ay [you know]
12  Thari        [oh right?]
13  Jill    I realize that just because someone's said
14          they're single doesn't necessarily mean
15          [that] they
16  Thari   [oh I see]
17  Jill    don't have a partner they might not be
18          living with them
19  Thari   right
20  Jill    but they might still think of someone
21          important in their lives as a partner
22  Thari   right
23  Jill    or they might have someone important in
24          their lives and say well no they're not a
25          partner but they're
26  Thari   yeah
27  Jill    my boyfriend and they ring me three times
28          a day
29  Thari   yeah
30  Jill    um (0.5) so I think I'm learning hhh
31          [what]
32  Thari   [mmm]
33  Jill    that (0.5) nothing is obvious
34  Thari   yeah
35  Jill    really
```

In Extract 3, where Thari simply answers Jill's question with 'no', the absence of accounting from either participant seems at its most stark, until Thari overlaps Jill's introduction to a new topic with 'But you wouldn't be interviewing me otherwise then would you?' and laughs. This acts as piece of face-work from Thari, to reassert her 'rightness' as fitting the category 'woman alone'. By her laughter she also minimizes any loss of face for Jill in having asked what appears to be a pointless and unnecessary question. She has also taken over the role of 'questioner' and the onus is now on Jill to do some accounting. Jill proceeds to account for her surprising question, and Thari joins in with overlapping responses and agreements before Jill has given much by way of explanation. This suggests more work from Thari to retract a possible threat to 'face' and to show accord.

I have suggested that the more equivocal and convoluted form of Jill's question about a partner is to explain what seems an odd question in the context of the overall subject of the interview, rather than oriented to the delicacy of the question. It can be seen as an attempt to pre-empt the kind of challenge that Thari produces in this interaction. However, it may also be worth considering that the equivocal form of the question avoids the situation seen in lines 1 to 6 of Extract 14. Here neither participant initially does any accounting work, and Jill is left with a preferred 'no' response to which she has no further comment to make by way of conclusion to this topic. She gives a token response and pauses awkwardly before what looks like an introduction to the next topic (line 6).

Conclusion

An aim of CA is to avoid being led by theory in analysis of the data, and I have tried to follow this tenet in my approach in this chapter. However, I do of course have an interest in social interaction and singleness, and this is what led me to consider looking at these particular aspects of data. My interest in what I call 'everyday trouble' arose from my own experience that beyond a certain (indeterminate) age, to be single is a social identity that requires explanation. At the same time it seemed to me there were no easy conversational routes that allowed for introduction of single status as an aspect of identity. How do we make personal information about ourselves known to others, and how do we find out about them?

Kitzinger has shown how normative assumptions about kinship, heterosexuality and family life are evident in the handling of calls to medical services. When a caller is ringing to ask for advice for someone who is not a member of their family, they become involved in explaining and accounting for their concern (Kitzinger 2005). When they are calling on behalf of a family member, explanations are not needed, the person is undertaking a category-bound activity that is 'natural', understood and oriented to immediately by the recipient of the call. These kinds of normative assumptions are indicative of the assumptions made in everyday social interaction. References to partners, husbands or children will be understood and oriented to by participants in the interaction as relationships within a category set of 'family', and contributing to an identity for the speaker. In my experience, part of the everyday routine for single women involves negotiating their way through and past category sets in which they either have no place, or need to explain in what ways they belong.

It might be assumed that any difficulties that single women have in everyday interactions flow from economic disadvantages or perhaps reproductive reasons: that society favours heterosexual couples because they more clearly contribute to the maintenance of society. However, what the data discussed in this chapter suggest is that the trouble in interactions does not follow in a logical way from problems that 'belong' to the incumbent of the category. As I have discussed, singleness is difficult to define, and the extracts considered here give evidence of the contested and imprecise meanings of singleness. Trouble persists across different and blurred meanings of singleness. This suggests that it is an ideological problem, and that the interactions shown in this data link to the everyday practices experienced by single women.

The detailed examination of interaction in these extracts from interviews shows that even in this context in which an attempt is being made to create a comfortable, stigma-free space for discussion, interactional trouble emerges. My theorizing on the preference organization of responses to questions about a partner is tentative, as the corpus is not large enough to demonstrate the pattern conclusively. The trouble in interaction is not dramatic stuff, and might not even be recalled as problematic by the participants involved. However, the data suggest that there is some trouble around the category 'singleness' and show how trouble occurs in the interactions of the interview.

7

CONCLUSIONS

Introduction

Throughout this book I've been investigating different meanings of singleness as understood by women who are alone. I have suggested that singleness is an important topic for feminism, yet in recent years there has been little sustained analysis of empirical data on the marginalization of single women. The different approaches to data taken in the preceding chapters show something of how women work with a 'single' identity in a social context in the west that is changing rapidly.

The social and cultural context is central as the arena in which discursive resources, that is, ways of thinking and talking about a subject, are developed and made widely available. Empirical social science studies regularly portray singleness as a problematic state. Although stigma is recognized and explored in social science literature, the problems are invariably dealt with at a personal level. This literature also contributes to the discursive context of singleness. The changing meanings of singleness are crucial resources drawn on by women in their narrative and identity work.

Popular media representations are an even more critical influence in creating a discursive context for singleness. For example, considerable media interest was generated in 2003 when *The Washington Post* decided not to publish a cartoon strip that suggested the single status of Condoleezza Rice, US National Security Advisor at that time, was contributing to the continuation of the war on terrorism: 'Find Condoleezza Rice a boyfriend?! [. . .]' asks one cartoon character. 'Maybe if there was a man in the world who Condoleezza truly loved, she wouldn't be so hell-bent to destroy it' responds the other (McGruder 2003).

This was not the first time that Rice's personal circumstances had been explored in less than positive descriptions by US media. In an interview on CNN's *Larry King Live*, Bob Woodward, journalist and author of a biography of Bush and his war on terrorism, described the key role that Rice played with the added comment: 'She has no personal life' (CNN 2002; DePaulo 2006: 193). This could be offered as an accolade for dedication to a critically important job, but somehow it doesn't read like this, instead appearing to undermine Rice's work by reference to lack of partner and family.

Interestingly, what made front page news of the decision not to print the cartoon was not so much its explicit sexism as the suggestion that the *Post* feared Rice would be offended at a possible interpretation of the cartoon as meaning that she was lesbian (Warn 2003). There is a double or even triple message of stigma for single women in this media debate: first, that singleness is so invisible that the censoring of sexist jokes about singleness attracts little attention as such; second, that the possibility of being lesbian is more reportable and scandalous (this was met with the media response that a suggestion that someone is lesbian should not be offensive so what was the fuss about (Blow 2003)? While this response appears to defend, it also gives publicity and credence to a rumour which can be damaging to a woman in a position of power); and third, that a strong, confident woman cannot be a 'real' woman, whether lesbian or straight, if she is not in a heterosexual relationship (Warn 2003).

Such competing categorizations of women as single or as lesbian have a long history, together with the resulting denigration of the category 'single'. Sheila Jeffreys (1985) comments that many spinsters in Britain, between the years of 1880 and the First World War, made a positive choice not to marry. However, she identifies different camps in the women's movement of this time: one advocating for sexual intercourse for women, in or outside marriage, the other seeing large differences of interest between men and women over issues of sexuality and advocating women's non-co-operation with the sexual desires of men. Jeffreys argues that the attack on those single women who defended their right not to have sexual intercourse with men in the earlier part of the twentieth century was in essence an attack on lesbians, and that this has important consequences: 'When lesbians are

stigmatised and reviled, so, also, are all women who live independently of men' (Jeffreys 1985: 100).

Jeffreys' comment can be extended with reference to women generally, whether partnered or not. When marriage and family life are viewed as the major proper occupation of women, such that Condoleezza Rice, a key figure in the US Administration, can have her status trivialized by discussions that imply she is incomplete without a male partner, this diminishes all women, not just those without partners or children.

The discursive context of singleness marks the identity of the single woman through the discursive resources that are available for making sense of life patterns. This book explores how single women respond to, and work with, the typical constructions of the identity available to them. In theorizing an approach to the single identity that draws on the discursive context, I have noted the prescriptive nature of some models of identity that can be detected in the empirical literature on singleness. In contrast, I consider the single identity to be a project that women work up through their social practices: in particular through their talk. Singleness is something that people *do*. The models of identity that emerge in the literature are also cultural resources that women may draw on in order to understand and explain their situation if they are alone. They are, in addition, notions of how things 'should' be, which women may use more by way of self-discipline. Alternatively, they may resist such implications in their discursive and narrative performances.

Much of the empirical literature on singleness predates the discursive turn in the social sciences. New perspectives on identity, subjectivity, categories, social action and practice that have emerged in recent years have not hitherto been fully integrated into the reporting of empirical research on singleness. Previously, literature on singleness has worked mainly within a realist framework and a potentially simplistic understanding of representation and rather simple, essentialist psychological models of identity.

Rather than add to this realist approach, I have brought the literature up to date by viewing singleness through the lens of the discursive turn. I have shifted the gaze from single women as problematic individuals, through consideration of the nature of the identity resources available. By taking a non-essentialist approach, and allowing meanings to emerge, I have drawn attention to variability and flexibility in my data. The subject negotiates her identity. She is not fixed by category membership, rather she is variable, dynamic and mobile. This subject, nonetheless, works within some cultural constraints. She cannot reinvent herself in just any way she chooses. Through this discursive approach, we get a better understanding of how trouble, problematic categories and personal deficit notions of singleness can be seen in social interaction. Instead of taking for granted that singleness is a problematic identity, I have explored how participants worked up their identities within the interview context.

A focus on the discursive context has also brought a sense of relativity, cultural change, history and contingency. It provides a way of studying shifts in meaning-making. This enables the recognition that there is no enduring, essential and fixed nature to singleness. Once this is recognized, it is possible to attend to the contribution of the 'social' in what might appear to be individual pathways and personalities. The social and the psychological are intertwined.

It is a common assumption that discourse is in some way ephemeral, and that an interest in how talk is carried out does not lead to an exploration of matters of intense personal significance. This is not the case: in talking of their lives my participants were talking about something deeply personal. They worked at making sense of their experiences. Any recognition of patterns should not diminish the personal significance of the sense-making undertaken by individual speakers. Rather it should be a resource for women to be able to gain a better understanding of how their personal articulations intersect with the available cultural resources.

This claim has application to my own disclosures on my experience of singleness. I have drawn on my own experience at times, to explain my interest in the topic, to contextualize the development of my thinking and to provide examples of my argument. I have also considered myself as a participant to the interviews I undertook. There are some pitfalls in taking a social constructionist approach to a topic under investigation and attempting to be self-reflexive. The researcher can appear to be placing herself above or outside the patterns observed in interactions, or claiming some special privileging of her argument as superior insight (for discussion of reflexivity and inherent contradictions, see Pels 2000; Lynch 2000). I have kept a focus on analysis of my data and what it can show of identity work, observing neutrality as to whether what people say provides a window onto some inner reality or an accurate account of events as they happened. However, my arguments become more 'realist' as I apply them to the cultural and discursive context of singleness and point to power differentials. This is in keeping with the theoretical commitments that I outlined in Chapter 1 and five linked claims: that the single state should be viewed as socially constructed, as a social category, as a discourse, as a set of personal narratives and subject positions, and finally singleness should also be a politics.

The importance of discourse and talk for a feminist politics of singleness

What are the implications of saying singleness should be a politics? The polarized and contradictory nature of resources for talking about singleness leads to difficulty in performing a 'single' identity that gives an empowered sense of self. Much of the literature on singleness focuses on internal and personal changes that single women should be encouraged to make as individuals. In contrast, my argument is that we need to develop the resources for talking about singleness. Discourse is not ephemeral and talk is not trivial. People do things with their talk: indeed, they build whole social worlds (Wetherell 2001). The categories for talking about the self that any culture makes available have a profound effect on people's lives. Paradoxically, individuals nonetheless talk and act as though their lives were the outcome of individual and unconstrained choices 'made in the furtherance of a biographical project of self-realization' (Rose 1991: 12).

If discourse is so powerful, how might some change be brought about in the discursive resources available? The matter of resources is not unconnected with individuals, since their use involves a social practice – talk – which is carried out by individuals. Clearly such practices do change over time, but in spite of many changes in relations between men and women, the notion of singleness as a deviant category seems remarkably enduring. I have drawn attention in this study to the continuing importance of gendered power relations and to notions of a woman's proper place. Is it inevitable that those who are single have to continue to orient to, and defend themselves against, an affinity between singleness and personal failure? What responsibility do those who are not single bear? Do marriage and singleness have to be seen as binary categories or can we recognize a more fluid set of possibilities of intimate relationships? My data suggest that since the early feminist work on such matters there has still been little progress in unsettling the privileging of the ability to make close and lasting relationships as the mark of emotional maturity (see Adams 1976).

There have been some changes in the discursive resources drawn on in other areas of stigma and oppression such as those relating to racism. Changing the ways in which it is thought acceptable and non-offensive to talk about matters does not necessarily transform social practices and there may still be resilient areas of oppressive discourse that remain. However, the relation between discourse, social structures and social practices is complex, and even ordinary interventions may have significant effects (Wetherell and Potter 1992). At any one moment the number of discourses in competition for meaning is finite, and the conflict between different discourses has been theorized as creating the possibilities for new ways of thinking, new subject positions (Weedon 1987). I suggest that the possibilities for a wider range of resources for talking and theorizing about singleness have hardly begun to develop, and attention to the discursive context of singleness is an important first step.

One of my interview questions was about whether participants recognized a 'politics of singleness'. This notion of a particular identity politics was not always easily articulated or delineated by participants, but ideas did emerge in response to this interview topic. Not all participants identified themselves as feminist, but some spoke of earlier feminist influences in their lives, or made links with feminist thinking on the family as a repressive structure.

There were some embryonic discourses of resistance intimated: some of it guided by other political discourses such as egalitarianism, humanism or anti-oppressive practice. For instance, participants sometimes expounded their ideas on 'correct' ways of talking about singleness. Several participants mentioned the British politician Ann Widdicombe as someone who is stereotyped in media representations as single and ageing, rather than criticized for her policies. The notion was that this was not the right way to talk about a person, and could be challenged in the same way that a racist or more overtly sexist reference might be.

One person drew on a humanist discourse in relation to herself, arguing that even if she was 'emotionally crippled' there still had to be a place for her as a woman on her own. She argued that the single person does less damage: 'you can be emotionally crippled and be on your own or you can be emotionally crippled and go into loads of relationships and make loads of other people really unhappy'. While I don't want to lend support to any suggestion that single women are in general emotionally deficient, or indeed that this was the case with this particular participant, her argument draws attention to the political nature of the high social value placed on marriage and partnership, which often pays scant consideration to the significant potential for emotional damage.

One issue in developing an identity politics of singleness is whether it is in women's interests to promote the idea of single women as a stigmatized group who should perceive some common cause and become recognized, appreciated and listened to more often. DePaulo and Morris (2005b) argue that all 'singles' are discriminated against and stigmatized, and refer to the 'Ideology of Marriage and the Family':

> As long as that ideology remains dominant and uncontested, all singles have something in common: Compared to married people, they are second rate. The term 'single' used to unite all adults who are outsiders to the ideological yellow brick road, has both theoretical and political potency.
>
> (DePaulo and Morris 2005b: 148)

They call in particular for the study of singles as a new and distinctive area for relationship researchers, or indeed any scholars. I support such developments as potentially contributing to a better understanding of singleness and correspondingly positive effects for the discursive context.

DePaulo and Morris (2005a) also make a case for a new social movement of singles, suggesting that group identification may give individuals emotional and instrumental support as well as validation of their emerging consciousness. They report research by Morris (DePaulo and Morris 2005a) to examine the effect of consciousness-raising on single participants in her study. Half her participants were assigned to read a news article showing that singles are discriminated against economically and socially. Those who read the article reported higher self-esteem than those who did not have this consciousness-raising induction. DePaulo and Morris argue that recognition of discrimination can help people to distinguish the social from the personal:

> Successful social movements can transform the hope of succeeding on the ideology's terms into a hope that is made of sterner stuff. Enlightened citizens come to realise that you don't need to be a man to be a leader, you don't need to be straight to be normal, you don't need to be white to be smart, and you don't need to be coupled to be happy.
>
> (DePaulo and Morris 2005a: 78)

I have more hesitation on whether a new social movement made up of single people is a valuable objective. While new social movements have undoubtedly had an important impact, and consciousness-raising among identified members is effective in raising public awareness more generally, my data suggest that singleness moves in and out of being a salient identity, even in an interview with a focus on this topic. How far might women who are on their own *want* to see some commonality with other women and men who are alone? Different circumstances and identifications may emphasize contradictions instead, for instance in relation to those 'others' who have either stayed single, are divorced, widowed, with or without children, or are straight or lesbian. Other specific identities may seem more obvious rallying points for individuals in an understanding of oppression. For instance, some of my participants saw single motherhood, race, sexuality, disability, or womanhood in general as more crucial to their self-image. Where participants had developed strategies that sought to challenge marginalizing expectations these were often drawn from their experience in relation to other oppressions. There may be limitations to how far such strategies can develop in relation to singleness.

Identity politics has been criticized as essentialist, reifying boundaries between groups, and undemocratic within groups, homogenizing difference (Cain and Yuval-Davis 1990). The boundaries are continually drawn up between 'us' and 'them', and people may be assigned to a group membership that is not of their choice (Sevenhuijsen 1998). In the case of an identity politics of singleness, if it developed in a way that required participants to meet some criteria of singleness then my current partnered status might debar me from engagement, which would be personally disappointing. Furthermore, the areas in which identity politics has been most effectively developed, such as disability or race, depend on a particular construct at the heart of them over which there is some shared understanding. A political move – a struggle to (re)articulate the meaning of experience in ways that make sense politically (Gill 1998) – is required if single women are to see a single identity as leading to a particular feminist standpoint.

Perhaps the meanings of singleness are so diverse, and the possibilities for moving in and out of the status so fluid, that a politics for single women may not have a similar trajectory to other areas of identity politics? What might a feminist new social movement look like if comprised solely of women who identify as single? Yvonne Roberts (1997), in her novel *The Trouble with Single Women*, gives a risible depiction with a character who leads a new organization 'Save our Spinsters' (SOS), and is appearing in a televised panel discussion (called *The Perfumed Pound*) about the new single woman.

> 'We want to reclaim the word "spinster" and make it synonymous with joy, celebration, pride, choice –' Chris Odell spoke as if she had written one too many mission statements.
>   'We believe that a woman's natural choice is to be single . . . roam free . . . to opt for no long-term partner.'
>
> (Roberts 1997: 376)

In this fictionalized version there are echoes of Mary Daly's (1987) ideas for changing the meaning of 'spinster' and 'old maid', contained in her 'wickedary': a project for reclaiming words for women in a different kind of dictionary. Her versions are compared with a more conventional dictionary definition at the head of this chapter. There is considerable power in changing the meanings of words, and this has been an effective strategy for feminists as well as in other spheres – for instance the appropriation of 'mad' by some mental health service users or 'survivor' to replace 'patient' as a positive self-description (Mad Chicks 2004; Read and Reynolds 1996).

The idea of devising more positive connotations for singleness, and indeed a social movement, is not a new one. Cicely Hamilton argued in *Marriage as a Trade* that marriage had been established as practically the only means that a woman had of 'earning her bread'; although she had to wait for the man to make advances rather than express any desire to enter that 'profession' (Hamilton [1909] 1981: 36–7). Hamilton was not unusual in her time in seeing marriage and employment as impossible for women to combine. She advocated the creation of a large class of spinsters who positively chose paid employment rather than marriage. Hamilton believed that spinsters might then gain respect and equality on male terms and this strategy would improve the lot of women generally (Jeffreys 1985).

Ideas of singleness as a positive choice, and one that brings freedom and satisfaction, are empowering for women. However, the binary formulations of Hamilton or of Roberts's fictional spinster organization also construct singleness as a choice for women that implies opposition to coupledom and marriage, and in particular opposition to men. In contrast, one of the dilemmas noted in my analysis is how women can have a positive notion of singleness that still allows them to articulate desire for a relationship. There are dangers in approaches that use binary oppositions. A strategy to reverse the oppositions, so that what was denigrated is upgraded, remains trapped in an oppositional logic (Sevenhuijsen 1998).

Another approach is to look for constructive developments that may emerge from wider recognition of the diversity of human relationships and the degree to which everyone moves in and out of intimate relationships, changes in the shape and make-up of families, different kinds of commitments. Participants to my study commonly drew on this line of thinking. As with the social category 'women' (Condor 1989), rather than being a rallying-point, singleness only becomes salient in particular contexts. From this perspective the multiplicity of meanings of singleness is its strength, rather than a problem. This kind of thinking was sometimes used by participants in my study to deny the existence of problems, as though an acceptance of diversity in relationships was already incontestably established. Yet at different points in the interview they would say things that indicated some continued wrestling with dilemmatic thinking. It is, of course, possible that the pace of social change in intimate relationships is moving so rapidly that the political tasks are also constantly shifting.

Active citizenship, feminism and singleness

There is more work for feminists to do in developing a committed politics of singleness. My own view is that this is not a responsibility solely for the single, not should it be enacted simply at the individual level of personal social interaction. We can learn on this from discussions on a feminist ethics of care (Budgeon and Roseneil 2002; Featherstone 2006; Parton 2003; Sevenhuijsen 1998; Trimberger 2002). The idea at the heart of these discussions is that of active citizenship. Identities are shaped through the exchange of narratives and opinions and participants revise and transcend their images of 'self' and 'other'; with 'what you do' being more important that 'what you are' (Sevenhuijsen 1998: 14). This process allows for an understanding of identity as open to change rather than fixed for all time.

The concept of active citizenship informed by an ethical dimension drawn from feminist insights is transferable to exploring the public issues of singleness and coupledom. For instance, Sevenhuijsen (1998) argues that a feminist ethics of care will not be framed solely in terms of the carer's experience and motivation, since consideration of diversity enables recognition that in the course of a lifetime almost everyone will assume the role of receiver as well as provider of care. In the same way, almost everyone is single at some point in their lives, and most people have some experience of being in a couple relationship. The task of a politics of singleness based on active citizenship would be to articulate and confront issues of stigma and exclusion in ways that transcend personal investment in the binaries of singleness and coupledom. This task is not a responsibility restricted to single women and men but becomes an issue for citizens whatever their relationship status.

The particular contribution of this book to a politics of singleness is to draw attention to the different discursive patterns and meaning-making of experiences employed by single women in western society. Attention to discourse provides useful resources for all women, and indeed all citizens, whether or not they consider themselves to be single. We need to develop our ability to recognize some of the repertoires that are being drawn on, that appear to be only common sense, and yet which construct a world in which single women are held to blame for their lack of fit with normative aspirations. We need to acknowledge the ideological dilemmas of single-ness, without making patronizing assumptions that those who are alone are struggling with circumstances that no one would choose. At the same time there is a need for some unravelling of the myth-making around coupledom and family life and the high importance attached in the public arena to being part of a couple.

Sara Mills (2003), in an article on anti-sexism and women's choices of Ms or Mrs in their naming practices, notes that a range of tactics were employed by her participants, and there was no uniformity in what women might claim to be a feminist approach:

> In thinking of the way that discursive change occurs [. . .] stra-tegically choosing particular options for particular contexts, and inflecting those choices positively is a more productive model than the Utopian notion that sexism can be reformed out of existence.
> (Mills 2003: 103)

Change does not come about simply by new, positive repertoires replacing old and defunct ones. Working with and exploring the contradictions in positionings, desires and practices, and thus in the subjectivity, which coexist in the old and the new (Hollway 1984), may open up the possibilities for change. A feminist politics of singleness will recognize that women make strategic decisions that do not have to be the same for everyone, but are based on some common understanding of issues of marginalization.

APPENDIX 1: METHODS

Selection of participants

My aim was to interview women who either thought of themselves as single, or who might be categorized in this way by others. Given the complexity of defining singleness, I did not want to fix the category too narrowly, nor to determine in advance of an interview process that a more inclusive range of women were 'really' single according to my own definition. I used the term 'women alone' (Bickerton 1983) for its applicability to a broad range of women in differing circumstances, and because (for me at least) it did not carry a set of stigmatizing associations.

My criteria for inclusion in the sample were that women had either remained single, or been divorced, separated or widowed for more than two years; were not living with anyone (male or female) in an intimate partnership at the time of making contact; and were aged between 30 and 60 years. Even with these quite broad parameters I was working within some commonly understood meanings of singleness, partnership and age: for instance that partnership generally requires cohabitation, and that singleness or aloneness 'matter' in an age-related way.

The sample was recruited through 'snowballing' (asking contacts to suggest possible participants) and through poster and handout advertisements. I contacted women known to me who I thought might fit my criteria and be willing to be interviewed, and asked them also to pass on an information handout to others. Handouts and posters were displayed in libraries, shops and other public places asking 'women alone' to participate in a study of meanings of 'singleness'. These notices explained that I was myself single, and that I was interested in knowing 'what being single means to you now, what it has meant to you in the past, what kind of choices you have made, and your hopes for the future'.

Roger Sapsford and Pamela Abbott advocate randomness in picking participants, and caution that reliance on snowball sampling risks the bias of only getting access to people who are already known to others through just one network. The researcher then does not reach those who are more isolated, or potentially excludes a whole set of people who might be linked in some different, but salient, way (Sapsford and Abbott 1992). I was not aiming to get a representative sample: this would be difficult in any case with a sample of the size I was able to work with. Indeed, my topic required considerable limitation, in terms of being women only, and women who were on their own. I was aiming for a 'typical' category of women with a broadly shared social position. There are arguments for snowballing as the most effective way to reach potential participants of this type who are not part of a formed, pre-existing group. In addition, the two-pronged approach of placing posters in public places as well as snowballing meant that there was also a degree of randomness built into my selection process.

Thirty women were included in the study. Of these, 21 were selected as a result of the snowballing process, 12 of whom had been contacted directly by me in the first place. Nine women were included who made contact because they had seen a poster, or picked up a handout. The typical demographic profile of the participants did not vary significantly across the two methods of recruiting, although the poster/handout approach was successful in reaching two black participants and two of the younger members of my sample. The research was carried out mainly in London, a city in south-west England, and in rural areas of the Cotswolds.

Table 1 shows the sample by age grouping, occupation, parenting status and by their status as 'always single' (19 participants) or 'single again' (which refers to those who have been married previously – 11 participants). The majority of women interviewed were white, owner-occupiers and British, with considerable variation in current employment and income. Ten of the sample were in the 45–49 years age band, and there were six each in the 5-year bands on either side of this one, so in terms of age people were clustered in the middle to upper age limits of my criteria. This was for-tuitous, rather than by design, and arguably may have been linked to the snowballing approach.

The aim was to work in depth and to develop a rich or 'thick' under-standing (Geertz 1973) of a relatively small sample with a broadly shared social position rather than, for example, conduct a questionnaire survey which would have allowed a 'thinner' exploration of a much more diverse sample. In my view the relative homogeneity of my sample was a strength, rather than a disadvantage, but there were also some distinctive differences in experience. Two participants had disabilities. Eight of the sample had children; in four cases these children were grown adults living in separate households at the time of the interview, and, apart from one person in the 35–39 bracket, all the mothers were over 45 years. Three of the mothers with children under ten years had never married. Two participants were black. Most participants referred to heterosexual experience, one person identified herself as lesbian and two referred to having had relationships with women as well as men.

Table 1 Participants showing occupation, age bands, marital status and parenting status

Name	Occupation	30–34	35–39	40–44	45–49	50–54	55–60
Shelley	Secretary				AS		
Val	Computer programmer					SAᶜ	
Sarah	Therapist					AS	
Milly	IT trainer	AS					
Josie	Teacher					SAᶜ	
Polly	Receptionist						AS
Thari	Teacher		ASᶜ				
Sue	Counsellor				AS		
Susie	Probation officer				SA		
Lucy	Lecturer				SA		
Mary	Nurse				SA		
Ruth	Student		AS				
Annie	Secretary				SA		
Margaret	Shop assistant				ASᶜ		
Marion	Service user consultant				SA		
Lyn	Lecturer					AS	
Pat	Lecturer						ASᶜ
Patsy	Management consultant			AS			
Rachel	Social work trainer					AS	
Pauline	Lecturer						AS
Maggie	Information work/ research				AS		
Mya	Racial equality officer				ASᶜ		
Jay	Housing manager					SAᶜ	
Alix	Lecturer			SA			
Claire	Therapist					SA	
Grace	Lecturer						AS
Molly	Social worker				AS		
Margot	Unemployed/trainer						SAᶜ
Jane	Student			AS			
Jennifer	Student			AS			

AS = 'Always single'; includes all those who have never married.
SA = 'Single again'; includes all those who are divorced or widowed.
ᶜ = Has a child or adult children.

There is a historic link between a class of rising professional women and singleness, and this is something of an argument for focusing predominantly on middle-class women. However, there are difficulties in making firm class categorizations of women who have remained single, which reflect both the degree to which class relates to male status and the financial difficulties associated with single motherhood. My aim was not to look for representativeness or comparability across different class or other boundaries; the most important aspect was to select women who fitted my broad description of 'women alone'. Like Ruthellen Josselson, in her follow-up study of college-educated women, I wanted to reach those who 'represent a group of women who are not studied, reported about, or understood often' (Josselson 1987: 41).

Interviews

I regarded my first two interviews as 'pilots', giving me an opportunity to find out whether I had identified fruitful areas for discussion, and to check how long the interviews took. These interviews highlighted the subjectivity and fluidity of self-definitions of singleness. One participant thought that she might not be single now, she could not be sure but things might be about to change. She had just made contact again with a former lover, and thought this might presage a revival of their relationship on what promised to be a better footing from her point of view. This later proved not to be the case. The other described herself as definitely single: 'a classic case', although she did see herself as having a partner. Their relationship was on a weekends-only basis because of the distance of their living and working arrangements. He later moved jobs and came to live with her, and they have since married.

The feedback that I got from one of the pilot participants helped me immensely in thinking about how I might avoid heteronormative assumptions in the interviews. The participant told me that she had not chosen to be single, but had not chosen an alternative: she had just stayed as she was. Later she referred to having always wanted to keep her options open. I asked about relationships that might have led to marriage or a long-term commitment and she spoke of relationships with men. When I checked with her at the end of the interview whether there was anything else she thought we should talk about, she spoke of having relationships with women as well as men. This was what keeping her options open had meant to her. My earlier question appeared to have been heard as a question about marriage and marriage-type partnerships, hence not an invitation to talk about same-sex relationships. It was very helpful to have my attention drawn to the unanticipated ways in which questions might be understood. As a result, in subsequent one-to-one interviews I asked each participant to tell me about important relationships in her life and to give her understanding of how she had got to where she was now.

I prepared a schedule of questions for use in the interview. This was refined after the two pilot interviews, which had helped me to decide on the central topic areas for my purposes. Participants were provided with information about the interviews in advance, and were asked to complete a form relating to personal details. The interview topics covered three broad areas, with some initial introductory questions. In order not to impose a definition of singleness on my participants who might not see themselves this way, I asked them first to give me a brief self-description: 'things you might want someone you have just met to know about you'. This allowed me to see what features they chose as salient, and where possible to use the terminology that they had used in relation to their marital status. I followed this up by asking directly what terms they preferred to use, offering some alternatives and asking whether there were other terms they might use.

I was interested in how participants dealt with self-presentation. My own experience of introducing myself was that I would rarely refer to being single. Asking my participants to say something about themselves by way of introduction meant I could note whether this was part of their self-description, although it was a somewhat contrived approach, particularly when I was talking to women I already knew. It framed the interview as 'serious business' where I was interested in the participant from my perspective as a researcher rather than simply as a friend. This verbal picture allowed for the possibility that any participants might have information unknown to me that they regarded as salient about themselves. It was also an opportunity to check whether they did consider themselves to be single.

The first substantive area of the interview involved interactional issues. I asked about the images participants held of singleness and how they perceived others' views of themselves. The second area focused on the participant's past and current relationships. The final questions aimed to revisit the participant's current feelings about her situation, and to elicit any political perspectives she might hold regarding the single state. While informal, it was a guided conversation with a particular purpose, and in this sense was in the tradition of ethnographic interviews (Burgess 1984). The interviewer asks questions designed to elicit talk from the person being interviewed.

My interviews were audio-recorded and transcribed. Transcripts were then made anonymous, with names changed and details removed such as place names or friends' names which might lead to identification of the participant. Although my focus is on resources used in talk, rather than the individual speakers, I also wished to recognize participants as persons with their own narratives and personal histories upon which they draw in the interview. I was concerned that if I made up a name for them, it might convey class or age-cohort associations that were misleading, and might be disliked by the participant concerned. I asked participants to choose a pseudonym for themselves for use with their transcript, thinking that this would allow them a degree of participation, albeit minimal, as well as providing names that had more authentic associations for the person concerned.

In my own approach to involvement in the process I wanted to provide participants with their own transcribed interviews and to give them an opportunity to correct or delete material. In part, this stemmed from the feminist orientation of my project. Participants were generous with their time, and this seemed to me one small thing that I could return to them. I was conscious of the research focus as a sensitive one, and was prepared for the possibility that participants might have qualms about their words being used for analysis and potential publication. Furthermore, interviewees own the copyright to their words under the 1988 Copyright, Designs and Patents Act and I needed their consent for quotation (Bornat 1994). I viewed consent to having interviews audio-recorded and permission to quote transcribed extracts as an ongoing process. I asked permission to record and explained the anonymizing process at the time of the interview. I later provided participants with a copy of the transcript of the interview and offered the opportunity to correct or delete material.

Transcription

Although I am discussing transcription following the interviews because this was the order in which processes took place, it can also be considered as part of generation of data, in this case the selection of what *counts* as data. It is important in discursive approaches to give detailed attention to what is said and how it is said: the fuller the transcript the more it is possible to capture how the interaction is a collaborative project organized around current activities (Potter and Wetherell 1995; Potter and Hepburn 2005). Transcription is both a theoretical activity and a selective process (Ochs 1979). Transcripts need to reflect the researcher's research goals. My main interest is in resources used at the level of phrases and the kind of positioning speakers achieve through such use. For the most part of this study the focus is on how meanings are jointly constructed and the words and kinds of descriptions employed rather than the detailed conversational moves. For this a fairly simple form of notation has been used and a list of transcription symbols is shown in Appendix 2.

The transcribed extracts shown in this book have the names of speakers listed down the side of the page with the transcribed speech laid out like a script. Lines have been numbered for ease of reference. The numbering is not continuous throughout an individual transcript, but restarts with each new extract. The exception is cases where a more extended length of speech has been split into smaller units for analysis. Numbering there is sequential over the larger speech unit, so that it is also possible to see if lines have been omitted (as in Chapter 4).

The transcription for Chapter 6 is dealt with differently in order to identify and bring out some trouble in the interaction in interviews. In this chapter I look at the sequential aspects of the interaction, and have used an extended and more detailed version of transcription so that it is possible to identify overlapping speech, interruptions or token responses and see an estimated length of pauses and gross changes of volume or emphasis (a list of symbols used in Chapter 6 is shown in Appendix 2).

Some researchers use initials in transcription, rather than participants' names: the initials may denote the role of the person speaking. For instance, Robin Wooffit, in research on psychic practitioners uses 'P' for psychic practitioner and 'S' for sitter in his transcription (Wooffitt 2001). This can have advantages in focusing attention on the talk as representative of patterns in conversation rather than 'belonging' to one or two identifiable people. However, all naming decisions bring their own implications, highlighting some features while disguising others (Billig 1999). The use of first names appears to be democratic, but there may be a power differential between one speaker and another. The use of initials appears to be gender-neutral, but gender differences may be important in the talk studied. My choice to use (anonymized) first names aims to retain a sense of persons, who while they may use a stock of common resources in patterned ways, are also individuals with personal lives and histories.

Methodical listening to the recordings of interviews is recommended as aiding later recall of the interaction that took place as well as accuracy of transcription (Psathas and Anderson 1990). Apart from the first two pilot interviews, which I transcribed myself, the initial transcription was done by secretaries. However, there were several rounds of checking that I went through. First, I listened to each recording again and checked the transcript for accuracy, before I sent a copy to the participant. At a later stage as I selected passages for fuller analysis, I checked again in more detail, inserting pauses and numbering the lines. A further layer of listening again to recordings and re-transcribing according to a modified version of the transcription system devised by Gail Jefferson (Atkinson and Heritage 1984b) was required for the extracts quoted in Chapter 6.

Data analysis

In any data analysis the first step is careful consideration of the data and familiarization: listening and re-listening to recordings, reading and re-reading of transcripts to get some overall sense of what might be of interest. Discourse or conversation analysts have contrasting ideas on how to move on to the next stage. Edwards (1997: 89) recommends 'unmotivated looking', in order to avoid reading into the data a set of analytic categories that may not work, and may leave the researcher disappointed in what has been identified. This advice comes originally from Sacks, who argues that data should not be used simply as evidence for problems that the researcher has defined prior to analysis. Instead 'The first rule is to be interested in what it is you've got' (Sacks 1992 Volume I: 471).

Wetherell and Potter (1992), in relation to their work on discursive practices and racism, describe their process involving series of codings, copying material into files according to different themes, and checking the source material again as understanding of particular themes developed. They point out that the process of arriving at a view of the social practices taking place may be very different to the way in which that conclusion is justified. Their own analysis was guided by 'the sorts of subtle knowledge that a cultural member possesses' (Wetherell and Potter 1992: 101). Wetherell and Potter recommend searching for variability as a signal that different ways of constructing events are being deployed.

My own experience was that I needed to do some preliminary sifting in order to get some sense of what it was I had got. I looked at a selection of manuscripts and noted major themes and topics that appeared. I copied material into large data files for the major areas of questioning. Passages were often replicated in more than one file as they might relate to different areas. I looked at the data files initially for specific aspects: for instance I mapped where I could detect different meanings being attached to single-ness in the 'images' data file, and noted strongly contrasting meanings involving stigma and independence. The approach has been somewhat different for each data file. In general it has involved movement from looking in detail at the data selected from one individual participant, back to checking across the corpus in the rest of the file for whether patterns identified are to be found elsewhere. What I searched for was some of the taken-for-granted ways of talking about singleness that were present in our talk, and areas of contradiction and variability in these. I looked for puzzles, for instance where a particular response might not be the antici-pated one.

Detecting regularities and patterns in participants' talk in relation to topic areas has been a slow process and has involved discussion of tentative hypotheses with colleagues. In order to develop my analysis I went through several rounds of looking for patterns for each area of questioning then, in extracts where I thought the pattern was evident, analysing it at a more micro-analytic level. The patterns came from my data, and were not predetermined hypotheses with which I approached the data. However, any pattern I initially identified was not necessarily the one I always ended up with as a 'finding'. A focus on one kind of pattern sometimes revealed additional interesting features when I analysed the pattern more closely. The particular process issues are discussed in more detail in Chapters 3, 4, 5 and 6, as they relate to the particular analytical concepts used.

APPENDIX 2: TRANSCRIPTION CONVENTIONS

Transcription symbols used in Chapters 3, 4 and 5

The transcription notation in these chapters is a very simplified version of that developed by Gail Jefferson (see Atkinson and Heritage 1984b: ix–xvi for a fuller account).

[. . .]	Material deliberately omitted.
[name] [place]	Identifying details removed.
(laughs)	Hearable laughter from the speaker.
<u>text</u>	Speaker emphasis.

Punctuation is given for ease of reading rather than to indicate speech patterns.

Additional transcription symbols used in Chapter 6

(0.5)	The number in brackets indicates a time gap within one speaker's talk or between speakers estimated to the nearest half second.
.hhh	A dot before an 'h' indicates speaker in-breath.
hhh	An 'h' indicates out-breath; the more 'h's the longer the breath.
=	The equals sign indicates that there is no interval between adjacent utterances.
co:lon	A colon indicates an extension of the sound or syllable it follows.
°text°	Degree signs indicate that the talk they encompass is noticeably quieter than the surrounding talk.
[ ]	Square brackets placed at the same position in lines above and below of different speakers indicate overlapping speech between the brackets.
-	A single hyphen indicates a halting cutoff. When multiple hyphens are used after several words as in 'wh- wh- how-' the speech has a stammering quality.

REFERENCES

Abell, J., Stokoe, E. and Billig, M. (2000) 'Narrative and the discursive (re)construction of events', in M. Andrews, S.D. Sclater, C. Squire and A. Treacher (eds) *Lines of Narrative: Psychosocial Perspectives*, London: Routledge.

Adams, M. (1976) *Single Blessedness: Observations on the Single Status in Married Society*, New York: Basic Books.

Adler, P.A. and Adler, P. (1987) *Membership Roles in Field Research*, London: Sage.

Agencies (2006) 'Lady Thatcher joins mourners at Profumo's funeral', *The Guardian*: 20 March 2006. Online. Available: <http://www.guardian.co.uk/uk_news/story/0,,1735280,00.html> (accessed 29 March 2006).

Allen, K.R. (1989) *Single Women/Family Ties: Life Histories of Older Women*, London: Sage.

Anderson, C.M. and Stewart, S., with Dimidjian, S. (1995) *Flying Solo: Single Women in Midlife*, London: W.W. Norton.

Andrews, M. (2002) 'Introduction: Counter-narratives and the power to oppose', *Narrative Inquiry*, 12, 1:1–6.

Andrews, M., Sclater, S.D., Squire, C. and Treacher, A. (eds) (2000) *Lines of Narrative: Psychosocial Perspectives*, London: Routledge.

Antaki, C., Condor, S. and Levine, M. (1996) 'Social identities in talk: speakers' own orientations', *British Journal of Social Psychology*, 35: 473–92.

Atkin, D. (1991) 'The evolution of television series addressing single women, 1966–1990', *Journal of Broadcasting & Electronic Media*, 35, 4: 517–23.

Atkinson, J.M. and Heritage, J. (1984a) 'Preference organisation', in J.M. Atkinson and J. Heritage (eds) *Structures of Social Action: Studies in Conversation Analysis*, Cambridge: Cambridge University Press.

Atkinson, J.M. and Heritage, J. (1984b) *Structures of Social Action: Studies in Conversation Analysis*, Cambridge: Cambridge University Press.

Atkinson, P. and Silverman, D. (1997) 'Kundera's *Immortality*: the interview society and the invention of the self', *Qualitative Inquiry*, 3, 3: 304–25.

Bainbridge, B. (2005) 'Waiting to grow up', *The Guardian*, Review, p. 4.

Bakhtin, M. (1981) 'Discourse in the novel', in M. Holquist (ed) *The Dialogic Imagination*, Austin, University of Texas Press.

Bamberg, M. (2004) 'Narrative discourse and identities', in J.C. Meister, T. Kindt, W. Schernus and M. Stein (eds) *Narratology Beyond Literary Criticism*, Berlin, New York: Walter de Gruyter.

167

Bankoff, E.A. (1994) 'Women in psychotherapy: their life circumstances and treatment needs', *Psychotherapy*, 31, 4: 610–19.

Barrett, M. and McIntosh, M. (1982) *The Anti-Social Family*, London: Verso.

Bauman, Z. (1998) 'On postmodern uses of sex', *Theory, Culture & Society*, 15, 3–4: 19–33.

Bauman, Z. (2001) 'Individually, together', in U. Beck and E. Beck-Gernsheim (eds) *Individualization*, London: Sage.

Bauman, Z. (2003) *Liquid Love: On the Frailty of Human Bonds*, Cambridge: Polity.

BBC (2007) *Book Club* (interview with Germaine Greer), Radio 4, 1 July 2007.

Beck, U. and Beck-Gernsheim, E. (1995) *The Normal Chaos of Love*, Cambridge: Polity.

Beck, U. and Beck-Gernsheim, E. (2001) *Individualization*, London: Sage.

Beck-Gernsheim, E. (1998) 'On the way to a post-familial family: from a community of need to elective affinities', *Theory, Culture & Society*, 15, 3–4: 53–70.

Berke, N. (2006) 'Single women at midlife: the always already dumped', in N. Bauer-Maglin (ed) *Cut Loose: (Mostly) Older Women Talk about the End of (Mostly) Long-term Relationships*, London: Rutgers University Press.

Bickerton, T. (1983) 'Women alone', in S. Cartledge and J. Ryan (eds) *Sex and Love: New Thoughts on Old Contradictions*, London: The Women's Press.

Billig, M. (1991) *Ideology and Opinions: Studies in Rhetorical Psychology*, London: Sage.

Billig, M. (1999) 'Whose terms? Whose ordinariness? Rhetoric and Ideology in conversation analysis', *Discourse & Society*, 10, 4: 543–82.

Billig, M., Condor, S., Edwards, D., Gane, M., Middleton, D. and Radley, A. (1988) *Ideological Dilemmas: A Social Psychology of Everyday Thinking*, London: Sage.

Bindel, J. (2005) The spinster passes away, *The Guardian*. Wednesday December 7, 2005. Online. Available: <http://www.guardian.co.uk/print/0,3858,5350096-103680,00.html> (accessed 15 March 2006).

Blow, R. (2003) 'Sex and politics'. Online. Available: <http://www.tompaine.com/Archive/scontent/9165.html> (accessed 1 October 2007).

Bornat, J. (1994) 'Recording oral history', in M. Drake and R. Finnegan (eds) *Sources and Methods: A Handbook*, Cambridge: Cambridge University Press.

Bristow, W. (2000) *Single and Loving it*, London: Thorsons.

Browne, J. and Frey, G. (1972) 'Take it easy' (song).

Bruner, J. (1990) *Acts of Meaning*, Cambridge, MA: Harvard University Press.

Bruner, J. (1991) 'The narrative construction of reality', *Critical Inquiry*, 18, 1: 1–21.

Budgeon, S. and Roseneil, S. (2002) 'Cultures of intimacy and care beyond "The Family": friendship and sexual/love relationships in the twenty-first century', paper presented at International Sociological Association World Congress of Sociology, Brisbane, July 2002.

Burgess, R.G. (1984) *In the Field: An Introduction to Field Research*, London: Allen and Unwin.

Burkitt, I. (1991) *Social Selves: Theories of the Formation of Personality*, London: Sage.

Bury, M. (1982) 'Chronic illness as biographical disruption', *Sociology of Health and Illness*, 4, 2: 167–82.

Bury, M. (2001) 'Illness narratives: fact or fiction?', *Sociology of Health and Illness*, 23, 3: 263–85.

Bushnell, C. (2005) *Lipstick Jungle*, London: Abacus.

Byrne, A. (2000) 'Singular identities: managing stigma, resisting voices', *Women's Studies Review*, 7: 13–24. Online. Available: <http://www.medusanet.ca/single-women/> (accessed 12 February 2004).

Byrne, A. (2003) 'Developing a sociological model for researching women's self and social identities', *The European Journal of Women's Studies*, 10, 4: 443–64.

Byrne, A. and Carr, D. (2005) 'Caught in the cultural lag: the stigma of singlehood', *Psychological Inquiry*, 16, 2–3: 84–91.

Cain, H. and Yuval-Davis, N. (1990) '"The equal opportunities community" and the anti-racist struggle', *Critical Social Policy*, 29: 5–26.

Carter, E. and McGoldrick, M. (1980) *The Family Life-cycle: A Framework for Family Therapy*, New York: Gardner.

Chandler, J. (1991) *Women Without Husbands: An Exploration of the Margins of Marriage*, Basingstoke: Macmillan.

Chasteen, A.L. (1994) '"The world around me": the environment and single women', *Sex Roles*, 31, 5/6: 309–28.

Chodorow, N.J. (1995) 'Individuality and difference in how women and men love', in A. Elliott and S. Frosh (eds) *Psychoanalysis in Contexts: Paths between Theory and Modern Culture*, London: Routledge.

Choi, N.G. (1996) 'Changes in the living arrangements, work patterns, and economic status of middle-aged single women: 1971–1991', *Affilia*, 11, 2: 164–78.

Clements, M. (1998) *The Improvised Woman: Single Women Reinventing Single Life*, London: Norton.

Cline, S. (1993) *Women, Celibacy and Passion*, London: Andre Deutsch.

CNN (2002) *Larry King Live* (interview with Bob Woodward), 11 December 2002.

Coates, J. (1996) *Women Talk: Conversation Between Women Friends*, Oxford: Blackwell.

Condor, S. (1989) '"Biting into the future": social change and the social identity of women', in S. Skevington and D. Baker (eds) *The Social Identity of Women*, London: Sage.

Connell, R.W. (1987) *Gender and Power: Society, the Person and Sexual Politics*, Oxford: Polity Press.

Craib, I. (2000) 'Narratives as bad faith', in M. Andrews, S.D. Sclater, C. Squire and A. Treacher (eds) *Lines of Narrative: Psychosocial Perspectives*, London: Routledge.

Crossley, M. (2000) *Introducing Narrative Psychology: Self, Trauma and the Construction of Meaning*, Buckingham: Open University Press.

Dallos, R. (1996) 'Change and transformations of relationships', in D. Miell and R. Dallos (eds) *Social Interaction and Personal Relationships*, London: Sage.

Dalton, S.T. (1992) 'Lived experience of never-married women', *Issues in Mental Health Nursing*, 13: 69–80.

Daly, M. with Caputi, J. (1987) *Websters' First New Intergalactic Wickedary of the English Language*, London: The Women's Press.

Davies, B. and Harré, R. (1990) 'Positioning: the discursive production of selves', *Journal for the Theory of Social Behaviour*, 20, 1: 43–63.

Davies, L. (1995) 'A closer look at gender and distress among the never married', *Women & Health*, 23, 2: 13–30.

DePaulo, B.M. (2006) *Singled Out: How Singles are Stereotyped, Stigmatized, and Ignored, and Still Live Happily Ever After*, New York: St Martin's Press.

DePaulo, B.M. and Morris, W.L. (2005a) 'Singles in society and in science', *Psychological Inquiry*, 16, 2–3: 57–83.

DePaulo, B.M. and Morris, W.L. (2005b) 'Should singles and the scholars who study them make their mark or stay in their place?', *Psychological Inquiry*, 16, 2–3: 142–9.

Dickens, C. (1920) *Great Expectations*, London, Caxton Publishing Company.

Dowling, C. (1982) *The Cinderella Complex: Women's Hidden Fear of Independence*, London: Michael Joseph.

Drew, P. (1984) 'Speakers' reportings in invitation sequences', in J.M. Atkinson and J. Heritage (eds) *Structures of Social Action: Studies in Conversation Analysis*, Cambridge: Cambridge University Press.

Dryden, C. (1999) *Being Married, Doing Gender*, London: Routledge.

Duck, S. (1994) *Meaningful Relationships: Talking Sense and Relating*, Thousand Oaks, CA: Sage.

Edley, N. (2001) 'Analysing masculinity: interpretative repertoires, ideological dilemmas and subject positions', in M. Wetherell, S. Taylor and S.J. Yates (eds) *Discourse as Data: a Guide to Analysis*, London: Sage.

Edley, N. (2002) 'The Loner, the Walk and the Beast Within: narrative fragments in the construction of masculinity', in W. Patterson (ed) *Strategic Narratives: New Perspectives on the Power of Personal and Cultural Stories*, Oxford: Lexington Books.

Edwards, D. (1997) *Discourse and Cognition*, London: Sage.

Edwards, D. (1999) 'Emotion discourse', *Culture and Psychology*, 5, 3: 271–91.

Edwards, D. and Potter, J. (1992) *Discursive Psychology*, London: Sage.

Eichenbaum, L. and Orbach, S. (1987) 'Separation and intimacy: crucial practice issues in working with women in therapy', in S. Ernst and M. Maguire (eds) *Living with the Sphinx: Papers from the Women's Therapy Centre*, London: The Women's Press.

Elliott, J. (2005) *Using Narrative in Social Research: Qualitative and Quantitative Approaches*, London: Sage.

Faludi, S. (1992) *Backlash: The Undeclared War Against Women*, London: Chatto and Windus.

Featherstone, B. (2006) 'Rethinking family support in the current policy context', *British Journal of Social Work*, 36: 5–19.

Fielding, H. (1996) *Bridget Jones's Diary*, London: Picador.

Fielding, H. (2000) *Bridget Jones: the Edge of Reason*, Basingstoke: Picador.

Fink, J. and Holden, K. (1999) 'Pictures from the margins of marriage: representations of spinsters and single mothers in the mid-Victorian novel, inter-war Hollywood melodrama and British film of the 1950s and 1960s', *Gender and History*, 11, 2: 233–55.

Fontana, B. (1994) 'Plastic sex and the sociologist: a comment on *The Transformation of Intimacy* by Anthony Giddens', *Economy and Society*, 23, 3: 374–83.

Forbat, L. (2005) *Talking about Care: Two Sides of the Story*, Bristol: Policy Press.

Foucault, M. (1972) *The Archaeology of Knowledge*, London: Tavistock.

170

Foucault, M. (1980) *Power/Knowledge: Selected Interviews and Other Writings 1972–77*, Brighton: Harvester.

Frosh, S. (1989) *Psychoanalysis and Psychology*, Basingstoke: Macmillan.

Geertz, C. (1973) *The Interpretation of Cultures*, New York: Basic Books.

Gergen, K.J. (1994) 'Self-narration in social life', in K.J. Gergen (ed) *Realities and Relationships: Soundings in Social Construction*, London: Harvard University Press.

Gergen, K.J. (1999) *An Invitation to Social Construction*, London: Sage.

Gergen, K.J. and Gergen, M.M. (1987) 'Narratives of relationship', in R. Burnett, P. McGhee and D.D. Clarke (eds) *Accounting for Relationships: Explanation, Representation and Knowledge*, London: Methuen.

Gergen, M. (1994) 'The social construction of personal histories: gendered lives in popular autobiographies', in T.R. Sarbin and J.I. Kitsuse (eds) *Constructing the Social*, London: Sage.

Giddens, A. (1992) *The Transformation of Intimacy: Sexuality, Love and Eroticism in Modern Societies*, Cambridge: Polity Press.

Giddens, A. (2005) *Modernity and Self-identity Revisited*, ESRC Identities and Social Action Research Programme Public Launch 14 April 2005, Royal Society of Arts, London. Online. Available: <http://www.open.ac.uk/socialsciences/identities/launch_transcripts.pdf> (accessed 28 March 2006).

Gilbert, G. N. and Mulkay, M. (1984) *Opening Pandora's Box: A Sociological Analysis of Scientists' Discourse*, Cambridge: Cambridge University Press.

Gill, R. (1998) 'Dialogues and differences: writing, reflexivity and the crisis of representation', in K. Henwood, C. Griffin and A. Phoenix (eds) *Standpoints and Differences: Essays in the Practice of Feminist Psychology*, London: Sage.

Gill, R. and Herdieckerhoff, E. (2006) 'Rewriting the romance: new feminities in Chick Lit?', *Feminist Media Studies*, 6, 4: 487–504.

Gilligan, C. (1982) *In a Different Voice: Psychological Theory and Women's Development*, London: Harvard University Press.

Gledhill, R. (2005) 'New marriage rules to split with spinster and bachelor', *Times Online*, 27 July 2005. Online. Available: <http://www.timesonline.co.uk/article/0,,2-1710342,00.html> (accessed 28 March 2006).

Goffman, E. (1955) 'On face work: an analysis of ritual elements in social interaction', *Psychiatry*, 18: 213–31.

Goffman, E. (1974) *Frame Analysis: An Essay on the Organization of Experience*, Harmondsworth: Penguin.

Gordon, T. (1994) *Single Women: On the Margins?*, Basingstoke: Macmillan.

Grafton, S. (1990) *A is for Alibi*, London: Pan Books.

Grafton, S. (2005) *R is for Ricochet*, London: Pan Books.

Greer, G. (1971) *The Female Eunuch*, London: Book Club Associates.

Gubrium, J.F. and Holstein, J.A. (1994) 'Grounding the postmodern self', *The Sociological Quarterly*, 35, 4: 685–703.

Gullette, M.M. (1988) *Safe at Last in the Middle Years: the Invention of the Midlife Progress Novel: Saul Bellow, Margaret Drabble, Anne Tyler, and John Updike*, London: University of California Press.

Gullette, M.M. (1997) *Declining to Decline: Cultural Combat and the Politics of the Midlife*, London: University Press of Virginia.

Habermas, J. (1981) 'New social movements', *Telos*, 49: 33–7.

Hall, S. (1988) 'Minimal selves', in ICA documents no. 6 (ed) *Identity: The Real Me*, London: Institute of the Contemporary Arts.

Hall, S. (1997a) 'The spectacle of the "other"', in S. Hall (ed) *Representation: Cultural Representations and Signifying Practices*, London: Sage.

Hall, S. (1997b) 'The work of representation', in S. Hall (ed) *Representation: Cultural Representations and Signifying Practices*, London: Sage.

Hall, S. (2000) 'Who needs 'identity'?', in P. du Gay, J. Evans and P. Redman (eds) *Identity: a Reader*, London: Sage.

Hamilton, C. (1981) *Marriage as a Trade*, London: The Women's Press (first published 1909).

Harré, R. (1995) 'Agentive discourse', in R. Harré and P. Stearns *Discursive Psychology in Practice*, London: Sage, pp. 120–36.

Harré, R. and van Langenhove, L. (1991) 'Varieties of positioning', *Journal for the Theory of Social Behaviour*, 21: 393–407.

Harris, A., Carney, S. and Fine, M. (2001) 'Counter work: introduction to "Under the Covers: Theorising the Politics of Counter Stories"', *Critical Psychology*, 4: 6–18.

Haskey, J. (2005) 'Living arrangements in contemporary Britain: Having a partner who usually lives elsewhere and Living Apart Together (LAT)', *Population Trends*, 122: 35–45. Office for National Statistics. Online. Available: <http://www.statistics.gov.uk/articles/population_trends/1351.pdf> (accessed 28 March 2006).

Heller, Z. (2004) *Notes on a Scandal*, London: Penguin.

Heritage, J. (2001) 'Goffman, Garfinkel and Conversation Analysis', in M. Wetherell, S. Taylor and S.J. Yates (eds) *Discourse Theory and Practice: a Reader*, London: Sage.

Hester, S. and Eglin, P. (eds) (1997) *Culture in Action: Membership Categorisation Analysis*, Boston: International Institute for Ethnomethodology and University Press of America.

Hilliard, M. (1956) *A Woman Doctor Looks at Love and Life*, New York: Permabook.

Hillis, M. (1936) *Live Alone and Like it: a Guide for the Extra Woman*, New York: Bobbs-Merrill.

Hite, S. (1993) *Women as Revolutionary Agents of Change: Selected Essays in Psychology and Gender, 1972–1993*, London: Bloomsbury.

Hodgkinson, L. (1993) *Happy to be Single: The Pleasures of Independence*, London: Thorsons.

Holden, K. (2005) 'Imaginary widows: spinsters, marriage, and the "lost generation" in Britain after the Great War', *Journal of Family History*, 30, 4: 388–409.

Holland, J., Ramazanoglu, C., Sharpe, S., and Thomson, R. (1996) 'Reputations: journeying into gendered power relations' in J. Weeks (ed) *Sexual Cultures, Communities, Values and Intimacy*, London: Macmillan.

Hollway, W. (1984) 'Gender difference and the production of subjectivity', in J. Henriques, V. Couze, W. Hollway, C. Urwin and V. Walkerdine (eds) *Changing the Subject*, London: Methuen.

ITV (2007) *Holly & Fearne Go Dating*. Online. Available: <http://www.itv.com/Lifestyle/Dating/HollyandFearneGoDating/default.html> (accessed 24 September 2007).

Jackson, S. (1995) 'Women and heterosexual love: complicity, resistance and change', in L. Pearce and J. Stacey (eds) *Romance Revisited*, London: Lawrence and Wishart.

Jackson, S. and Cram, F. (2003) 'Disrupting the sexual double standard: young women's talk about heterosexuality', *British Journal of Social Psychology*, 42: 113–27.

Jacobs, R.N. (2000) 'Narrative, civil society and public culture', in M. Andrews, S.D. Sclater, C. Squire and A. Treacher (eds) *Lines of Narrative: Psychosocial Perspectives*, London: Routledge.

Jamieson, L. (1998) *Intimacy: Personal Relationships in Modern Societies*, Oxford: Polity.

Jamieson, L. (1999) 'Intimacy transformed? A critical look at the "pure relationship"', *Sociology*, 33, 3: 477–94.

Jamieson, L., Stewart, R., Yaojun, L., Anderson, M., Bechhofer, F. and McCrone, D. (2002) 'Single, twenty-something and seeking?', in G. Allen and G. Jones (eds) *Time and the Life Course: Age, Generation and Social Change*, Buckingham: Palgrave.

Jeffreys, S. (1985) *The Spinster and her Enemies: Feminism and Sexuality 1880–1930*, London: Pandora.

Jiminez, M.E. (1993) 'Book review: The Transformation of Intimacy: Sexuality, Love and Eroticism in Modern Societies', *Social Forces*, 72, 1: 271–2.

Jones, R.L. (2002) '"That's very rude, I shouldn't be telling you that": older women talking about sex', *Narrative Inquiry*, 12, 1: 121–43.

Josselson, R. (1987) *Finding Herself: Pathways to Identity Development in Women*, London: Jossey-Bass.

Josselson, R. (1996) *Revising Herself: The Story of Women's Identity from College to Midlife*, New York: Oxford University Press.

Juska, J. (2003) *A Round-Heeled Woman: My Late-Life Adventures in Sex and Romance*, London: Chatto and Windus.

Kettle, M. and Kennedy, M. (2006) 'Sex, lies and charity – end of Britain's greatest scandal', *The Guardian* 11 March 2006: 6.

Kitzinger, C. (2005) 'Heteronormativity in action: reproducing the heterosexual nuclear family in after-hours medical calls', *Social Problems*, 52, 4: 477–98.

Labov, W. (1972) 'The transformation of experience in narrative syntax', in W. Labov (ed) *Language in the Inner City: Studies in the Black English Vernacular*, Oxford: Blackwell.

Labov, W. and Waletzky, J. (1967) 'Narrative analysis: oral versions of personal experience', in J. Helm (ed) *Essays on the Verbal and Visual Arts*, Seattle, WA: University of Washington Press.

Lee, Y-J., and Roth, W-M. (2004) 'Making a scientist: discursive "doing" of identity and self-presentation in research interviews', *Forum: Qualitative Social Research*, 5, 1: Article 12.

Lees, S. (1993) *Sugar and Spice*, London: Penguin.

Lette, K. (2003) *Dead Sexy*, London: Pocket Books.

Lewis, J. (2001) *The End of Marriage? Individualism and Intimate Relations*, Cheltenham: Edward Elgar.

Lewis, K. G. (1994) 'Heterosexual women through the life cycle', in M. Mirkin (ed)

Women in Context: Towards a Feminist Reconstruction of Psychotherapy, New York: Guilford Press.

Lewis, K.G. (2000) 'The four pillars of wisdom: helping singles counteract conflicting cultural messages', *Family Therapy Networker*: 75–82.

Lewis, K.G. (2001) *With or Without a Man: Single Women Taking Control of Their Lives*, Palo Alto, CA: Bull Publishing Company.

Lewis, K.G. and Moon, S. (1997) 'Always single and single again women: a qualitative study', *Journal of Marital and Family Therapy*, 23, 2: 115–34.

Loewenstein, S.F. (1983) 'A feminist perspective', in A. Rosenblatt and D. Waldfogel (eds) *Handbook of Clinical Social Work*, San Francisco: Jossey-Bass.

Loewenstein, S.F., Ebin Bloch, N., Campion, J., Sproule Epstein, J., Gale, P. and Salvatore, M. (1981) 'A study of satisfactions and stresses of single women in midlife', *Sex Roles*, 7, 11: 1127–41.

Lupton, D. (1998) *The Emotional Self: a Sociocultural Exploration*, London: Sage.

Lynch, M. (2000) 'Against reflexivity as an academic virtue and source of privileged knowledge', *Theory, Culture & Society*, 17, 3: 26–54.

McGruder, A. (2003) 'The Boondocks', reproduced in Warn, S. (2003) 'Condoleezza and the Comic Strip controversy', *After Ellen: News, Reviews and Commentary on Lesbian and Bisexual Women in Entertainment and the Media*. Online. Available: <http://www.afterellen.com/archive/ellen/Print/boondocks.html> (accessed 28 September 2007).

Mad Chicks (2004) Online. Available: <www.mad-chicks.org.uk> (accessed 28 September 2007).

Mangan, L. (2007) 'The cruel truth about love', *The Guardian Weekend*, 18 August 2007: 28–32.

Marshall, H. and Wetherell, M. (1989) 'Talking about career and gender identities: a discourse analysis perspective', in S. Skevington and D. Baker (eds) *The Social Identity of Women*, London: Sage.

May, V. (2003) 'Lone motherhood and identity construction: an interplay between dominant and counter narratives', paper presented at Narrative, Ideology and Myth, The Second Tampere Conference on Narrative, Tampere, June 2003.

Maybin, J. (2001) 'Language, struggle and voice: the Bakhtin/Volosinov writings', in M. Wetherell, S. Taylor and S.J. Yates (eds) *Discourse Theory and Practice: a Reader*, London: Sage.

Mills, S. (2003) 'Caught between sexism, anti-sexism and 'political correctness': feminist women's negotiations with naming practices', *Discourse & Society*, 14, 1: 87–110.

Mishler, E. (1999) *Storylines: Craftartists' Narratives of Identity*, London: Harvard University Press.

Nikander, P. (1995) 'The turn to the text: the critical potential of discursive social psychology', *Nordiske Udkast*, 2: 3–15.

Norwood, R. (1990) *Women Who Love Too Much*, London: Arrow Books.

Ochs, E. (1979) 'Transcription as theory', in E. Ochs and B.B. Schieffelin (eds) *Developmental Pragmatics*, London: Academic Press.

Office for National Statistics (2006a) *General Household Survey 2005 Data*. Online. Available: <http://www.statistics.gov.uk/StatBase/Product.asp?vlnk=5756> (accessed 5 December 2007).

Office for National Statistics (2006b) *General Household Survey 2005, Overview*

Report. Online. Available: <http://www.statistics.gov.uk/downloads/theme_compendia/GHS05/GHS05_%20Overview_report.pdf> (accessed 5 December 2007).

Paretsky, S. (1987) *Indemnity Only*, London: Penguin Books.

Paretsky, S. (2002) *Total Recall*, London: Penguin Books.

Parris, M. (2006) 'Just one look', *The Sunday Times*, March 12, News Review 4: 1–2.

Parton, N. (2003) 'Rethinking *professional* practice: the contributions of social constructionism and the feminist "ethics of care"', *British Journal of Social Work*, 33: 1–16.

Payne, D. (1983) *Singleness,* Philadelphia: The Westminster Press.

Pearsall, J. and Trumble, B., (eds) (1996) *The Oxford English Reference Dictionary*, Oxford: Oxford University Press.

Pels, D. (2000) 'Reflexivity: one step up', *Theory, Culture & Society*, 17, 3:1–25.

Peterson, N.L. (1981) *Our Lives For Ourselves: Women who have Never Married*, New York: Putnam's Sons.

Plummer, K. (2001) *Documents of Life 2: an Invitation to a Critical Humanism*, London: Sage.

Pomerantz, A. (1984) 'Agreeing and disagreeing with assessments: some features of preferred/dispreferred turn shapes', in J. Heritage and J.M. Atkinson (eds) *Structures of Social Action: Studies in Conversation Analysis*, Cambridge: Cambridge University Press.

Pomerantz, A. and Fehr, B.J. (1997) 'Conversation analysis: an approach to the study of social action as sense making practices', in T.A. van Dijk (ed) *Discourse Studies: a Multidisciplinary Introduction, Volume 2, Discourse as Social Interaction*, London: Sage.

Potter, J. (1996) *Representing Reality: Discourse, Rhetoric and Social Construction*, London: Sage.

Potter, J. and Hepburn, A. (2005) 'Qualitative interviews in psychology: problems and possibilities', *Qualitative Research in Psychology*, 2: 238–307.

Potter, J. and Wetherell, M. (1987) *Discourse and Social Psychology: Beyond Attitudes and Behaviour*, London: Sage.

Potter, J. and Wetherell, M. (1995) 'Discourse analysis', in J. Smith, R. Harré and L. van Langenhove (eds) *Rethinking Methds in Psychology*, London: Sage, pp. 80–92.

Psathas, G. and Anderson, T. (1990) 'The "practices" of transcription in conversation analysis', *Semiotica*, 78, 1/2: 75–99.

Rapley, T.J. (2001) 'The art(fulness) of open-ended interviewing: some considerations on analysing interviews', *Qualitative Research*, 1, 3: 303–23.

Read, J. and Reynolds, J. (1996) 'Working for change: Introduction' in J. Read and J. Reynolds (eds) *Speaking Our Minds: An Anthology of Personal Experiences of Mental Distress and its Consequences*, Basingstoke, Macmillan.

Reilly, L. (1996) *Women Living Single: Thirty Women Share Their Stories of Navigating Through a Married World*, London: Faber and Faber.

Reynolds, J. (2002) 'Constructing the single woman in therapy', *The Journal of Critical Psychology, Counselling and Psychotherapy*, 2, 1: 20–31.

Reynolds, J. (2006) 'Patterns in the telling: single women's intimate relationships with men', *Sociological Research Online*, 11, 3. Online. Available: <http://www.socresonline.org.uk/11/3/reynolds.html> (accessed 14 December 2006).

REFERENCES

Reynolds, J. and Taylor, S. (2005) 'Narrating singleness: life stories and deficit identities', *Narrative Inquiry*, 15, 2: 197–215.

Reynolds, J. and Wetherell, M. (2003) 'The discursive climate of singleness: the consequences for women's negotiation of a single identity', *Feminism & Psychology*, 13, 4: 489–510.

Reynolds, J., Wetherell, M. and Taylor, S. (2007) 'Choice and chance: negotiating agency in narratives of singleness', *Sociological Review*, 55, 2: 331–51.

Rice, M. (2002) 'Live-out lovers', *The Observer Magazine*, 16 June. Online. Available: <http://observer.guardian.co.uk/magazine/story/0,,738207,00.html#article_continue> (accessed 9 January 2007).

Rich, A. (1980) 'Compulsory sexuality and lesbian existence', *Signs*, 5: 631–60.

Richardson, L. (1988) 'Secrecy and status: the social construction of forbidden relationships', *American Sociological Review*, 53, April: 209–19.

Ricoeur, P. (1992) 'Life in quest of narrative', in D. Wood *On Paul Ricoeur: Narrative and Interpretation*, London: Routledge.

Riessman, C. (1990) *Divorce Talk: Women and Men Make Sense of Personal Relationships*, London: Rutgers University Press.

Riessman, C.K. (1993) *Narrative Analysis*, London: Sage.

Riessman, C.K. (2002) 'Analysis of personal narratives', in J.F. Gubrium and J.A. Holstein (eds) *Handbook of Interview Research: Context and Method*, London: Sage.

Roberts, Y. (1997) *The Trouble with Single Women*, Basingstoke: Macmillan.

Robinson, I. (1990) 'Personal narratives, social careers and medical courses: analysing life trajectories in autobiographies of people with multiple sclerosis', *Social Science and Medicine*, 30, 11: 1173–86.

Rosa, B. (1994) 'Anti-monogamy: a radical challenge to compulsory heterosexuality', in G. Griffin, M. Hester, S. Rai and S. Roseneil (eds) *Stirring it: Challenges for Feminism*, Portsmouth: Taylor and Francis.

Rose, N. (1991) *Governing the Soul: the Shaping of the Private Self*, London: Routledge.

Roseneil, S. (2006) 'On not living with a partner: unpicking coupledom and cohabitation', *Sociological Research Online*, 11, 3: Online. Available: <http://www.socresonline.org.uk/11/3/roseneil.html> (accessed 14 December 2006).

Roulston, M.H. (1951) *You Can Start All Over: A Guide for the Widow and Divorcee*, New York: Harper and Brothers.

Sacks, H. (1992) *Lectures on Conversation, Volumes I and II*, Oxford: Blackwell.

Sapsford, R. and Abbott, P. (1992) *Research Methods for Nurses and the Caring Professions*, Buckingham: Open University Press.

Saussure, F. de (1974) (Revised edition) *Course in General Linguistics*, London: Peter Owen.

Scase, R. (2000) *Britain in 2010: The New Business Landscape*, Oxford: Capstone.

Schegloff, E.A. (1997a) '"Narrative Analysis" thirty years later', *Journal of Narrative and Life History*, 7, 1–4: 97–106.

Schegloff, E.A. (1997b) 'Whose text? Whose context?', *Discourse & Society*, 8, 2: 165–87.

Schegloff, E.A. (1998) 'Reply to Wetherell', *Discourse & Society*, 9, 3: 413–16.

Schegloff, E.A. (1999) '"Schegloff's texts" as "Billig's data"', *Discourse & Society*, 10, 4: 558–72.

REFERENCES

Schwartzberg, N., Berliner, K. and Jacob, D. (1995) *Single in a Married World: A Life Cycle Framework for Working with the Unmarried Adult*, London: Norton.

Scott, J.W. (1991) 'The evidence of experience', *Critical Inquiry*, 17, Summer 1991: 773–97.

Seale, C.F. (1988) 'Qualitative interviewing', in C.F. Seale (ed) *Researching Society and Culture*, London: Sage.

Sevenhuijsen, S. (1998) *Citizenship and the Ethics of Care*, London: Routledge.

Shakespeare, P. (1998) *Aspects of Confused Speech: A Study of Verbal Interaction Between Confused and Normal Speakers*, London: Lawrence Erlbaum.

Siegel, J.M. (1995) 'Looking for Mr. Right? Older single women who become mothers', *Journal of Family Issues*, 16, 2: 194–211.

Silverman, D. (1973) 'Interview talk: bringing off a research instrument', *Sociology*, 7, 1: 31–48.

Silverman, D. (1997) 'The construction of "delicate" objects in counselling', *Discourses of Counselling: HIV Counselling as Social Interaction*, London: Sage.

Simpson, R. (2003) *Contemporary Spinsters in the New Millennium: Changing Notions of Family and Kinship*, London: London School of Economics, Gender Institute.

Simpson, R. (2006) 'The intimate relationships of contemporary spinsters', *Sociological Research Online*, 11, 3. Online. Available: <http://www.socresonline.org.uk/11/3/simpson.html> (accessed 14 December 2006).

Small, J. (1982) 'The family maiden aunt', song, *The Best of Judy Small*, Victoria, Australia: Crafty Maid Music.

Smith, M.B. (1952) *The Single Woman of Today: Her Problems and Adjustment*, London: Watts.

Speer, S.A. (2005) *Gender Talk: Feminism, Discourse and Conversation Analysis*, London: Routledge.

Stein, P.J. (1976) *Single*, Englewood Cliffs, NJ: Prentice-Hall.

Stein, P.J. (1981) 'Understanding single adulthood', in P.J. Stein (ed) *Single Life: Unmarried Adults in Social Context*, New York: St Martin's Press.

Stevens, R. (ed) (1996) *Understanding the Self*, London: Sage.

Stokoe, E. and Edwards, D. (2006) 'Story formulation in talk-in-interaction', *Narrative Inquiry*, 16, 1: 56–65.

Suchman, L. and Jordan, B. (1990) 'Interactional troubles in face-to-face survey interviews', *Journal of the American Statistical Association*, 85, 409: 232–41.

Tannen, D. (1995) *Talking from 9 to 5: How Women's and Men's Conversational Styles Affect who gets Heard, who gets Credit, and what gets Done at Work*, London: Virago.

Taylor, S. (2003a) 'Narrative analysis in social psychology', paper presented at British Psychological Society Social Section Conference, London School of Economics, September 2003.

Taylor, S. (2003b) 'A place for the future? Residence and continuity in women's narratives of their lives', *Narrative Inquiry*, 13, 1: 192–215.

Taylor, S. (2004) 'Narratives of remembered places', paper presented at Narrative, Memory and Everyday Life Conference, Huddersfield, April 2004.

Taylor, S. (2006) 'Narrative as construction and discursive resource', *Narrative Inquiry*, 16, 1: 94–102.

REFERENCES

Tennyson, A. L. (1998) *The Lady of Shalott*, Oxford: Oxford University Press. (Poem first published 1833.)

The Hen Co-op (1993) *Growing Old Disgracefully: New Ideas for Getting the Most out of Life*, London: Piatkus.

Thomas, K. (1996) 'The defensive self: a psychodynamic perspective', in R. Stevens (ed) *Understanding the Self*, London: Sage.

Throsby, K. (2002) 'Negotiating "normality" when IVF fails', *Narrative Inquiry*, 12, 1: 43–66.

Todorov, T. (1990) 'The origin of genres', in T. Todorov (ed) *Genres in Discourse*, Cambridge: Cambridge University Press.

Trimberger, E.K. (2002) *Friendship Networks and Care*, Berkeley: Center for Working Families.

Trimberger, E.K. (2005) *The New Single Woman*, Boston: Beacon Press.

Turner, B.S. (1993) 'Book review: *The Transformation of Intimacy: Sexuality, Love and Eroticism in Modern Societies*', *British Journal of Sociology*, 44, 4: 728–9.

Vernon, P. (2005, 7 August) 'Does Bridget still speak for single women?', *Observer*. Online. Available: <http://books.guardian.co.uk/print/0,,5256789-99930,00.html> (accessed 15 March 2006).

Walby, S. (1989) *Theorising Patriarchy*, Oxford: Basil Blackwell.

Walkerdine, V. (1990) *Schoolgirl Fictions*, London: Verso.

Warn, S. (2003) 'Condoleezza and the Comic Strip controversy', *After Ellen: News, Reviews and Commentary on Lesbian and Bisexual Women in Entertainment and the Media*. Online. Available: <http://www.afterellen.com/archive/ellen/Print/boondocks.html> (accessed 28 September 2007).

Weedon, C. (1987) *Feminist Practice and Poststructuralist Theory*, Oxford: Blackwell.

Wetherell, M. (1998) 'Positioning and interpretative repertoires: conversation analysis and post-structuralism in dialogue', *Discourse & Society*, 9, 3: 387–412.

Wetherell, M. (2001) 'Themes in discourse research: the case of Diana', in M. Wetherell, S. Taylor and S.J. Yates (eds) *Discourse Theory and Practice: a Reader*, London: Sage.

Wetherell, M. and Edley, N. (1998) 'Gender practices: steps in the analysis of men and masculinities', in K. Henwood, C. Griffin and A. Phoenix (eds) *Standpoints and Differences: Essays in the Practice of Feminist Psychology*, London: Sage.

Wetherell, M. and Edley, N. (1999) 'Negotiating hegemonic masculinity: imaginary positions and psycho-discursive practices', *Feminism & Psychology*, 9, 3: 335–56.

Wetherell, M. and Maybin, J. (1996) 'The distributed self: a social constructionist perspective', in R. Stevens (ed) *Understanding the Self*, London: Sage.

Wetherell, M. and Potter, J. (1988) 'Discourse analysis and the identification of interpretative repertoires', in C. Antaki (ed) *Analysing Everyday Explanation: A Casebook of Methods*, London: Sage.

Wetherell, M. and Potter, J. (1992) *Mapping the Language of Racism*, London: Harvester Wheatsheaf.

Wetherell, M., Taylor, S. and Yates, S.J. (eds) (2001) *Discourse Theory and Practice: A Reader*, London: Sage.

Widdicombe, S. (1993) 'Autobiography and change: rhetoric and authenticity of "Gothic" style', in E. Burman and I. Parker (eds) *Discourse Analytic Research: Repertoires and Readings of Texts in Action*, London: Routledge.

Widdicombe, S. (1998) '"But you don't class yourself": the interactional management of category membership and non-membership', in C. Antaki and S. Widdicombe (eds) *Identities in Talk*, London: Sage.

Widdicombe, S. and Wooffitt, R. (1995) *The Language of Youth Subcultures: Social Identity in Action*, London: Harvester Wheatsheaf.

Wile, I.S., (ed) (1940) *The Sex Life of the Unmarried Adult: An Inquiry into and an Interpretation of Current Sex Practices*, New York: Garden City.

Williams, F. (2004) *Rethinking Families*, London: Calouste Gulbenkian Foundation.

Woehrle Blong, L. (1980) 'I ain't gonna be the woman that you left behind', song, personal communication from the author's sister.

Women and Equality Unit (2003) *Responses to Civil Partnership: a Framework for the Legal Recognition of Same-sex Couples*, London: Department of Trade and Industry.

Wooffitt, R. (2001) 'Researching psychic practitioners: conversation analysis', in M. Wetherell, S. Taylor and S.J. Yates (eds) *Discourse as Data: a Guide for Analysis*, London: Sage.

Wooffitt, R. (2005) *Conversation Analysis and Discourse Analysis: A Comparative and Critical Introduction*, London: Sage.

Zimmerman, D.H. (1998) 'Identity, context and interaction', in C. Antaki and S. Widdicombe (eds) *Identities in Talk*, London: Sage.

INDEX

active citizenship 156–7
affairs 33, 93, 116, 117, 130, 134
agency 19, 23, 82, 84, 88, 93, 96, 98,
    101–3, 107, 109–11, 114, 117,
    120–1, 124
analytic process 51, 79–80, 126–7

'bachelor' 15, 17, 22, 63–4
Bainbridge, Beryl 50
biographical disruption 87
Bridget Jones's Diary 1, 5, 25, 43,
    75
Bushnell, Candace 1, 2

Cagney and Lacey 4
chance 98, 107, 109–11, 118–21
children 1–2, 11, 14, 16, 26–8, 30, 34,
    53, 59, 72, 73, 75–6, 102, 103, 108,
    120, 123, 146, 148, 150, 154, 159,
    160
choice 97–100, 103, 110–11, 119
cohabitation 8–9, 13, 14, 17
commitment 2, 3, 11, 14, 66, 83, 90,
    117, 161
consciousness-raising 36, 153–4
contraception 9, 10
conversation analysis 45, 124–6
cultural repertoire 75
cultural representations 36, 41–2, 98

Daly, Mary 148, 155
data analysis 164–5
Dead Sexy 44
demographic changes 8–9, 11
Dickens, Charles 87
discourse 2, 18–20, 47, 48, 51, 152;
    emotion 113
discourse analysis 44–51, 124, 150

discursive events 23
discursive formations 19
discursive psychology 15, 45, 163
divorce 8–9, 87
double standard 4, 82
dreams 78

Eagles, the 4
egalitarianism 153
empowerment 3, 34, 35, 96, 151,
    155
ethnomethodology 45
existential perspectives 35, 36
experiential models 26, 35–9

'face' 139, 140, 146
female deviance 17
Female Eunuch, The 2
feminism 3, 6, 10, 21–2, 35, 100, 109,
    115, 151–7; challenges for 11–13,
    156
Fielding, Helen 1, 5, 25, 43, 75
First World War 6, 87, 149
Foucault, Michel 16, 18, 19, 23, 45, 50,
    124
frames 78–9, 91, 95
Freud, Sigmund 30
friendships, same-sex 2, 28

Grafton, Sue 25
Great Expectations 87
Greer, Germaine 2–3, 21
grieving 28

Heller, Zöe 33
heterosexuality 146; compulsory 13,
    95, 105
humanistic perspectives 35, 36, 153

180

identity 25–6, 49–50, 150, 154; fixed 29–30; fluid 40, 41, 146; formation of 35, 77, 79, 150; gendered 35; management of 20, 50, 51; models of 25; single 2, 25, 151; as 'task' 9; 'troubled' 3, 50
identity performances 78
identity politics 61, 152–5
identity projects 40, 41
identity work 141–2, 148
ideological dilemmas 48, 49, 51
ideological fields 19–20, 78
individualization 9–11
interpretative repertoires 47–9, 51–61, 63, 65, 98–9, 104–11, 119–20, 157
interview process 2, 23, 44 46–9, 66–8, 74–80, 120, 124, 126–8, 137–8, 140–7, 150–2, 158–63
intimacy 11, 12, 34, 82, 97, 105, 107

Keeler, Christine 18

'Lady of Shallott, The' 82
language 2, 13, 14, 45; use of 2, 19, 44, 48
Larry King Live 149
lesbians 13, 22, 103, 105, 149, 154, 159
Lette, Kathy 44
life cycle 25, 26–30, 40, 68, 80–7, 95
life events 77, 80, 87–90, 95
linguistic analysis 48
lone parenthood 8
love 9, 11, 50, 63, 75, 77, 94, 96, 109, 113, 149; confluent 10; 'liquid' 84; romantic 10, 119; and sex 105
Lipstick Jungle 1, 2
literary construction 77
L-Shaped Room, The (film) 17

Mary Tyler Moore Show, The 4
Marxism 49
monogamy 105, 119; serial 139
mother–daughter relationship 32–3, 42

narrative 10, 29, 30, 37–9, 41, 43, 74–95, 148; canonical 76; co-construction of 77; counter- 76; hetero-normative 101; master 76; personal 16, 20–1; progressive 76–8, 90–2, 95; regressive 76–8, 90; tragic 90

narrative analysis 75–6
narrative genres 76
narrative traditions 39, 75–6
normality 3; construction of 12
Notes on a Scandal 33
nuclear family 9, 27

old age 28
one-person households 8
'otherness' 14, 18

Paretsky, Sara 25
participants, selection of 158–61
personal deficit repertoire 40, 49, 52–3, 56, 60, 62, 63, 65, 67, 94, 150
personal histories 162, 164
phenomenological perspectives 35–6
positioning 50, 60–2, 65–6, 84, 107, 114
poverty 12
power relations 11, 13, 19–23, 39, 45–6, 56, 94, 110, 117–19, 151, 152, 164
Profumo, John 18
'progress novels' 95
psychoanalysis 31
psycho-discursive practice 42
psychodynamic models 26, 30–5
psychotherapy 34, 38

racism 152, 153, 164
reflexivity 151
relationships 10, 21, 29, 32, 40, 66–7, 74–95, 101, 105–7, 114, 119, 124, 141, 152, 156, 162; changing practices in 8–9; female/male 3–4, 6, 111, 117, 120, 134; multiple 4; power in 13, 22; same-sex 8; sexual 2, 34; theories of 9–11
'revirginization' 43–4
Rhoda 4
Rice, Condoleezza 149, 150
Roberts, Yvonne 155
romantic fiction 1–2, 25, 43–4
Rubens, Bernice 50

self 41, 103, 140; construction of 61–6; differentiation of 27; narrative of 10, 20, 68, 74–95, 96, 98, 114, 120; and 'other' 156; sense of 31, 75, 151
self-help literature 5–7, 32, 38

self-narrative *see* self, narrative of
sense-making 26, 45, 151
separation 8
Sex and the City 1, 2
sexual feelings 28–9
sexual revolution 10
sexuality 4, 10, 17, 61, 82, 149, 154;
  compulsory 95, 105; 'plastic' 10;
  portrayal in fiction and films 17
single women: marginalization of 3; and
  'troubled identity' 3
singleness 1–6, 13–14, 20, 23, 26–7,
  30, 32, 36–7, 39, 41, 42, 44, 46,
  51–61, 72–3, 96, 121, 122, 128,
  132–3, 150, 153, 155–6, 162; and
  age 15; choosing 101, 156; definitions
  of 18, 158; as deviance 152; discourse
  of 18–20, 48, 70, 150; feminist
  discursive analysis of 15–23, 46, 150;
  images of 80, 162; as independence
  and choice 56–8; meanings of 2, 13,
  15, 21, 22, 148; models of 25–42; as
  personal deficit 52–3, 65, 101, 150;
  politics of 6, 21–3, 61, 143, 151–3,
  156–7; as 'problem' 2, 5, 7, 49, 97,
  123, 142, 148–50; 'public issues' of
  6; repertoires of 68, 94, 101, 110;
  representations of 12, 15; as self-
  development and achievement 58–60;
  social construction of 15–17, 51; as a
  social category 17–18; as social
  exclusion 49, 53–6, 60, 65, 69, 95,
  122; statistics on 8–9; and theory of
  language 13
singlism 122–3
'snowballing' 158–9
social constructionism 15–17, 151
social psychology 15, 45
social sciences 150
'spinster' 15, 17, 19, 22, 49, 50, 52–3,
  63–5, 105, 122, 148, 149, 155
step-families 8
stereotypes 25, 50, 53, 56, 95, 122

stigma 7, 21, 23, 29, 74, 122, 144,
  147–50, 152, 153, 157, 158, 165
stories 38, 41, 53, 57, 74–80, 95–7,
  111, 114, 119–20; public 11–12
subject positions 13, 16, 20–1, 41, 42,
  48, 49–51, 53, 56, 59–60, 67,
  69–70, 79–80, 82, 91–5, 99, 103,
  105, 107, 117, 120, 151, 152

Tennyson, Alfred 82
Thelma and Louise 3
theoretical commitments 15–23
theory 39, 46, 125, 146; of
  contemporary relationships 9–11; of
  discourse analysis 44–5; feminist
  12–13, 35; lack of 4, 37, 39; of
  language 13; psychoanalytic 31;
  psychodynamic 33; psychological 15;
  sex-role 31; of single identity 25, 37,
  40; social 9, 12; of social construction
  16
transcription 47, 126, 163–4
transcription conventions 166–7
trouble 2, 32, 40, 50–1, 63–4, 66–8,
  72, 75, 76, 82, 91–2, 99, 107, 117,
  120, 122, 140–4, 146, 147, 150, 163
Trouble with Single Women, The 155
troubled desire 66–70
troubled identity 3
troubled subject position 82, 91, 101,
  103, 105
'truth effects' 19

Victorian era 17
violence 111–14, 120

Washington Post, The 149
'wickedary' 148, 155
Widdicombe, Ann 154
'woman's place' 2, 152
'women alone' 158
Women's Therapy Centre 32
Woodward, Bob 149